# POPULAR DIMENSIONS
# OF THE
# 'ABBASID REVOLUTION

# ROBERTO MARÍN-GUZMÁN

# POPULAR DIMENSIONS
# OF THE 'ABBASID REVOLUTION

## *A Case Study of Medieval Islamic Social History*

**FULBRIGHT-LASPAU**

*Affiliated with Harvard University*

**Cambridge, Massachusetts**

**1990**

Published by Fulbright-LASPAU, affiliated with Harvard
University
25 Mt. Auburn Street
Cambridge, Massachusetts 02138
United States of America

Marín-Guzmán, Roberto,
*Popular Dimensions of the 'Abbasid Revolution.*
*A Case Study of Medieval Islamic Social History*

I. Islamic History ('Abbasid Revolution) -- Civilization
II. Title.

ISBN  9977-88-004-2

Printed in the United States of America
by Fulbright-LASPAU,
affiliated with Harvard University
Cambridge, Massachusetts
1990

*To*
**SILVIA LEAL CARRETERO**
*and*
**RAÚL FERNÁNDEZ GONZÁLEZ**
*as a remembrance of our*
*happy and fruitful years*
*at El Colegio de México*

# TABLE OF CONTENTS

# ACKNOWLEDGMENTS

For this kind of essay much help is received from various institutions and individuals. First of all I want to thank **FULBRIGHT-LASPAU** for the scholarship granted for carrying out studies in Islamic history and culture at The University of Texas at Austin from 1986 to 1990. During those fruitful years of academic research I was able to complete and discuss this essay with professors expert in the area and with collegues in Austin. Special thanks to Julie Leitman at **LASPAU** for her help in acquiring most of the sources and materials needed for this research. I also appreciate her help in obtaining a **FULBRIGHT** grant to attend a seminar at the prestigious **Schloss Leopolskron** in Salzburg, Austria, in the summer of 1988. This seminar gave me a new perspective in understanding more widely the current problems of the Middle East. This essay on the 'Abbasid revolution offers a projection into the Modern Middle East and proves the continuity of several relevant aspects of the Islamic culture. This trip to Austria also gave me the opportunity to study several Arabic sources at the Österreichischen National-Bibliothek in Vienna.

To the authorities of the Universidad de Costa Rica I want to express my gratefulness for agreeing to my leave of absence for this long period. Special mention to Dr. Manuel Araya Incera, Dr. Luis Fernando Sibaja, Dr. Enrique Martínez A., all part of the Department of History. To Hilda Chen Apuy E., Professor Emeritus of the Universidad de Costa Rica, my deepest gratefulness for all her advice, support and encouragement in dedicating my academic research and studies to the Muslim World.

I am indebted to Dr. Manuel Ruiz Figueroa, Dr. Rubén Chuaqui and María Chuary, all of them from El Colegio de México, for their teaching, and scholarly responses to my countless questions.

Special thanks to my professors at The University of Texas at Austin, Dr. Abraham Marcus and Dr. Hafez Farmayan, both from the Department of History, for their scholarly discussions, and for carefully reading this work. Their advice and numerous corrections of the manuscript considerably improved this research. I also want to thank Dr. Peter 'Abboud and Dr. Aman 'Attieh, from the Department of Arabic of The University of Texas at Austin, for their patient teaching and for suggesting my use of Medieval Arabic sources.

To my collegues and friends of The University of Texas at Austin, especially Pio Schurti, Michael Begala, Brent Neely, Najib and Catherine Ahmad, Douglas Haldane, Caroline 'Attieh and James Grehan, my sincere gratitude.

To my friends Silvia Leal Carretero and Raúl Fernández González of El Colegio de México my deepest gratefulness for their friendship, advice and constant encouragement for my studies of the Muslim World.

To my mother, brothers and sisters I give my deepest gratefulness for their love, encouragement and constant support of my academic life.

Finally, my gratitute to David Everett for all his help, for his superb editing of the whole manuscript and for the typesetting.

To err is human, and it is needless to say that all the mistakes in content or in form in this research are the exclusive responsibility of the author.

Roberto Marín-Guzmán,
Austin, Texas,
February 21, 1990.

# PREFACE

This essay is the result of many years of research, reflections and academic discussions. It does not pretend to show the whole history of the Umayyad period, of the origins of the 'Abbasid revolution and the beginning of the second dynasty of Islam, or a detailed description of all the political, social and religious events, but rather a critical approach to the problem, raising important questions leading to the analytical understanding of the major features of the period. History is not understood as a mere description of events anymore, but as a critical and scientific study of the various activities and creations of men of the past, in a particular time and society. For this reason the study and understanding of the proper elements of each society in each particular epoch is extremely important, Islam being no exception in this respect.

Descriptions of wars, revolts and other political events have been generally avoided in pursuit of clarity and conciseness, although the major upheavals and other political events are discussed in this essay with the purpose of exemplifying and supporting the explanations. The projections of the various political issues serve the purpose of helping in understanding this period. For the study of the countless details and descriptions of the political events the reader is sent to both Arabic primary sources and secondary works.

However, this essay is addressed not only to specialists on the topic, but also to students specializing in Middle Eastern history, as well as to the general public interested in this period and the projections of these issues into the modern Middle East.

Because this work was written over many years, several editions of the Arabic sources have been used. However, the indication of those editions are placed in parentheses to avoid confusion and to facilitate the reader a quick look of those references. Major Arabic sources such as al-Tabari's *Ta'rikh al-Rusul wa al-Muluk* have been consulted in several libraries such as the Biblioteca Daniel Cosío Villegas of El Colegio de México, The Middle Eastern Collection at The University of Texas at Austin, and the Österreichischen National-Bibliothek in Vienna, Austria, where different editions are kept. The indication of the Leiden or the Egyptian Edition is provided in the footnotes as well as in the bibliography. A different name of al-Tabari's chronicle has been preserved as *Ta'rikh al-Umam wa al-Muluk,* which is the title of most of the Egyptian editions of this source. The indication of this title and the place of printing  helps the reader who wants to consult those particular references. Something similar is given to other Arabic sources such as al-Ya'qubi's *Ta'rikh al-Ya'qubi,* and Yaqut's *Mu'jam al-Buldan,* when the indication of the edition is provided when other than the first one quoted was used. On certain ocassions a source is quoted in the original Arabic, but later is also quoted in the translation, such as Ibn Khaldun's *al-Muqaddimah,* al-Maqqari's *Nafh al-Tibb* and Ibn Hisham's *Sirat al-Rasul.* The reader is warned that ocassionally translations to other languages were used; such as the English and the Spanish translations of Ibn Khaldun's *al-Muqaddimah.* The indication of which translation and which language is cited appears in the footnotes.

The Library of Congress system of Arabic transliteration is followed throughout this work, with a few changes for some proper names and long structures of the *idafah.* For common proper names of cities and regions, the common word has been preferred. For example, Damascus instead of Dimashq, Kufa and Basra over al-Kufah and al-Basrah, Mecca instead of Makkah, Transoxiana over Ma wara' al-Nahr, Jerusalem over al-Quds, and so on.

# Introduction:

## A Methodological Approach

### I- Identification of the problem

The Umayyads caused serious problems to various ethnic, religious and political groups during their administration of the Empire. On many occasions Arabs, *mawali* (non-Arab new converts to Islam), Shi'ites, Khawarij and other groups revolted against the leading dynasty. These rebellions were violently repressed by the Umayyads who were able to keep control of the Empire for around ninety years. Several leading questions can be raised at this point. Their answers are the main purpose of this research:

1) The first one is concerned with the reasons why the 'Abbasid revolution was successful, in contrast to all the other revolts which ended in fiascos for their leaders and followers and became definite victories for the Umayyads.

2) Why was the 'Abbasid revolution so popular?

3) How did the 'Abbasids manage to organize an opposition movement unifying the various groups which had grievances and were against the Umayyads for different political, religious, economic, ethnic and social reasons?

4) Which groups supported the 'Abbasid revolution?

5) Which other groups might have participated in the struggles against the Umayyads in the time of the 'Abbasid revolution, although there is no evidence in the Arabic sources? By trying to answer these key questions one has, first of all, to identify the various groups, their particular grievances, and the reasons for their opposition to the Umayyads. At the same time, it is important to study the 'Abbasid ideology and propaganda, which is also relevant to under-

*1*

standing what the 'Abbasids offered to each group to gain their support in the rebellion and armed struggle against the ruling dynasty. When one tries to comprehend the reasons for the 'Abbasids' success, it is absolutely necessary to deal with their army, propaganda, ideology, organization and leadership of the war, as well as with the tough and ruthless people who led the revolution.

## II- Identification of the various groups in the 'Abbasid revolution

A picture of Khurasan and Iraq in the year 747 when the 'Abbasid revolution started openly would reveal the presence of various groups fighting against the Umayyads: big armies of Khurasanis, comprising Arabs as well, mainly from the Southern confederation of tribes; discontent religious factionsprotesting, opposing and fighting against the first dynasty of Islam; and the existence of different ethnic groups, mainly *mawali* vs. Arabs. This part is dedicated to identifying each one of these groups, their grievances and the reasons for their participation in the 'Abbasid revolution. In the following chapters of this work I will also trace back through the Umayyad period for the various and numerous problems and grievances of these groups and how they stirred a strong anti-Umayyad feeling. This anti-Umayyad feeling was skillfully and intelligently harnessed by the 'Abbasid propaganda and ideology into the main stream of the 'Abbasid cause.

By identifying these groups we can note the different reasons for the opposition to the first dynasty of Islam. These motives were mainly political, religious, ethnic, tribal, economic and social.

The various groups which participated in the 'Abbasid revolution against the Umayyads were the following:

1) The Arab tribes. The Southern tribes (Yemenites, Kalb, Qahtan) participated in the 'Abbasid revolution against the Umayyads because the rulers supported more frequently the Qahtans' traditional enemies, the Northern confederation of tribes (Qays, Mudar, Tamim, etc.). The traditional and ancient tribal rivalries and disputes were used advantageously by the 'Abbasids who, despite being members of the Northern confederation of tribes, fought against the Umayyads, also members of the Qays group. The 'Abbasids helped and supported the Yemenites against the Mudar. In return, the Southern tribes joined the 'Abbasid revolution against the Umayyads. The reasons for their participation in favor of the 'Abbasids were mainly economic, political, and also for power, status and prestige.

2) Religious groups. Various religious groups opposed, attacked and revolted against the Umayyads persistently during their rule. These groups considered the Umayyads usurpers and people with a weak commitment to Islam. They revolted against the Umayyads hoping to improve the Muslim community after ousting the bad rulers. The religious issue was always an important element for the various ideologies and justifications of opposition to the Umayyads, the 'Abbasid revolution not being an exception in this respect. The most important religious groups were the following:

a) The Shi'ah, which on numerous occasions revolted against the Umayyads. The Shi'ites also participated very actively in the 'Abbasid revolution against the Umayyads. The *Hashimiyyah*, one of the many groups split from the Shi'ah, was taken by the 'Abbasids as one of their major supporters, as well as one of the main pillars for the development of their ideology and their claims for legitimacy to the caliphate.

b) The Khawarij. They saw the Umayyads as usurpers and sinners. The Khawarij called for rebellion, not only as a right, but also as a duty, of every Muslim to oust the sinners. There is, however, no evidence in the Arabic sources that the 'Abbasids supported them or that the 'Abbasids managed to draw the Khawarij into their revolution, despite the mention in the *Akhbar al-Dawlah al-'Abbasiyyah* of a Khawarij revolt as partial fulfillment of a prophecy about the fall of the Umayyads and the 'Abbasid success. However, it is possible to infer that if the Khawarij were actively hostile to the dynasty in power in previous years, they could also have allied with the 'Abbasids in their struggles against the Umayyads. This hypothesis needs further research.

c) The *Qadariyyah*. This religious school, which believes in Free Will in opposition to the *Jabariyyah*, that forwards the notion of Predestination, was very active politically. The *Qadariyyah* fought and opposed the Umayyads on various occasions, especially in the time of the caliph Hisham, who reacted strongly by expelling several of the leaders and imprisoning many of the followers. In the Arabic sources there is no evidence, however, that the *Qadariyyah* joined the 'Abbasid revolution against the Umayyads. However, again it is valid to speculate that if they were politically active against the Umayyads in early years, it is likely that they were also active during the 'Abbasid revolution.

3) Taxation and the conversion process; ethnic rivalries and discrimination. Very closely related with the issue of discrimination against the *mawali* (non Arab Muslim converts) and against the *dhimmis* (non-Muslim protected religious minorities; i.e., Jews, Christians and later on Zoroastrians as well) was the whole Umayyad taxation system. To avoid heavy taxation the Persian population of Iraq and Khurasan had two choices. Either convert to Islam or, as *mawali*, once they have accepted the new religion, revolt

against the Umayyads. The offer to new converts(*mawali*) of not paying the *jizyah*, but to paying the pious Muslim *zakah* instead, was an important incentive for many to convert to Islam. This is why conversion was so closely related to taxation in Iraq, Khurasan and other parts of the Muslim Empire, Persia and al-Andalus being the most clear examples. However, conversion to Islam did not automatically bring equality (*musawah*) of treatment and opportunities to all Muslims. It has been already explained the Umayyad discrimination against the *mawali*, as well as their responses through rebellion, and arguments through the *Shu'ubiyyah* school, whose purpose was to obtain equality for all Muslims. However, the *Shu'ubiyyah* in many instances portrayed the non-Arab Muslims as being superior to the Arabs, a reaction to the discrimination that they so often faced, and possibly one of the best examples of ethnic rivalries. The *mawali* joined the 'Abbasid revolution in the hope of gaining equality (*musawah*). However, the 'Abbasid revolution can not be understood as an exclusive *mawali* reaction to the Arab domination, despite the fact that this was until recently a very common and far spread belief. An enumeration of the various groups that joined or could have joined the revolution reveals the complexities of this movement and the popular dimensions of the 'Abbasid revolution.

## III- Some notes about the sources

### 1- Arabic primary sources

In this essay many Arabic primary sources have been consulted. These works are of various kinds: chronicles, general history books (*Ta'rikh*), biographies, collections of biographies, religious works (*Qur'an* and *Fiqh*), histories of the caliphs (*Ta'rikh al-Khulafa'*), histories of the Islamic sects (*al-Firaq, al-Nihal, al-Milal*), books on taxation in Islam (*Kitab al-Kharaj*), descriptions of the Muslim conquests (*Futuh al-Buldan*), history of the administration of the Empire (*al-Ishraf*), geographical descriptions (*Masalik al-Mamalik*), accounts of Muslim travelers (*al-Rihlah*), literary works (*al-Adab*), genealogical books, etc. Names of famous Muslim historians and scholars such as al-Tabari, al-Baladhuri, Ibn Qutaybah, Ibn al-Athir, Ibn 'Abd al-Hakam, al-Mas'udi, al-Mawardi, al-Hamdani, Ibn 'Abd Rabbihi, Ibn Khaldun, Ibn Rustah, Ibn Khurdadhbih, Ibn Hisham, Ibn Khallikan, al-Baghdadi, al-Jahiz, al-Suyuti, al-Maqrizi, and others are mentioned and their opinions analysed through this essay.

However, many problems are encountered when one deals with the Arabic sources. The first one to be explained refers to the reliability of the Arabic sources. Some sources are to a certain extent reliable and supported by other previous works. These previous sources are mainly the *isnad* chain which, for a modern historian, raises many doubts. If one keeps in mind that several of the available Arabic sources about the Umayyad period and the 'Abbasid revolution were written during the 'Abbasid time, it is possible to doubt the reliability of several issues, since some of those works tend to be very biased. Moreover, for certain topics, the quotation of *ahadith* (singular *hadith*) is not totally reliable, since some of them are only valuable for Shi'ite Muslims and not for Sunnis.

Some of the chronicles were written many years after the events. These historians were obviously not eyewitnesses to the events they wrote about. Despite the fact that they supported their works with previous accounts and other sources, there is no doubt that the eyewitness was in most cases in a better position and closer to the truth. This does not mean that the eyewitness always wrote about what he saw. Often they wrote for rulers, commanders, and governors, and for obvious reasons they frequently exaggerated their master's strength and bravery, the sizes of armies, and the booty conquered. Even Ibn Khaldun, the famous Muslim historian, who wrote the first scientific approach to history, recommended a cautious and critical eye to the accounts of armies and treasures provided by many historians.

Another problem with the chronicles is that most of them concentrate mainly on political issues. Little information about daily life, the economy, the geography or other aspects is provided. Thus it is necessary to consult different sources on various topics, to bring a more complete understanding to the period under investigation.

Another major difficulty: the Arabic sources often have different accounts of the same event. For various reasons the writers had different understanding of those events, with descriptions of a battle or a revolt varying from one author to another. For this reason the study of a variety of chronicles and other sources is absolutely necessary, as well as a critical comparison of them. This is why in this essay I frequently mention the Muslim historian or the source from which the information has been taken.

Another problem with the Arabic sources is that of generalizations, which are sometimes extremely dangerous. For instance, on the conversion of the Arab tribes to Islam one of the major sources is 'Abd al-Malik Ibn Hisham's *Sirat Rasul Allah*. In this book, Ibn Hisham, following Ibn Ishaq's work, described in detail how the leaders of different tribes went to the Prophet to submit to Islam. Al-Tabari's *Ta'rikh al-Rusul wa al-Muluk* also provided details about these conversions. However, these sources must be taken very cautiously, since in many cases when a leader of a family, a clan or a tribe went to the Prophet to accept Islam, it did not follow that all his clan or his tribe also submitted to Muhammad. Some followed the leader, but some others opposed him. Proof of this opposition is found in the historical event of the war of the Riddah (which can be studied in the various *Ta'rikh al-Khulafa'* books and al-Baladhuri's *Ansab al-Ashraf*), shortly after the Prophet's death when Abu Bakr was appointed the first caliph.

The same is also true for the various traditions about the Umayyad rule, about the 'Abbasids, about Abu Muslim, etc. When one deals with all these various sources one has to comparecarefully the informations they provide. By comparing them one approaches a balanced account of these events and avoids flawed generalizations.

## 2- Secondary works

Based upon most of the Arabic sources already mentioned, several European and Arab scholars have written their own interpretations of the origins and development of the 'Abbasid revolution. One of the first European works, *Das Arabische Reich und sein Sturz (The Arab Kingdom and its Fall)* (1902), by Julius Wellhausen is still a classic work. Wellhausen emphasized the Arab tribal dimensions and especially the role of the *mawali* as the major reasons (besides religious, political and ethnic motives) for the fall of the Umayyad dynasty and the rise of the 'Abbasids. A more recent work by the French scholar Claude Cahen, "Points de vue sur la 'Révolution 'Abbaside'" (1963) keeps a more balanced view of the reasons of the 'Abbasid revolution. He points out that the revolution cannot be understood as only a family affair, although it was a major element of the 'Abbasid propaganda. The 'Abbasids gave to Islam a universal dimension, incorporating Arabs and *mawali* as members of the same *ummah*. The Shi'ah, on the other hand, because of its numerous subdivisions, was unable to give such a dimension to the *Dar al-Islam*.

Another more recent book is M.A. Shaban's *The 'Abbasid Revolution* (1970) in which he denies the importance and traditional rivalries of the Arab tribes; i.e., Qays versus Qahtan. Instead, he analyses them as political parties in favor of the expansion wars and the acquisition of booty (the Qays) and in favor of assimilation and integration of the Muslim territories and peoples already submitted to Islam (the Yemenites).

The thought-provoking book by Elton Daniel, *The Political History of Khurasan under 'Abbasid Rule, 747-820* (1979), has been a major contribution to the understanding of the political history of this important province of the Islamic Empire, where the 'Abbasid revolution started. Daniel emphasizes the socio-economic issues of the 'Abbasid revolution, which had been neglected by most scholars, but are the major contribution of his work.

Some other general works, also important for the study of the 'Abbasid revolution and its background are Bertold Spuler's *Iran in Früh Islamischer Zeit* (1952) and *Geschichte der Islamischen Länder* (1959); Francesco Gabrieli, ''La rivolta dei Muhallabati nel 'Iraq e il nuovo Baladuri'', (1938). Faruq 'Omar's *Al-'Abbasiyun al-Awa'il* (1977), and *Al-Khilafah al-'Abbasiyyah* (1977), are also relevant, offering a profound study of the Arabic sources and providing very original interpretations.

Specific works about the actors in the 'Abbasid revolution: Sabatino Moscati's ''Studi su Abu Muslim'' (1949-1950), one of the most detailed and complete studies on Abu Muslim, Moshe Sharon's *Black Banners from the East* (1983) (undoubtedly one of the major works about the 'Abbasid *da'wah*), and Jacob Lassner's *Islamic Revolution and Historical Memory* (1986) (a profound study of the various traditions and their differences concerning the 'Abbasid revolution). These works are extremely important and useful for the study of these events. These last authors have studied and reviewed very carefully the Arabic sources and the major secondary works in order to draw their own conclusions.

However, a specific study of the popular dimensions of the 'Abbasid revolution, the anti-Umayyad feelings, and the identification of the various groups that participated, or could have participated, in favor of the 'Abbasids, is still lacking. The purpose of this essay is to bridge that gap, based upon both primary and secondary sources. This essay will analyse the reasons, the grievances, and the various groups that supported the 'Abbasids against the Umayyads, which gave a popular dimension to this revolution that changed the face of the *Dar al-Islam*.

# Chapter I

## The role of the Arab tribes in the origins of the 'Abbasid revolution

### I- The Arab tribes: rivalries and divisions

The Umayyads controlled the power by exploiting the tribal disputes. However, the same practice, skillfully used by the 'Abbasids, expelled the Umayyads from power and brought a new dynasty to rule the Muslim Empire. The traditional rivalries between the different Arab tribes played a major role in the decline and fall of the Umayyads and in the rise of the 'Abbasids, which are the major points to be developed in this section.

In general terms, the Arab tribes fall into two major groups or confederations: the Northern tribes, also known as Mudar, Ma'add, Qays 'Aylan and Syrians, comprising a great number of different tribes; and the Southern tribes, also known as Qahtan, Kahlan, Kalb, Himyar and Yemenites, which also had several tribal subdivisions. These two confederations of tribes were in a state of almost constant rivalry dating back to the early history of the Arab people. Their rivalries were mainly economic and political. When they had to share the same territories, the same space and water, the problems arose. The location of Southern tribes in northern territories even before the origins of Islam -- for example, the Lakhmids in al-Hirah on the Euphrates[1] and the settlements of Northern tribes in the south -- were motives for dispute, as when members of the other confederation invaded what they considered their own territory, or when nomads moved in.

The tribal conflicts were between confederations and also between tribes within a confederation, as portrayed in the legends of the Arabs, in their literature and in their history. In many cases, the rivalries between two tribes of the Northern group were so profound that one of the two would unite and ask for help from their enemies, the Qahtan, to defeat the other Northern group. Islam did not overcome these social and ethnic tribal rivalries which, as it has been pointed out, were due mainly to economics and politics. However, social, ethnic and racial motives have also been mentioned and put into consideration.[2] The process of alliances between different groups of tribes, even between their traditional enemies, has been explained by many Muslim historians as well as by several Western scholars, who described how the wars between the Tamim and the Azd in Central Asia and Khurasan generated a major problem between the Mudar and the Yemenites.[3] This process of alliances and their rupture took place in both regions, the West and the East of the Muslim Empire, and became for the 'Abbasid revolution one of the major reasons for its success. In al-Andalus, for example, on many occasions some Arab tribes even allied themselves with traditional enemies to fight another tribe from the same confederation or *sha'b* to improve and defend their own position. The economic interest was one of the reasons of these strange but not unusual alliances occurring all over the Muslim Empire.[4]

The different Arab tribes accepted Islam, as explained by 'Abd al-Malik Ibn Hisham in his *Sirat Rasul Allah*.[5] Both the Northern and the Southern tribes participated eagerly in the Islamic expansion which had, along with religious motives, economic and political reasons.[6] Perhaps the main reason for their eager participation was the share of booty.[7] The disputes between Qahtan and Qays tribes were increased during the Muslim conquests for economic and political reasons. In the analysis and in the general explanations of the expansion of the Arab tribes with the expansion of Islam (*Intishar al-Islam*), one has to keep in mind various elements of this process. The following three are the most important:

1. The first process of Islamic expansion was directed towards the north and the east of the *al-Jazirah al-'Arabiyyah* (The Arabian Peninsula). This first stage of the expansion, which was successful in the conquest of Syria and Palestine (after the battle of Yarmuk, in 636) and *Jazirah* (Iraq), with the famous battle of Qadisiyyah, in 637,[8] was mainly performed by members of the Northern tribes, especially Arabs from Mecca and the surrounding areas. Moreover, al-Asat Ibn Qays, a hero of the war of the Riddah, was the one who conquered Iraq.[9] For this reason they obtained a big share of the booty as well as the best lands over the Qahtan, who were a minority in the expansion wars at that time. According to al-Baladhuri, the Qahtan, the Southern tribes, or *Ahl al-Yaman*, also demanded equal treatment in privileges and land ownership, although their role in the expansion wars was inferior to that of the Mudar.[10] These conquests opened the doors for further expansion towards the east. They were led by members of the Northern tribes, who were the beneficiaries of the booty and wealth garnered in those regions. The Southern tribes also participated but in lesser numbers, and their share of the booty and the revenues obtained were much less than those of their traditional tribal enemies. The Northern tribes also occupied the land, and very soon after they settled down they engaged in trade, which brought them considerable benefits.

2. When the Southern tribes saw their opportunities of benefit, land, trade, and especially booty, closed in the east and in certain way blocked by their enemies, the Northern tribes, they enrolled in those same activities westward, mainly toward North Africa and al-Andalus, two regions that they conquered with great benefit. A close reading of 'Abd al-Rahman Ibn 'Abd al-Hakam's *Futuh Misr wa Akhbaruha* reveals that the main positions in the army and the governorship of provinces and cities were in the hands of the Southern tribes. Abu 'Abbas Ahmad Ibn Muhammad al-Maqqari (d. 1632) asserted in his *Kitab*

*Nafh al-Tibb* that the Qahtan had settled in al-Andalus in great numbers and that they had carried there the same hereditary hatred against the Mudar and the other tribes of the line of 'Adnan.[11] Al-Maqqari also asserted that the Qahtan tribes were more numerous in al-Andalus than their adversaries and always obtained a greater share of power and influence.[12] This is probably one of the reasons why the 'Abbasid revolution was not well received in al-Andalus as it was in the East. Moreover, al-Andalus was far from the centers of power of the caliphate. Although not totally apart from the caliph's main policies, al-Andalus faced other problems, such as the struggles against the Christians and the Franks; also the Berber revolts in both al-Andalus and North Africa, which distracted the Qahtan from the 'Abbasid propaganda centered mainly in Khurasan.

The opposite occurred in the East, which is understood by looking at the tribal origin of those in important administrative and military positions, who were mainly from the Northern tribes. This information is provided by the major Arabic sources, such as al-Tabari, al-Baladhuri, Ibn Majah, and later Arabic works such as al-Suyuti's *Ta'rikh al-Khulafa'*.[13]

However, one should not think that the Northern tribes settled exclusively in the east, or the Southern only in the west of the *Dar al-Islam*. Both groups of tribes expanded in both directions and settled everywhere in the Muslim Empire, a situation that aggravated their traditional rivalries.

3. The Arab expansion should not be understood only as a religious motivation. This process was not only an expansion of Islam, nor it was one single movement which stopped as soon as the tribes settled. The process was quite the contrary. The expansion of Islam also led the Arab tribes to undertake one of the biggest expansions that history records. The Arab tribes spread from the Arabian Peninsula towards the east to Iraq, Khurasan, and the frontiers (*Hudud*) of the Chinese Empire, and towards the west to North Africa and Spain (al-Andalus).

Arabic became the official and religious language in the vast empire, although some languages were also kept for religious purposes (Coptic, Greek, Latin, Persian, etc.) and some others remained spoken in various regions, including Berber, Romance (Spanish), Aramaic, Turkish, and Persian. The Arabic culture was adopted by the conquered peoples in this vast empire.[14] The Arabization process took several centuries and finally prevailed in the Mashriq of the Empire (with the exception of Iran) and in North Africa. The case of al-Andalus is totally different, since Islam and the Arabic culture, language and customs were replaced by those of the Christian Spaniards[15] after the Reconquista wars.[16]

The various expansions of the Arab tribes to different places of the Muslim Empire proves several things. First of all, it shows the interest that the tribes had in the acquisition of booty, wealth and land in places outside the Arabian Peninsula. In fact, the Arab tribes spread all over the Muslim Empire, which was a process of many years. These Peninsular tribes were seeking better conditions. The statement of al-Baladhuri, that there were more Arabs in Iraq than in Syria, proves the extent of the Arab migrations out of the *al-Jazirah al-'Arabiyyah* into the north and east.[17] For many Arabs at the time of the expansion of Islam, that was an excellent opportunity to leave the Peninsula in search of better economic conditions. The share of the booty was always an important incentive. An interesting speculation, although little evidence exists, since the Arabic sources do not deal with it, is that there was an excess of population in the Arabian Peninsula and that it was one of the major reasons for the expansion of the Arab tribes.

Another proof that the Arab migrations were not undertaken in a single wave is the fact that Arabic sources speak of the problems between "old" and "new" Arabs settled in different regions, whether they were in al-Andalus, in Khurasan or in *Ma wara' al-Nahr*. These migrations brought new struggles and fighting between the "new" and the "old" Arabs wherever new migrations of Arabs took place, especially if the newcomers belonged to the opposite confederation of tribes of those already settled in those particular regions.

The system of land ownership and the establishment of the institution of the *junds* also caused an increase in their rivalries. The rapid Arab expansion from Arabia to Syria, Mesopotamia, Iran, Egypt, North Africa and al-Andalus made Muslims adopt the existing institutions of the ancient Empires (Byzantium and Persia) that had controlled most of those territories. Lacking experience in administration as well as the institutions to control and keep together the conquered areas, the Arabs transformed the basic division of spoils and territories from the three categories explained by al-Baladhuri in *Muhajirun, Ansar* and the wives of the Prophet,[18] to a major and better organized one following the ancient Roman practice of the *limitanei*. The *limitanei* were soldiers who received land in return for their services to defend the frontiers of the Empire. The same practices were adopted by Muslims through the institution of the *junds* in the frontier areas (*hudud*) of the *Dar al-Islam*, where fortresses (*amsar*, singular *misr*) were also established for the defense of the Empire.[19]

Al-Baladhuri explained the organization of the *junds* in Syria[20] and in Egypt,[21] as well as the divisions of the spoils of war and territories among Muslim soldiers. For the case of Egypt, Ibn 'Abd al-Hakam explained the creation of a *diwan* for the division of the conquered territories.[22] For Jerusalem, the *'Ahd al-'Umariyyah* also included in the capitulation of the city the way to divide the territories.[23] The presence of these armed groups of various tribes led to more disputes and rivalries between them, especially in Khurasan and Iraq.[24] The traditional struggles and disputes between Qays and Qahtan also had an economic context in Khurasan as well as in other regions of the Muslim Empire, expressed in the territorial divisions and the role played by the *junds* with very clear economic interests and socio-economic status.

Religious and political issues were also important. Both confederations of tribes claimed superiority on different grounds. The Qahtan, due to the prestige of their southern kingdoms and culture before Islam, felt that they were superior to their enemies the Qays. However, the origins of Islam and the preponderance of the Quraysh tribe (a tribe of the Ma'add group) gave the Northern tribes a more prestigious position among Arabs and all Muslims. The Northern tribes frequently asserted that the *Jahiliyyah*, (the period of ignorance; i.e., the period before Islam) is associated with the Yemenites, while Islam is associated with the Mudar.[25] They also said very proudly that the Prophet arose from their group to transmit the revelation contained in the Qur'an and that the expected caliph will rise from among them.[26]

The information provided by Abu Mansur al-Baghdadi (d. 1037) in his *al-Farq bayna al-Firaq* explains the pride of the Quraysh tribe for receiving the revelation. Furthermore, the Quraysh asserted that "The imamate must not be, save among the Quraysh." They also frequently repeated the *hadith* (pl. *ahadith*) of the Prophet Muhammad referring to them: "The Imams are of the Quraysh",[27] as well as the tradition attributed to Abu Bakr that the Quraysh were the most noble of all Arabs.[28] They also kept in mind what Abu Bakr said in one occasion concerning the leadership of the Quraysh and the submission of others, even the *Ansar*: *"Nahnu al-'Umara' wa antum al-Ansar."* ("We are the *Amirs* and you are the helpers [supporters].") All these ideas made the Northern tribes feel proud and superior to the Southerners. The fact that the Qur'an was transmitted in Arabic to a member of the Quraysh tribe was also emphasized throughout the centuries, especially for the importance of the Arabic language in maintaining the unity of all Muslims and the integrity of the *al-Ummah al-Islamiyyah*. Concerning the importance of the Arabic language and the prestige of the Quraysh tribe in Islam, several Muslim scholars wrote their opinions throughout the centuries. Suffice it with few examples. `Abd Allah Ibn Muslim Ibn Qutaybah (d. 889?) wrote in his *Ta'wil al-Qur'an* about the importance of the Arabic language for the revelation and the unity that it gave to the Muslims.[29] Some centuries later, Jalal al-Din `Abd al-Rahman b. Abi Bakr al-Suyuti (d.1505) in his *Al-Itqan fi `ulum al-Qur'an* emphasized the importance of the Arabic language and the revelation of the *Qur'an* to a member of the Quraysh tribe. He also referred to the importance of the use of one language for the sake of unity.[30]

The Yemenites responded in several ways to these important facts pointed out by the Qays, as the Muslim sources explained. The Southern tribes described the greatness of their past, and they made Qahtan a son of the Prophet Hud and gave him some other special genealogical origins. They also claimed that Qahtan was a direct descendant of Isma'il, "father of all Arabs", ideas which Ibn Hisham, al-Tabari and other Muslim historians explained in their works.[31] Ibn Hisham not only mentioned what the Yemenites, the Southern tribes, believed and thought about their own origins, but also their opinions about being direct descendants of Isma'il. He wrote:

> *All Arabs are descended from Isma'il and Qahtan. Some of the people of Yamam claim that Qahtan was a son of Isma'il and so according to them Isma'il is the father of all Arabs.*[32]

The Arab tribes played an important role in the politics of the Umayyad period. Despite the fact that Islam preached equality (*musawah*) of all men in which supposedly the tribal origin would have no effect, the tribes in fact were always important. Belonging to a particular tribe at that time could have meant either a prestigious position or a severe social limitation.

The caliph's policies over the years had a direct impact upon Arab tribal power and land ownership. Either the Mudar or the Qahtan could improve their position, depending on the support and help received from the ruling caliph. However, the local administration of certain parts of Khurasan was left to the *dahaqin*, the Persian aristocracy. According to the terms of surrender between 'Umar and the conquered Persians, the local *dahaqin* levied the tributes without direct Arab interference and paid them to the ruling Arabs after keeping for themselves a considerable part. Despite this local administration in those territories, the Arabs were undoubtedly in control of the whole region, especially the Northern tribes, who were most of the time well connected with the ruling class in Damascus (a good example of this was the government of Ibn Zur'ah, who had the support of the Qaysites in the capital of the Empire) and managed to have more privileges and a better position than the Qahtan tribes. On different occasions some tribes were granted special privileges and leading positions, a situation detrimental to other groups. For the privileges and patronage many things were expected in return, such as participation in a better control of the Muslim frontiers and the collection of taxes. The major privileges granted were land, administrative positions of cities andprovinces, command in the army of expedition wars, allotment from the booty conquered, patronage, tax exemption, favoritism in trade, industry, minery. On certain occasions and to certain specific governors, the rulers granted permission to mint coins. The rulers also granted some other political-religious administrative positions, such as *Qadi al-Islam, Qadi* of a city, *Shaykh al-Balad, Sahib al-Madinah, Sahib al-Saqiyyah, Sahib al-Suq,* and *Muhtasib*. These positions gave power and prestige. Through favoritism and the grant of privileges, some people indeed improved their economic and social situation. Although the Arabic sources speak about two social classes, the *khassah* and the *'ammah,* favoritism and privileges granted in patronage helped develop a middle class, which proves social mobility. It was possible to become a member of the middle class through education (be a member of the *'ulama',* the learned people) and through success in trade, industry and agriculture.

Throughout Islamic history the opposite process also occurred. In many instances, for various reasons, some middle class people lost their patrons or their property, or were not successful in their businesses any longer; and for these reasons their social status was jeopardized and they were impoverished. They fell from the middle class and became part of the *'ammah (ra'yah* in the Ottoman period). Those tribes not favored by the system fought against it, hoping to gain the same privileges from a new government. The betterment of those favored stirred the envy, the opposition and the anger of the tribes not favored, who then fought against their traditional enemies and against the Umayyad caliph in turn, the major supporter of their enemies. The tribal disputes, although ancient and traditional, had during the Umayyad period very clear political and socio-economic causes.

The possession and use of land brought many benefits to those in charge. It did not mean that the owners cultivated the land with their own hands; instead they used peasants or hired others through various agricultural contracts (*muzara'ah, mugharasah, musaqah*) to do their work, but they benefited from the revenues. However, they were supposed to respect and follow the tradition of *ihya' al-ard al-mayyitah* ("The revivification of the dead land", meaning the reclamation of land.) In an agricultural society, and the revenues that the land produced, the possession of parcels (*qati'ah,* pl. *qata'i'*) was extremely important.

In dealing with all these issues of land ownership, agriculture, parcels, etc., one has to remember that at the beginning of the Islamic expansion, the Arab tribes were not supposed to settle down, but to live in the garrison-cities (*misr*, pl. *amsar*). However, they did settle down and acquire land, and privileges were granted them by the caliph in power. After this process they cohabited with the *mawali* and the Persian population in Khurasan and Iraq. The Arab tribes even adopted some Persian religious celebrations, speaking

Persian in the daily transactions in the markets (*suq*, pl. *aswaq*) and dressing like the Persians in that part of the Muslim Empire. Shortly afterwards, they were engaged in trade activities between Khurasan and *Ma wara' al-Nahr* (Transoxiana). Those granted important political administrative positions benefited a great deal from them. In most cases they were in charge of tax collection, and in many instances they benefited personally from the revenues. The case of Yazid Ibn al-Muhallab in Iraq and Khurasan, whether or not he illegally acquired personal benefits from the collection of taxes, is a clear example of this situation. He was jailed by the caliph 'Umar II allegedly for stealing from the public treasury. This is only one example of the many instances throughout the Umayyad period.

Those appointed to important provinces had tremendous administrative power and often chose members of their own tribes to rule smaller provinces and cities and to raise and command armies in the wars of expansion. For example, Khalid b. 'Abd Allah al-Qasri, governor of Iraq (724-738) in the time of the caliph Hisham, appointed his brother Asad al-Qasri on two occasions (724-726 and 734-738) as governor of Khurasan.

Some tribes occupying administrative positions became extremely powerful. The best example is the Thaqafi tribe with al-Hajjaj Ibn Yusuf in the time of the caliphs 'Abd al-Malik and al-Walid I. Another case was the already mentioned Yazid Ibn al-Muhallab from the Azd Southern tribe.

In the administrative positions the governors and the commanders of armies benefited considerably both in their persons and in their tribes. Some became extremely powerful and rich to the point of defying and challenging the central authority through revolt. The examples of these rebellions are numerous, such as the one led by 'Abd al-Rahman Ibn al-Ash'ath. Some other governors became so powerful that the caliph removed them from office before they could challenge the central authority and establish independent states. Examples of this are the removal of Musa Ibn Nusayr in Ifriqiyyah and al-Andalus, and also his client Tariq b. Ziyad in the time of the caliph al-Walid I.[33] The case of the removal of Yazid Ibn al-Muhallab by 'Umar II can be interpreted the same way.

Some other governors were also removed for inter-tribal fighting and rivalries, such as Yazid Ibn al-Muhallab who was replaced by Qutaybah Ibn Muslim.

It is important to remember that if the governors of provinces and rulers of cities were members of the same family in power in Damascus during the time of the Umayyad dynasty, they also benefited extensively from the properties (real estate) and luxurious houses built with public money and given to members of the Marwanid family.

Those chosen by the caliph or his representatives (*na'ib* pl. *nuwwab*) in the provinces as governors (*'amil*, pl *'ummal*) to lead military expeditions for new conquests also greatly benefited. In most cases not only the leaders, but their tribes as well, profited from the booty captured. In the expansionist wars there was, since the beginning of the spread of Islam, the promise of sharing the booty among those who had participated in the expedition wars. This promise was an important incentive for the Arab tribes to enroll in those campaigns. In this respect one has to bear in mind two important issues.

The first one is that the Northern tribes, which had conducted and benefited from the conquests and the expansion of Islam since the time of the caliph 'Umar, were always in favor of new expansionist wars as a way to benefit themselves economically. The Southern tribes, perhaps because they had participated in those expansions mainly towards the east in a more limited way than the Qays, favored the consolidation of those territories already conquered. They also shared with the *Shu'ubiyyah* the projects for assimilation; i.e., acceptance and equal treatment to the non-Arab converts (*mawali*). It is relevant, as well, to keep in mind that the Southern tribes also organized and participated in expansionist wars (again the case of Yazid Ibn al-Muhallab is a good example in this respect). Although they mainly favored assimilation and consolidation of the frontiers (*hudud*) and peoples of the Muslim Empire, that commitment did not block their desire for booty and revenues obtained in the campaigns. In fact, the inter-tribal rivalries and fighting in Iraq and Khurasan were sparked on numerous occasions by the expansionist wars and the share of booty and the selfish way the Mudar blocked the Yemenites from participating in such campaigns.

Second, despite the great number of Arabs who had moved to Iraq, Khurasan, as well as to North Africa and al-Andalus, they were always a minority (although the ruling group) among the local population, whether Iranian or Berber. For the expansionist wars Arabs had to enroll and organize armies of local people to be able to face successfully their enemies. The armies that Tariq Ibn Ziyad and Musa Ibn Nusayr organized for the conquest of al-Andalus were mainly Berber.[34] In the East, (*al-Mashriq*) Qutaybah Ibn Muslim drafted into his army local Persians who participated in the conquest of Central Asia as far away as Farghana. His army, like many other armies organized for the expansionist wars by different Arab military leaders in the East, was composed mainly of *mawali*. However, the *mawali* were not treated equally to Arab Muslims, receiving a lesser share of the booty. Arabic sources are explicit about this and show how much discrimination took place in the allotment of the booty. This unjust treatment of the Iranian and the Berber populations drafted into the armies was an important reason for the *mawali* to revolt against the Arabs, both in the east and in the west, in North Africa and al-Andalus.[35]

## II- Umayyad politics and government: Administration of the Empire and tribal divisions

The numerous privileges in various levels, granted by the Umayyads to the Northern tribes, of land ownership, commanding and leading positions, tax exemption, and others, upset the Qahtan. The Southerners opposed both the Mudar and the Umayyads and strongly fought against their enemies in Iraq and Khurasan, which led to the fall of the Umayyads and the rise of the 'Abbasids. The analysis of their disputes in other parts of the Empire, although mentioned for North Africa and al-Andalus, is beyond the scope of this research, since the 'Abbasid revolution had little impact on the West.

The first three Umayyad caliphs, Mu'awiyah Ibn Abi Sufyan (661-680)[36], Yazid Ibn Mu'awiyah (680-683)[37] and Mu'awiyah II (683-684)[38], who formed the Sufyaniyyah Umayyad family, supported the Southern tribes. Mu'awiyah Ibn Abi Sufyan encouraged and even ordered the settlement of 50,000 Azd families in Khurasan, according to al-Tabari.[39] These families settled mainly in Merv (Marw) and its surrounding areas. The caliph Mu'awiyah helped them since they joined Talhah and al-Zubayr in their struggles against 'Ali. These events had gained them the reputation of anti-'Alids at that time.[40] The Northern tribes opposed these measures in favor of the Azd tribe. However, no fighting took place, either in Jazirah (Iraq) or in Syria, probably because of fear of the caliph and his tight administration. The problems between Mudar and Qahtan were reactivated in those areas after Mu'awiyah's death, especially during the time of Yazid, who was challenged by the *fitnah* (civil war) of 'Abd Allah Ibn al-Zubayr. In his *khilafah*, Yazid had to face the opposition of some Northern tribes which supported Ibn al-Zubayr in the Hijaz, because of his pro-Qahtan policy.[41]

Marwan I (684-685) succeeded Mu'awiyah Ibn Yazid

in 684 [42] and started the Marwaniyyah Umayyad family, the second and last Umayyad family to rule Islam. Marwan's mother was also Kalbi, and because of this situation he relied on the Qahtan tribes again. The Qays did not like the predominant position of their enemies, the Kalbis, and opposed the rulers. Some Qays tribes, especially the Sulaym, the 'Amir and the Ghatafan, supported the claims of 'Abd Allah Ibn al-Zubayr in the Hijaz.[43] Al-Baladhuri even explained that Ibn Ziyad, governor of the Khurasan province that included Sistan, did not have the respect and acceptance of the Arab tribes in his governorship. Due to these reasons, he fled that region and joined Ibn al-Zubayr in the Hijaz.[44]

However, it is important to bear in mind that a large percentage of Southern Arabs moved and settled in Khurasan, following Mu'awiyah's order. In this region the Northern tribes had already occupied the best land. These facts explain in part the inter-tribal rivalries in both places, especially for economic and political reasons. The Yemenites fought against the Mudar in Iraq because the Northern tribes monopolized the best lands and also blocked the Southern tribes from participating in the profitable expansionist wars in Armenia.[45] On the other hand, the Mudar opposed and fought the Qahtan who had settled in Khurasan, a region where there were more Northern than Southern tribes. Aside from this, the former claimed more rights for having participated directly in the conquest.[46]

Contrary to the Sufyanids' more indirect way of governing, the Marwanids always tried to keep a balance between the *ashraf*, the tribal leaders, and the governors through a centralized system of government. The Marwanids also established an army responsible to the *Amir al-Mu'minin* and to the governors. This army was the main instrument for centralization, defense and administration of the Empire, and for the first time it was loyal to the caliph.[47] Syrian troops, which formed the imperial army, were sent to different parts of the Muslim Empire to stop revolts, centralize the administration, and keep direct control of the Empire. However, the presence of Syrian troops in Iraq and Khurasan caused further problems as a result of the antagonism between Syria and Iraq. Syrian troops were also sent on various occasions to North Africa and al-Andalus to stop the Berber revolts.

In the Marwanid period the caliphs started relying on military men as governors. Al-Hajjaj Ibn Yusuf is a clear example of a person of humble origin reaching important positions through military services, which he began in the *shurtah* of Damascus. He was also to become the architect of the military, political and economic reforms of the caliph 'Abd al-Malik b. Marwan.[48]   As part of the centralization program, the Marwanids started new institutions with that clear purpose. The *barid* (a postal system) was very well organized both as an efficient communication system and as an excellent way to keep the government informed about any possible problems or revolts in the provinces. The writing and sealing of documents were developed through the institutions of *diwan al-rasa'il* and *diwan al-khatam*.

The Marwanids also introduced a specific Muslim coinage in the Muslim lands, replacing the old Sasanid and Byzantine coins. It was in the time of 'Abd al-Malik and his governor al-Hajjaj Ibn Yusuf that real Muslim coins were minted. These coins were purely epigraphic and without portraits of the rulers, following the Muslim doctrine prohibiting representation of human or animal figures.[49] Having their own coins, along with the Syrian army and the centralization plans, gave the Umayyads, during the time of the Marwanids, a great power and an efficient control of the Empire.

The caliph 'Abd al-Malik b. Marwan (685-705) succeeded the brief government of Marwan I.[50] He married a Qaysi woman of the 'Abs, and for this reason he supported and relied on the Qays confederation of tribes, especially through the support he gave the Thaqafi tribe by appointing al-Hajjaj Ibn Yusuf as governor of Iraq. Al-Hajjaj at that time had already defeated Ibn al-Zubayr in the Hijaz. Al-Hajjaj Ibn Yusuf consolidated the Qays power in Iraq and Khurasan.

His mission was not easy, and numerous struggles against him took place. It is possible to infer that the caliph was aware of the difficulties and the problems in controlling the tribes, and to convince him to move to that area, the caliph even offered al-Hajjaj the city of Kufa as a gift (*sadaqah*) in a letter that al-Baladhuri quoted in his *Ansab al-Ashraf*, which says: *"Ya Hajjaj qad a`taituka al-Kufah sadaqah fa-ta'ha wata't yatada'al minha ahl al-Basrah."* ("Oh Hajjaj, I have given you al-Kufah as a gift, therefore, control it so firmly that the people of al-Basrah will be intimidated [they will be fearful and they won't revolt against you]". [51] The caliph `Abd al-Malik appointed him in order to control Iraq in an effective way and to stop all rebellions. Al-Hajjaj had very difficult tasks to carry out. To accomplish them he obliged Arabs to join the army to defeat the Khawarij resistance and to participate in new wars of expansion for Islam. He was obviously in favor of the expansion policies. If someone refused to join the army, the punishment was decapitation, an effective threat, although some Arabs complained about his tyrannical methods. In such a decree one can easily see what caused so many Arabs to accuse the Umayyads of brutality and despotism.

Al-Hajjaj was able to control the tribes in Iraq because of their weak position. Their internal problems and the Khawarij threat had weakened them to the point that, despite occasional and poor resistance, they accepted him, especially in the major garrison-cities (*amsar*) of Kufa and Basra. He faced a more serious Khawarij opposition in Iraq, not only in the countryside, but also in the cities such as in Basra where the *Azariqah* opposed very strongly the Umayyad control of the city. In Kufa, Shahib Ibn Yazid was the leader of the Khawarij resistance to al-Hajjaj.[52] To quell the Khawarij revolts, Syrian forces were sent to Iraq. It is at this time that the city of

Wasit was founded. According to the sources, the main purpose of Wasit was to station the Syrian troops.[53]

Although al-Hajjaj tried to balance the Arab tribal disputes and their struggles for power, and although he appointed as governors of Khurasan al-Muhallab b. Sufrah and Yazid Ibn al-Muhallab of the Azd tribe and kept them there for several years; in the long run what he favored most was the Qays' power. Later on al-Hajjaj dismissed Yazid Ibn al-Muhallab and appointed Qutaybah Ibn Muslim, who was a Qaysite but from the weak clan of Bahilah. These political measures were opposed by the Southern tribes, and new tensions and problems arose between the two confederations of tribes.

Qutaybah Ibn Muslim was governor of Khurasan for ten years, from 705 to 715, and as a Northerner he favored the expansionist wars, as proved by his numerous successful conquests in Central Asia. He was the one who conquered those important cities that contributed so much to the greatness of Islam: Samarqand,[54] Bukhara,[55] Paykand,[56] and Khwarizm.[57] His armies went as far as Farghana, according to the Arabic sources.[58] However, a change of caliphs, al-Walid I (705-715) who succeeded 'Abd al-Malik, had a direct impact upon Khurasan and the administration of Central Asia. Al-Walid I was very careful not to irritate the Kalbis in those campaigns organized by Qutaybah Ibn Muslim.[59] At this point the caliph al-Walid I was also concerned that neither the Syrian nor the Iraqi armies were strong enough to participate in long and dangerous campaigns in Central Asia. This is one of the major reasons why Qutaybah Ibn Muslim drafted local people into his army.[60]

The sudden death of al-Walid I and the predominance of the opposite party, since Sulayman (715-717) [61] supported the Yemenites and tried to balance the Qays' power, made Qutaybah Ibn Muslim fear for his position. In the hope that his army would support him, he revolted against the caliph Sulayman in 715. However, his army deserted him, and that same year his own army killed him.

This revolt exemplifies the political instability of those eastern regions and their inter-tribal struggle for power, prestige and influence.

Furthermore, one has to keep in mind that while al-Hajjaj's policies encouraged land ownership and other privileges for the Northern tribes, the Yemenites (*Ahl al-Yaman*) demanded equal treatment.[62] 'Izz al-Din Ibn al-Athir in his *Al-Kamil fi al-Ta'rikh* also described these problems between the tribes and the opposition of the Azd tribe to the final *aman* of al-Hajjaj. Again the problems and rivalries between the tribes broke out for the same old economic and political reasons, even before al-Hajjaj dismissed Yazid Ibn al-Muhallab, the Azd governor of Khurasan, and replaced him with Qutaybah Ibn Muslim.[63] It is at this point that a new alliance between the Azd and the Rabi'ah took place to defend their own interests and to oppose the Tamim.

The problems among the different tribes were exacerbated by the Marwanids' ways of appropriating land and dividing it among the members of their family and their tribal allies. This policy, clearly developed in the practice of the *sawafi* (gain land capable of cultivation from deserts, marshes and the sea), which was forwarded by 'Abd al-Malik and al-Walid I, really angered the Southern tribes for two major reasons: first because the Marwanids used public funds to gain those lands; and second because they were allotted only to members of the Marwanid family. Discontent spread among many people, especially among the Yemenites in Khurasan, who noted that the Marwanids in most cases excluded them from public positions with only few exceptions, and from many projects of land distribution and land ownership.

More social, ethnic and economic problems arose when al-Hajjaj Ibn Yusuf supported the Arabs over the *mawali*. This situation also aggravated the new converts' grievances. The *mawali* were ready to revolt or to join and support any rebellion against the Umayyads to stop the heavy taxation, the discrimination policies, and the tyrannical ways of ruling. For very similar reasons the *dahaqin* (the traditional Persian aristocracy) of Iraq and the Eastern provinces of Iran were also in a difficult economic situation and were discouraged by the Umayyad administration. Even the *dahaqin* were eager to support a rebellion against al-Hajjaj. With all these economic, political, and social grievances, along with the reduction of the stipends *('ata')* to the army and the presence of Syrian troops in the Eastern provinces, the rebellion of 'Abd al-Rahman Ibn al-Ash'ath broke out, although the Azdite Yazid Ibn al-Muhallab had not yet been replaced by the Qaysite Qutaybah Ibn Muslim. There is evidence in the Arabic sources that after Ibn al-Ash'ath was defeated in Iraq and fled with some of his followers to Khurasan, the Azdite governor of that province, Ibn al-Muhallab, sent back to al-Hajjaj in Wasit only the Mudarite supporters of the revolt. Ibn al-Muhallab treated the Yemenites with respect and consideration.[64] It is by this understanding and perspective that this revolt should be analysed. For the grievances already mentioned it is possible to note the reasons for the popular, although limited support, that this revolt gained from the different social and ethnic groups, the major supporters being the Southern tribes and the *mawali*.

    This revolt also had religious overtones. The appeals to God, to the true religion, and to other religious aspects were used in the language of both groups. The rebels against the Umayyads even called al-Hajjaj "The enemy of God".[65] No wonder that the revolt was supported by most religious people, the `*ulama*' (learned people, religious leaders) and the *qurra*' (the *Qur'an* readers), with the exception of the celebrated al-Hasan al-Basri, as explained by Hans Heinrich Schaeder[66] and Hellmut Ritter.[67]

    The revolt led by Ibn al-Ash'ath lost some popular support with al-Hajjaj's promises of pardon for those who renounced the revolt and submitted to the central administration, which was understood as the Umayyad rule. The

Syrian army was also more powerful than that of Ibn al-Ash'ath. There is no doubt that the presence of Syrian troops imposed respect on those in revolt, and their mere presence convinced many to submit. Al-Hajjaj was able to enter Kufa and forgive those who had laid their arms aside. Moreover, the religious propaganda also played a major role for many to revolt against the so called infidel Umayyads and for many to submit to al-Hajjaj, who skillfully spread the idea that those revolting had renounced Islam. The role played by al-Hasan al-Basri was also influential for many.[68]

The role played by the *mawali* in this revolt was also of great relevance, since in the general Umayyad policy, the new converts were not fairly treated, because they were not Arabs. The revolt of Ibn al-Ash'ath had the *mawali* support because they saw in this rebellion a way to fight against the unjust Umayyad rule, the discrimination which considered them inferior, and the Umayyad heavy taxation. For the same reasons the *dahaqin* (the Persian aristocracy) also supported this rebellion. After the revolt was suppressed they faced serious consequences. They were removed by al-Hajjaj from their previous position of tax collectors.

Other rebellions throughout the history of Islam had very similar causes. Their appeals for change and equality in the Muslim society were important aspirations that resurfaced frequently, the 'Abbasid revolution being no exception in this respect.

It is important to note in the long run that the Umayyad dynasty favored the Northern confederation over the Southerners. The revolt of Yazid Ibn al-Muhallab against the caliph Yazid II exemplifies these inter-tribal rivalries, as well as the opposition to the Umayyads.[69] It is with this perspective of inter-tribal disputes and enmity against the Umayyad rule that this revolt should be analyzed. The popular support Ibn al-Muhallab gained in Basra and other places of Iraq, both from the Northern and Southern tribes, is proof of the anti-Umayyad feeling. However, he obtained more support from the Southern tribes, despite the fact that his own tribe the Azd did not support him entirely.

The ideology, the appeals to religion, freedom from the Umayyad control, and the Syrian troops (he called a *Jihad* against the Syrians) could make one think about his proto- or semi-independent aspirations for Iraq and possibly for Khurasan. Again the celebrated al-Hasan al-Basri opposed this movement as he did earlier against Ibn al-Ash'ath.[70]    Although he did not favor the Umayyads openly, neither did al-Hasan al-Basri accept Yazid Ibn al-Muhallab's aspirations and claims for the caliphate.[71]

The revolt of Ibn al-Muhallab was extremely important and enjoyed popular support. It may be considered a precursor of the 'Abbasid revolution. Besides the Arab tribal help, Ibn al-Muhallab gained the *mawali* support. Although there is no evidence in the sources that the *dahaqin* helped him, it is reasonable to infer that they did since they had supported the revolt of Ibn al-Ash'ath against the Umayyads a few years earlier. It is reasonable to speculate that they backed this revolt against the Umayyads in the hope of recapturing their previous position as tax collectors, which they had lost for having helped Ibn al-Ash'ath. They could also have helped Ibn al-Muhallab in his revolt in 720 because they were interested in the expansionist wars to keep the Arabs away and avoid the important assimilation programs forwarded in the famous Fiscal Rescript of the recently disappeared caliph 'Umar II (717-720). For the *dahaqin*, Yazid Ibn al-Muhallab was portrayed as an expansionist, due to his involvement in several campaigns in Transoxiana while governor of Khurasan in the time of the caliph Sulayman.[72]

His revolt had a catastrophic end when he faced the Umayyad army;[73] however, his impact was considerable, because the 'Abbasids took several of the traditions developed after this revolt:

a) Ibn al-Muhallab repudiated the Umayyads and asserted that a member of the Banu Hashim would be appointed as *Amir al-Mu'minin*.[74] This tradition was taken by the *Hashimiyyah* and through this group by the 'Abbasids.

b) Yazid Ibn al-Muhallab called himself *Qahtani*, which could be understood as the one who raised the black flag (the color taken by the 'Abbasids), the symbol of opposition to the Umayyads, whose banner was white.

The inter-tribal fighting characterizing the Umayyad period increased in the last twenty-five to thirty years of the Umayyad rule because the major two of the last four caliphs, Hisham (724-743) and Marwan II, (744-750) had openly relied on the Mudar, despite the fact that 'Umar II (717-720) had kept a balance between the tribes. When the caliphs favored the Mudar, the Yemenites considered this situation detrimental to their own interests. The support of a particular confederation of tribes was in most cases crucial for the caliph to stay in power.

The Southern tribes joined the 'Abbasid revolution against the Umayyads in the hope with a new government to change their political and social status, so unfavored in the last two decades of the Umayyad rule. The 'Abbasids in their famous call (*da'wah*) to revolution were very skillful in maneuvering the inter-tribal disputes for their own interests and objectives. In this call the 'Abbasids appeared to join the *Shu'ubiyyah* movement, appealing to equality (*musawah*) of all Muslims. The Yemenites responded positively to this call since they wanted justice to prevail. The 'Abbasids also managed to transform the Yemenites' grievances into an extremely active political and military force of opposition to the Umayyads. Undoubtedly, deep at the bottom of the 'Abbasid strategy, the constant of the Arab inter-tribal rivalries was always present and played a significant role in the popular dimensions of the 'Abbasid revolution.

## Endnotes to Chapter I

(1) About the kings of al-Hirah see Abu Muhammad 'Abd Allah Ibn Qutaybah, *Al-Ma'arif,* edited by Tharwat 'Ukasha, Cairo, 1969, pp.645-650. Cf. Philip Hitti, *History of the Arabs,* New York, 1951, pp.81-83. Abu 'Umar Ahmad b. Muhammad Ibn 'Abd Rabbihi, *Al-'Iqd al-Farid,* Cairo, 1948-1953, II, p.85. Montgomery Watt, *Mahoma, Profeta y Hombre de Estado,* Buenos Aires, 1973, p.20. Naji Hasan, *Al-Qaba'il al-'Arabiyyah fi al-Mashriq Khilal al'Asr al-Umawi,* Beirut, 1980, pp.36-37. Abu Muhammad al-Hasan Ahmad b. Ya'qub b. Yusuf b. Dawd al-Hamdani, *Kitab Sifah Jazirat al-'Arab,* edited by David Heinrich Müller, Leiden, 1968, pp.129-131, and pp.205-206. Abu al-Hasan Ahmad b. Yahya Al-Baladhuri, *Futuh al-Buldan,* edited by M.J. de Goeje, Leiden, 1866, (second edition, Leiden, 1968) p.59 and p.136. Abu Hanifah Ahmad b. Dawd al-Dinawari, *Al-Akhbar al-Tiwal,* Cairo, 1960, pp.54-55. Al-Mas'udi, *Muruj al-Dhahab wa Ma'adin al-Jawhar,* edited by C. Barbier de Meynard and Pavet de Courteille, Paris, 1917, IV, p.353. Ahmad b. Abi al-Ya'qubi, *Ta'rikh al-Ya'qubi,* edited by Th. Houtsma, Leiden, 1883, (reprinted in Beirut, 1960) I, p.229 and p.264. Muhammad Ibn Jarir al-Tabari, *Ta'rikh al-Rusul wa al-Muluk,* edited by M.J. de Goeje, Leiden, 1879-1901, passim, especially I, p.1102, I, pp.1555-1556, and I, pp.1604-1605. Roberto Marín-Guzmán, *Introducción a los Estudios Islámicos,* San José, Costa Rica, 1983, passim. Roberto Marín-Guzmán, "Las causas de la expansión islámica y los fundamentos del Imperio Musulmán", in *Revista Estudios,* Number 5, 1984, pp.39-67. Roberto Marín-Guzmán, *El Islam: Ideología e Historia,* San José, Costa Rica, 1986, p.136. See also Roberto Marín-Guzmán, "Algunas notas sobre el origen, desarrollo y expansión del Islam", in *Tiempo Actual,* Vol. VIII, Number 32, 1984, pp.71-79. Carl Brockelmann, *History of the Islamic Peoples,* English translation by Joel Carmichael and Moshe Perlman, New York, 1960, pp.8-10. H. Lammens, "Lakhm", in *Encyclopaedia of Islam* (1), Vol. III, Leyden, 1928, pp.11-12. H. Lammens, "Djudham", in *Encyclopaedia of Islam* (1), Vol. I, Leyden, 1913, pp.1058-1059. Irfan Shahid, "Lakhmids", in *Encyclopaedia of Islam* (2), Vol. V, Leiden, 1986, pp.632-634. G. Rothstein, *Die Dynastie der Lakhmiden in al-Hira,* Berlin, 1899, passim.

(2) A. Fischer, "Kays 'Aylan", in *Encyclopaedia of Islam* (1), Vol. II, Leyden, 1927, pp.652-657. A. Fischer, "Kahtan", in *Encyclopaedia of Islam* (1), Vol. II, Leyden, 1927, pp.628-630. Julius Wellhausen, *The Arab Kingdom and its Fall,* translated by Margaret Graham Weir,

Beirut, 1963, passim. For the study of the settlements of the various Arab tribes see Dinawari, *Al-Akhbar al-Tiwal,* passim, especially pp.16-17 for the Rabi`ah settlements in Yamamah and Bahrayn. For the Rabi`ah and the Mudar see also Abu Ishaq Ibrahim b. Muhammad al-Farisi al-Istakhri, *Kitab Masalik al-Mamalik,* edited by M.J. de Goeje, Leiden, 1927, p.14. For the Ghassan and the Asad tribes and for the Yemenite settlements in *al-Jazirah al-`Arabiyyah* see al-Istakhri, *Kitab Masalik al-Mamalik,* p.14. See also Ibn Qutaybah, *Al-Ma`arif,* pp.626-637 for a detailed study of the Yemenites and their kings.

(3)   Cf. Tabari, *Ta'rikh al-Rusul wa al-Muluk,* II, p.1895, p.1899, pp.1924-1925, pp.1934-1935, p.1937, pp.1970-1971, pp.1986-1987 and p.1996 (Leiden Edition). Shihab al-Din Abu 'Abd Allah Yaqut, *Mu'jam al-Buldan,* edited by F. Wüstenfeld, Leipzig, 1866-1873, III, p.530. Ibn 'Abd Rabbihi, *Al-'Iqd al-Farid,* III, p.345. Dinawari, *Al-Akhbar al-Tiwal,* p.7. See also Istakhri, *Kitab Masalik al-Mamalik,* p.14. Reinhart Dozy, *Historia de los Musulmanes de España,* Buenos Aires, 1946, I, pp.115-121. Hugh Kennedy, *The Prophet and the Age of the Caliphates,* London and New York, 1986, pp.86-87. For a detailed description of the struggles between the Yemenites and the Mudar, and of the *'asabiyyah* of these tribes see Thuraya Hafiz 'Arafah, *Al-Khurasaniyun wa Dawruhum al-Siyasi fi al-'Asr al-'Abbasi al-Awwal,* Jiddah, 1982, pp.20-28. Moshe Sharon, *Black Banners from the East. The Establishment of the 'Abbasid State. Incubation of a Revolt,* Jerusalem and Leiden, 1983, passim, p.15.

(4) Cf. G.R. Hawting, *The First Dynasty of Islam,* London and Sydney, 1987, p.36. See Tabari, *Ta'rikh al-Rusul wa al-Muluk,* II, p.1497 (Leiden Edition) for a good study of the alliance between the Azd and the Rabi'ah. See also Sharon, *Black Banners,* pp.54-55, and p.58 where he explained that in Khurasan the term Yaman meant the alliance between Azd and Rabi'ah. About this see Tabari, *Ta'rikh al-Rusul wa al-Muluk,* II, p.1290 (Leiden Edition). Ya'qubi, *Ta'rikh al-Ya'qubi,* II, p.399, quoted by Sharon, *Black Banners,* p.58. The famous historian Ibn Hayyan dealt with these strange, but by no means unusual, alliances between different groups. He mentioned the alliance of the Shi'ite Husaynids and Hasanids of North Africa with 'Abd al-Rahman III, the Umayyad caliph of al-Andalus. See: Ibn Hayyan, *Al-Muqtabis fi Akhbar Balad al-Andalus. Crónica del Califa 'Abdar-rahman III an-Nasir entre los años 912 y 942,* Spanish translation by Ma. Jesús Viguera and Federico Corriente, Zaragoza, 1981, Vol. V, pp.217-226. See also: Ibn Hayyan, "Al-Hakam II y los Bereberes según un texto inédito de Ibn Hayyan", edited and Spanish translation by Emilio García Gómez, in *Al-Andalus,* XIII, 1948, pp.209-226.

(5) 'Abd al-Malik Ibn Hisham, *Sirat Rasul Allah, The Life of Muhammad,* English translation by A. Guillaume, London, 1955, passim, especially pp.450-451. For the Northerners' conversion to Islam see: pp.3-107, pp.450-451 and p.620. However, the Southern tribes also sent delegations to the Prophet and accepted Islam. About the important Southern tribe of al-Kindah: Ibn Hisham wrote: "Al-Ash'ath Ibn Qays came to the Prophet with the deputation of Kinda (and accepted Islam)" (p.641). About the Azdi he wrote: "Surad came to the apostle and became a good Muslim with the deputation from al-Azd. The apostle put him in command of those of his people who had accepted Islam and ordered him to fight the neighbouring polytheists from the tribes of the Yaman with them". (p.642) About the Kindah tribe see: Hamdani, *Kitab Sifah Jazirat al-'Arab,* p.86. For the study and understanding of al-Kindah's expansion from Yemen (Hadramawt) northward, dominating important parts of the Arabian Peninsula see: Hamdani, *Kitab Sifah Jazirat al-'Arab,* p.169. For their location between al-Sham and Iraq see: Yaqut, *Mu'jam al-Buldan,* III, p.421. See also: F. Krenkow, "Kinda", in *Encyclopaedia of Islam* (1), Vol. II, Leyden, 1927, pp.1018-1019. For a general explanation of the Arab conversion to Islam see 'Arafah, *Al-Khurasaniyun wa Dawruhum,* p.21. For a detailed description of the religions of the Arabs before Islam see Ibn Qutaybah, *Al-Ma'arif,* p.621, where he explained that Christianity was among some members of Rabi'ah, Ghassan, and Quda'ah; and Judaism among some Himyar, Banu Kinanah, Banu al-Harith b. Ka'b and Kindah. The rest were polytheists.

(6) Cf. Dinawari, *Al-Akhbar al-Tiwal,* pp.113-119. A. Fischer, "Kahtan", p.655.

(7) The Qur'an has the explanation of the spoils of war *(al-Anfal)* in *Surat al-Anfal,* VII, 1 and 41. The spoils of war have also been explained in the *Sunnah.* See: Al-Sayyid Sabiq, *Fiqh al-Sunnah,* Beirut, 1969, pp.691-692.

(8) Marín-Guzmán, "Las causas", p.39-67. Marín-Guzmán, *El Islam: Ideología e Historia,* p.144. Brockelmann, *History,* p.54. About the conquest of Iraq see: Al-Tabari, *Ta'rikh al-Umam wa al-Muluk,* Cairo, n.d. IV, p.72 (Egyptian Edition). Baladhuri, *Futuh al-Buldan,* pp.255-262. Dinawari, *Al-Akhbar al-Tiwal,* pp.119-127. Hasan, *Al-Qaba'il al-'Arabiyyah,* p.163. Francesco Gabrieli, *Mahoma y las Conquistas del Islam,* Madrid, 1967, passim. Al-Mas'udi, *Al-Tanbih wa al-Ishraf,* Beirut, 1981, pp.266-269. Abu al-'Abbas Shams al-Din b. Abi Bakr Ibn Khallikan, *Wafayat al-A'yan wa Anba' Abna' al-Zaman,* edited by Ihsan 'Abbas, Beirut, 1972, IV, pp.233 and ff. Leone

Caetani, *Annali Dell'Islam,* Milano, 1905-1926, II (2), pp.831-861. For an account of the conquest of Iraq and the taxation imposed there during the time of 'Umar Ibn al-Khattab see: Ya'qub b. Ibrahim Abu Yusuf, *Kitab al-Kharaj,* Cairo, 1392 H., pp.30-31. Baladhuri, *Futuh al-Buldan,* pp.448-449, where he asserted that the taxation impossed in Iraq by the caliph 'Umar Ibn al-Khattab was according to the Prophet's practices. See also: pp.300-301. Ya'qubi, *Ta'rikh al-Ya'qubi,* II, pp.143-144. For the *jund* administration of Iraq (Basra and Kufa) see Tabari, *Ta'rikh al-Umam wa al-Muluk,* IV, p.115 (Egyptian Edition). Ya'qubi, *Ta'rikh al-Ya'qubi,* II, pp.142-147. Ibn Qutaybah, *Al-Ma'arif,* pp.182-183.

(9) Marín-Guzmán, "Las causas", pp.39-67. Marín-Guzmán, *El Islam: Ideología e Historia,* pp.72-73. About the war of the *Riddah* and the life of the caliph Abu Bakr see Baladhuri, *Futuh al-Buldan,* pp.94-100. Jalal al-Din 'Abd al-Rahman b. Abi Bakr al-Suyuti, *Ta'rikh al-Khulafa',* edited by Muhammad Muhiy al-Din 'Abd al-Hamid, Cairo, 1964, pp.27-108. Ibn Qutaybah, *Al-Ma'arif,* pp.167-178. Ya'qubi, *Ta'rikh al-Ya'qubi,* II, pp.123-138. Abu 'Abd Allah Muhammad Ibn Yazid Ibn Majah, *Ta'rikh al-Khulafa',* edited by Muhammad Muti' al-Hafiz, Damascus, 1979, p.22. Mas'udi, *Al-Tanbih wa al-Ishraf,* pp.263-266. Leone Caetani, *Annali Dell'Islam,* II (1), pp.510-518. About the war of the *Riddah* see II (1) pp.553-561. See especially pp.727-728.

(10) Al-Baladhuri, *Ansab al-Ashraf,* edited by W. Ahlwardt, Griefswald, 1883, Vol. XI, p.282. See also Hasan, *Al-Qaba'il al-'Arabiyyah,* p.142.

(11) Abu al-'Abbas Ahmad b. Muhammad al-Maqqari, *Kitab Nafh al-Tibb,* edited by Reinhart Dozy and Guztave Dugat, Leiden, 1855-1861 (Reimpression, Amsterdam, 1967), *Muhammedan Dynasties in Spain,* English translation by Pascual de Gayangos, New York, 1964, II, p.24. It is important to bear in mind that this translation of al-Maqqari's work is poor, defficient and impreciste. The reading of the original Arabic is not only basic but absolutely necessary. In this essay most of the references to *Kitab Nafh al-Tibb* are from the original Arabic, although for some general information, and when the translation is reliable, the reader is suggested to consult the English version. See also Hasan, *Al-Qaba'il al-'Arabiyyah,* pp.39-60.

(12) Maqqari, *Nafh al-Tibb,* II, p.24. See also *Kitab al-'Uyun wa al-Hada'iq fi Akhbar al-Haqa'iq,* edited by M.J. de Goeje and P. de Jong, Leiden, 1869, Vol. III, p.3.

(13) See the major Arabic sources quoted in this essay: Tabari,

*Ta'rikh al-Rusul wa al-Muluk,* Baladhuri, *Ansab al-Ashraf,* Baladhuri, *Futuh al-Buldan,* Ibn Majah, *Ta'rikh al-Khulafa',* Suyuti, *Ta'rikh al-Khulafa',* Ibn al-Athir, *Al-Kamil fi al-Ta'rikh,* Cairo, 1290 H. (See also the Leiden-Beirut Edition, 1965). See also Istakhri, *Kitab Masalik al-Mamalik,* pp.7-9 for a good description of the extensions and the frontiers of the *Dar al-Islam.* For the settlements of the Arab tribes see pp.12-14, pp.36-55, and pp.78-88.

(14) About the importance of the various languages in the Muslim Empire, with special emphasis on Persian and Turkish in the Eastern provinces see Richard Frye, *The Golden Age of Persia,* New York, 1975, pp.202-207 and p.212. See Wellhausen, *The Arab Kingdom,* pp.492 ff., where he explained the predominance of the Persian language in Khurasan and in *Ma wara' al-Nahr,* where Arabs were forced to learn and practice the Persian language for daily activities such as the inter-relations in the market (*suq*). This fact proves that the Arabization process was slow and took many years to be completed. See also Crone, *Slaves on Horses,* p.61. For the Western provinces, especially for al-Andalus, see Ramón Menéndez Pidal, *El español en sus primeros tiempos,* Buenos Aires, 1942, pp.33-56 and pp.118-119. Ramón Menéndez Pidal, *Orígenes del español. Estado lingüístico de la Península Ibérica hasta el siglo XI,* Madrid, 1950, pp.415-440. Montgomery Watt, *Historia de la España Islámica,* Madrid, 1980, pp.173-174. E. Levi-Provençal, *España Musulmana. Instituciones y vida social e intelectual,* in Ramón Menéndez Pidal, *Historia de España,* Madrid, 1957, Vol. V, pp.118-126. Claudio Sánchez Albornoz, *El Islam de España y el Occidente,* Madrid, 1974, pp.52-56. Américo Castro, *España en su Historia: Cristianos, Moros y Judíos,* Buenos Aires, 1948, *La Realidad Histórica de España,* México, 1954. passim. Thomas Glick, *Islamic and Christian Spain in the Early Middle Ages,* Princeton, 1979, pp.135-164, and p.175. Armand Abel, "Spain: Internal Division", in Gustav von Grunebaum, *Unity and Variety in Muslim Civilization,* Chicago, 1979, pp.207-230. José Angel García de Cortázar, *La Epoca Medieval,* Madrid, 1973-1974, pp.26-32. Vicente Cantarino, *Entre Monjes y Musulmanes. El Conflicto que fue España,* Madrid, 1978, pp.96-109.

(15) For lack of a better term, I have chosen to use "Spaniards". However, the reader has to keep in mind that there was no consciousness of being "Spaniards" in the early Middle Ages, nor a clear idea of nationality. "Spaniards" implies the Christian inhabitants of the Northern Kingdoms of the Peninsula Ibérica, those descendants of the Hispano-Romans and the Visigoths.

(16) About the Reconquista wars see: Ramón Menéndez Pidal,

*La España del Cid,* Buenos Aires, 1939, passim, especially pp.23-70, pp.96-100 and pp. 483-491. Cantarino, *Entre Monjes y Musulmanes,* passim, especially pp.116-128. Watt, *Historia de la España Islámica,* passim, especially pp.123-124.

(17) Al-Baladhuri, *Ansab al-Ashraf,* edited by S.D. Goitein, Jerusalem, 1936, Vol. V, p.167. See also Ihsan Sidqi al-'Amad, *Al-Hajjaj Ibn Yusuf al-Thaqafi. Hayatuhu wa Ara'uhu al-Siyasiyyah,* Beirut, 1981, p.168. This author also asserted that Iraq became the site of the highest concentration of Arab population especially in the garrison-cities of Basra and Kufa. Riyad Mahmud Ruwayhah, *Jabbar Thaqif: Al-Hajjaj Ibn Yusuf,* Beirut, 1963, p.129. Ruwayhah asserted that Iraq was the most rebellious (*mutamarrid*) of all the provinces in the whole history of the Muslim Empire (*Dar al-Islam*). For more details about the important cities of Basra and Kufa see Ibn Qutaybah, *Al-Ma'arif,* pp.563-565.

(18) Baladhuri, *Futuh al-Buldan,* Beirut, 1957, p.636. (Beirut Edition).

(19) Maurice Gaudefroy-Demombynes, *Muslim Institutions,* London, 1954, pp.108 and ff. Marín-Guzmán, "Las causas", pp.39-67. Marín-Guzmán, *El Islam: Ideología e Historia,* pp.159-160.

(20) Baladhuri, *Futuh al-Buldan,* pp.163-165.

(21) Baladhuri, *Futuh al-Buldan,* p.212-220. (pp.298-314 of the Beirut Edition).

(22) Abu al-Qasim 'Abd al-Rahman b. 'Abd Allah Ibn 'Abd al-Hakam, *Futuh Misr wa Akhbaruha,* edited by Charles C. Torrey, Leiden, 1920, passim, especially pp.55-84, pp. 151-156 and also pp.158-161.

(23) Cf. Maqqari, *Kitab Nafh al-Tibb,* I, pp.140-141. Ya'qubi, *Ta'rikh al-Ya'qubi,* II, pp.147 ff. Ibn Qutaybah, *Al-Ma'arif,* pp.182-183, and also p.569. See Ibn Khurdadhbah, *Kitab al-Masalik wa al-Mamalik,* p.118, where he explained the conquest of Jerusalem by the caliph 'Umar Ibn al-Khattab. 'Abd al-Hamid al-Sa'ih, *Ahammiyyat al-Quds fi al-Islam,* 'Amman, 1979, pp.8-10. See also: Mu'in Ahmad Mahmud, *Ta'rikh Madinat al-Quds,* n.p., 1979, pp.54-61. For the case of al-Andalus see: Joaquín Vallvé, "España en el siglo VIII: Ejército y Sociedad", in *Al-Andalus,* XLIII, 1978, pp.51-112. E. Levi-Provençal, *España Musulmana. Hasta la caída del Califato de Córdoba (711-1031),* in Ramón Menéndez Pidal, *Historia de España,* Madrid, 1950,

Vol. IV, pp.13-19. Dozy, *Historia de los Musulmanes de España,* I, pp.190-194. Glick, *Islamic and Christian Spain,* pp.19-33. Anwar Chejne, *Muslim Spain. Its History and Culture,* Minneapolis, 1974, pp.6-10. García de Cortázar, *La Epoca Medieval,* pp.51-56. S.M. Imamuddin, *A Political History of Muslim Spain,* Karachi, 1984, pp.16-31.

(24) Tabari, *Ta'rikh al-Rusul wa al-Muluk,* passim, especially II, pp.1924-1925, pp.1934-1935, p.1937, pp.1970-1971, and p.1996 (Leiden Edition). Wellhausen, *The Arab Kingdom,* pp.397-491.

(25) Quoted by Hasan, *Al-Qaba'il al-'Arabiyyah,* p.145.

(26) Ibn 'Abd Rabbihi, *Al-'Iqd al-Farid,* III, p.330, quoted by Hasan, *Al-Qaba'il al-'Arabiyyah,* p.145.

(27) Abu Mansur 'Abd al-Qahir Ibn Tahir Ibn Muhammad al-Baghdadi, *Al-Farq bayna al-Firaq, Moslem Schisms and Sects,* English translation by Kate Chambers Seelye, New York, 1966, p.32.

(28) Quoted by Manuel Ruiz Figueroa, "Imamah o autoridad en los primeros tiempos del Islam", in *Estudios Orientales,* Vol. IX, Numbers 1-2 (24-25), 1974, pp.61-82. 'Abd Rabbihi, in his *Al-'Iqd al-Farid* (IV, p.258) quoted what Abu Bakr said to the participants in the Saqifah affair: "We the Muhajirun were the first to accept Islam; we possess the most noble pedrigree; our abode is the most central; we have the best leaders, we are nearest in kin to the Prophet of Allah." (quoted by Sharon, *Black Banners,* p.37.)

(29) 'Abd Allah Ibn Muslim Ibn Qutaybah, *Ta'wil al-Qur'an,* Cairo, 1973, p.30, quoted by Muhammad Husayn 'Ali al-Saghir, *Ta'rikh al-Qur'an,* Beirut, 1983, p.105.

(30) Al-Hafiz Jalal al-Din 'Abd al-Rahman b. Abi Bakr al-Suyuti, *Al-Itqan fi 'Ulum al-Qur'an,* edited by Muhammad Abu al-Fadl Ibrahim, Cairo, 1967, I, p.47, quoted by Muhammad Husayn 'Ali al-Saghir, *Ta'rikh al-Qur'an,* p.105.

(31) Ibn Hisham, *Sirat Rasul Allah,* p.691. See also p.642 where Ibn Hisham explained how the Qahtan accepted and submitted to Islam. In various chapters of his work Ibn Hisham quoted several leaders who came to the Prophet to express their submission to Islam. See Hasan, *Al-Qaba'il al-'Arabiyyah,* pp.13-14.

(32) Ibn Hisham, *Sirat Rasul Allah,* p.691.

(33) Ibn 'Abd al-Hakam, *Futuh Ifriqiyyah wa al-Andalus, La Conquista de Africa del Norte y de España,* Spanish translation by Eliseo Vidal Beltrán, Valencia, 1966, pp.49-50. It is important to bear in mind that this translation into Spanish is only one section of Ibn 'Abd al-Hakam's *Futuh Misr wa Akhbaruha.* Ibn al-Athir, *Al-Kamil fi al-Ta'rikh,* IV, pp.539-540, and for particular information about the conquest of al-Andalus see IV, pp.556-567. (Leiden-Beirut Edition). *Akhbar Majmu'ah,* edited and Spanish translation by Emilio Lafuente y Alcántara, Madrid, 1867, pp.18-20 (pp.30-31 of the Spanish translation). 'Abd Allah Ibn Muslim Ibn Qutaybah, *Al-Imamah wa al-Siyasah,* edited by Taha Muhammad al-Zayni, n.p., 1967, II, pp.69-70, pp.71-77 and pp.82-86. Ya'qubi, *Ta'rikh al-Ya'qubi,* II, p.285, see also II, pp.294 ff. Ibn Qutiyyah al-Qurtubi, *Ta'rikh Iftitah al-Andalus,* edited and Spanish translation (*Historia de la Conquista de España*) by Julián Ribera, Madrid, 1926, pp.10-11 (pp.7-8 of the Spanish translation). In this respect the chronicles vary, since in Ibn Qutiyyah's work Musa Ibn Nusayr entered the court of al-Walid before the caliph's death. About the caliph al-Walid I see *Al-'Uyun wa al-Hada'iq fi Akhbar al-Haqa'iq,* III, pp.2-16. Ya'qubi, *Ta'rikh al-Ya'qubi,* II, pp.283-292. Ibn Qutaybah, *Al-Ma'arif,* p.359. Regarding al-Walid's building of several mosques and other public constructions see *Al-'Uyun wa al-Hada'iq fi Akhbar al-Haqa'iq,* III, pp.4-5 and also III, p.12. Angel González Palencia, *Historia de la España Musulmana,* Barcelona, 1925, p.9. Dozy, *Historia de los Musulmanes de España,* I, pp.339-357. Levi-Provençal, *España Musulmana. Hasta la Caída del Califato,* pp.18-19. Chejne, *Muslim Spain,* p.9.

(34) *Akhbar Majmu'ah,* passim, especially pp.6-7 (p.21 of the Spanish translation). Ibn Qutiyyah, *Ta'rikh Iftitah al-Andalus,* pp.4-6 (pp.2-3 of the Spanish translation). Ibn 'Abd al-Hakam, *Futuh Ifriqiyyah wa al-Andalus,* pp.41-42. Ibn Qutaybah, *Al-Imamah wa al-Siyasah,* II, pp.60-62. Baladhuri, *Futuh al-Buldan,* pp.230-235. For a study of the *mawali* formation of the armies which conquered al-Andalus see Crone, *Slaves on Horses,* p.53.

(35) See Ibn Khallikan, *Wafayat al-A'yan,* IV, pp.86-87. *Akhbar Majmu'ah,* pp.6-7 (pp.20-21 of the Spanish translation). Crone, *Slaves on Horses,* p.53. About the discrimination against the *mawali* who were not being paid for their services in the armies which they enlisted, see Tabari, *Ta'rikh al-Rusul wa al-Muluk,* II, p.1354. (Leiden Edition).

(36) About the origin of the Umayyad dynasty and Mu'awiyah Ibn Abi Sufyan see Ibn Majah, Ta'rikh al-Khulafa', p.27. Suyuti, *Ta'rikh al-*

*Khulafa'*, pp.194-205. See also Ibn Qutaybah, *Al-Ma'arif*, pp.344-345 and also pp.349-350. Ya'qubi, *Ta'rikh al-Ya'qubi*, II, pp.216-224. See also 'Amad, *Al-Hajjaj Ibn Yusuf al-Thaqafi*, pp.43-48. Kennedy, *Prophet*, pp.83 ff. The people of Syria gave Mu'awiyah the *bay'ah*. See Ibn Qutaybah, *Al-Imamah wa al-Siyasah*, I, p.74. For a detailed description of Mu'awiyah Ibn Abi Sufyan's life and activities see Abu al-Hasan Ahmad b. Yahya al-Baladhuri, *Ansab al-Ashraf*, edited by Max Schloessinger, Jerusalem, 1971, Vol. IV A, pp.11-138. For the *bay'ah* to Yazid Ibn Mu'awiyah and the actual practice of a dynastic system see Al-Baladhuri, *Ansab al-Ashraf*, edited by Max Schloessinger, Jerusalem, 1938, Vol. IV B, pp.12-13. Ibn Qutaybah, *Al-Imamah wa al-Siyasah*, I, pp.174-175. It is important to underline the fact that Arabic sources are not objective when dealing with the Umayyad dynasty, especially those written during the 'Abbasid period. Some early Arabic sources do not consider the Umayyads as legitimite rulers. On the contrary, they are considered usurpers. A clear example of such sources is Abu al-Hasan 'Ali b. Husayn b. 'Ali al-Mas'udi, who in his *Al-Tanbih wa al-Ishraf* explained the government of the *Rashidun* caliphs as *khilafah*, i.e. caliphate, as well as those of the 'Abbasids up to al-Mustakfi and al-Muti' al-Fadl, his contemporaries. In al-Mas'udi's opinion, all the Umayyad rulers were not caliphs but kings, with the only exception of 'Umar Ibn 'Abd al-'Aziz. Al-Mas'udi did not explain their tenures as rulers as *khilafahs*, but instead he used the term *ayyam* (the days or the period) of each one of the Umayyad rulers, with the exception already mentioned. For example, the biography of Mu'awiyah is introduced with the title *Ayyam Mu'awiyah Ibn Abi Sufyan*. Al-Mas'udi also considered al-Hasan b. 'Ali Ibn Abi Talib a caliph, and his biography is introduced with the title *Khilafat al-Hasan b. 'Ali 'alaihi al-Salam*. For more details see Mas'udi, *Al-Tanbih wa al-Ishraf*, pp.276-278.

(37) Ibn Majah, *Ta'rikh al-Khulafa'*, p.28. Suyuti, *Ta'rikh al-Khulafa'*, pp.205-210. Mas'udi, *Al-Tanbih wa al-Ishraf*, pp.278-281. For a general account of Yazid Ibn Mu'awiyah see Baladhuri, *Ansab al-Ashraf*, IV B, pp.1-11. Ya'qubi, *Ta'rikh al-Ya'qubi*, II, pp.241-242. Ibn Qutaybah, *Al-Ma'arif*, pp.351-352.

(38) Ibn Majah, *Ta'rikh al-Khulafa'*, pp.28-29. Suyuti, *Ta'rikh al-Khulafa'*, pp.210-211. Mas'udi, *Al-Tanbih wa al-Ishraf*, p.281. Baladhuri, *Ansab al-Ashraf*, IV B, pp.62-65. 'Amad, *Al-Hajjaj Ibn Yusuf al-Thaqafi*, p.114. About the Banu of Abu Sufyan see Baladhuri, *Ansab al-Ashraf*, IV B, passim, especially pp.124-149. H. Lammens,"Mo'awiya II ou le dernier Sofianides", in *Rivista degli Studi Orientali*, Vol. VII, Fascicolo 1, 1916, pp.1-49.

(39) Al-Tabari, *Ta'rikh al-Umam wa al-Muluk*, II, p.161 (Egyptian Edition).

(40) Michael Morony, *Iraq after the Muslim Conquest*, Princeton,1984, pp.248-249. Hasan, *Al-Qaba'il al-'Arabiyyah*, pp.21-38. The Azd was one of the most important Arab tribes, with more than 27 subdivisions, that are currently called Qahtan. See Hasan, *Al-Qaba'il al-'Arabiyyah*, p.22. About these subdivisions see also Yaqut, *Mu'jam al-Buldan*, III, pp. 330 and ff. About their mobilization from the areas they previously inhabitated, especially near Mecca and the Northern parts of the Hijaz, to al-Sham, see 'Abd al-Rahman Ibn Khaldun, *Kitab al-'Ibar wa Diwan al-Mubtada wa al-Khabar*, Beirut, 1956, II, pp.524-528. About Khurasan as a frontier of the Muslim Empire see Hamdani, *Kitab Sifah Jazirat al-'Arab*, p.32. For a clear description of Khurasan as a frontier region near the Turkish land (*Ard al-Turk*) see p.38 and p.43.

(41) Baladhuri, *Ansab al-Ashraf*, V, pp.132-133 and also pp.136-140. Tabari, *Ta'rikh al-Rusul wa al- Muluk*, II, pp.468-483. (Leiden Edition). See also Ibn Qutaybah, *Al-Imamah wa al-Siyasah*, II, pp.12-13. Hasan, *Al-Qaba'il al-'Arabiyyah*, p.179. 'Amad, *Al-Hajjaj Ibn Yusuf al-Thaqafi*, p.113. Ya'qubi, *Ta'rikh al-Ya'qubi*, II, pp.255-256 explained that after Yazid Ibn Mu'awiyah's death several tribes supported Ibn al-Zubayr in the Hijaz and in many other places of the Muslim Empire. Al-Ya'qubi provided a list of the various representatives of Ibn al-Zubayr in such places as Hims, Kufa, Basra, Damascus, Filastin (Palestine), Qinnasrin, Khurasan and in Egypt. Al-Ya'qubi even mentioned that the people of Egypt were in submission ( lit. obedience) to Ibn al-Zubayr. He wrote: "*Wa Ahl Misr fi Ta'atihi [Ibn al-Zubayr]*." For more details see Ya'qubi, *Ta'rikh al-Ya'qubi*, II, pp.255 ff. See also Ibn Qutaybah, *Al-Ma'arif*, pp.356 ff. Kennedy, *Prophet*, p.87, p.91 and p.93. Crone, *Slaves on Horses*, pp.34-36.

(42) About Marwan b. al-Hakam see Ibn Majah, *Ta'rikh al-Khulafa'*, p.29. Mas'udi, *Al-Tanbih wa al-Ishraf*, pp.282-286. About Mu'awiyya Ibn Yazid see Suyuti, *Ta'rikh al-Khulafa'*, pp.210-211. Mas'udi, *Al-Tanbih wa al-Ishraf*, p.281. Ibn Qutaybah, *Al-Imamah wa al-Siyasah*, II, pp.10-11. Ibn Qutaybah, *Al-Ma'arif*, pp.353-358. Brockelmann, *History*, pp.76-78.

(43) Roberto Marín-Guzmán, "La Escatología Musulmana: Análisis del Mahdismo", *Cuadernos de Historia,* Number 44, University of Costa Rica, San José, Costa Rica, 1982, passim. Marín-Guzmán, *El Islam: Ideología e Historia*, pp.170-172. Wellhausen, *The Arab King-*

*dom,* passim, especially pp.159-160 and p.181.

(44) Baladhuri, *Futuh al-Buldan,* p.414. About the support of the Northern tribes to the revolt of Ibn al-Zubayr see Baladhuri, *Ansab al-Ashraf,* V, pp.136-140. See also 'Amad, *Al-Hajjaj Ibn Yusuf al-Thaqafi,* p.113, where he makes the interesting observation that the Northern tribes joined and supported Ibn al-Zubayr for fear of the power the Yemenites were gaining through the Umayyads' support.

(45) M.A. Shaban, *El Islam,* Madrid, 1976, I, pp.106-107. Marín-Guzmán, *El Islam: Ideología e Historia,* pp.135-162.

(46) Hasan, *Al-Qaba'il al-'Arabiyyah,* pp.179-182 and pp.183-189.

(47) Muhammad Diya' al-Din al-Rayyis, *'Abd al-Malik b. Marwan wa al-Dawlat al-Umawiyyah,* Cairo, 1969?, pp.46-48. 'Abd al-Wahid Dhannun Taha, *Al-'Iraq fi 'Ahd al-Hajjaj Ibn Yusuf al-Thaqafi,* Mosul, 1985, pp.204-205. Crone, *Slaves on Horses,* pp.37-39.

(48) About al-Hajjaj's role in taxation in Iraq and the development of the institution of the *Iqta'* see Abu Yusuf, *Kitab al-Kharaj,* p.63 'Amad, *Al-Hajjaj Ibn Yusuf al-Thaqafi,* passim, especially pp.23-24 and pp.85-87. Ihsan Sidqi al-'Amad discusses in his book (pp.85-87 and also p.101) the origins and development of the relations between the Thaqafi tribe (mainly located in Ta'if) and the Umayyads. These relations were improved mainly in the *Khilafah* of Marwan b. al-Hakam, when al-Hajjaj Ibn Yusuf and his father participated in the administration of Fustat in Egypt. The Arabic sources are contradictory about the time when al-Hajjaj and his father left Egypt for Syria, either in the time of Marwan b. al-Hakam or 'Abd al-Malik b. Marwan. However, the sources coincide in the point that both, al-Hajjaj and his father, joined in Syria the military expedition that the caliph Marwan b. al-Hakam had organized to stop the *fitnah* led by 'Abd Allah Ibn al-Zubayr in the Hijaz. Whether or not that meant that they moved to al-Sham is still a point under discussion. Later on, a Thaqafi, (al-Hajjaj Ibn Yusuf) working for the Umayyads defeated 'Abd Allah Ibn al-Zubayr in the Hijaz. Al-Hajjaj was also the architect of the caliph 'Abd al-Malik's reforms. For al-Hajjaj's activities in Ta'if see also Ibn Qutaybah, *Al-Ma'arif,* p.548. See also the following sources: 'Amad, *Al-Hajjaj Ibn Yusuf al-Thaqafi,* pp.385-386. Ibn 'Abd al-Hakam, *Futuh Misr wa Akhbaruha,* pp.109 and ff. Ruwayhah, *Jabbar Thaqif: Al-Hajjaj Ibn Yusuf,* passim, especially p.112 and pp.128-142. Taha, *Al-'Iraq fi 'Ahd al-Hajjaj Ibn Yusuf al-Thaqafi,* pp.26-27. See also Ibn Qutaybah, *Al-Ma'arif,* pp.396-397. For al-Hajjaj Ibn Yusuf's *bay'ah* to

'Abd al-Malik b. Marwan see *Al-'Uyun wa al-Hada'iq fi Akhbar al-Haqa'iq,* III, p.9; see III, pp.10-11 for al-Hajjaj's administrative positions. Kennedy, *Prophet,* p.100. Crone, *Slaves on Horses,* pp.42 ff. 'Umar Ibn 'Abd al-'Aziz followed the *Iqta'* Institution. See Yahya Ibn Adam al-Qurashi, *Kitab al-Kharaj,* Lahore, 1395 H. pp.83-89. Rayyis, *'Abd al-Malik b. Marwan,* pp. 187-193. Morony, *Iraq after the Muslim Conquest,* pp.37-38 and also p.95. About al-Hajjaj's role in the *shurtah* of Damascus see Ibn 'Abd Rabbihi, *Al-'Iqd al-Farid,* V, p.14. For a general study of the *iqta'* and its evolution see Cahen, *Les peuples musulmans,* pp.231-269. About al-Hajjaj's governorship of Iraq see: Ibn al-Athir, *Al-Kamil fi al-Ta'rikh,* IV, pp.374-380. About his position in Basra see: IV, pp.380-387. (Leiden-Beirut Edition).

(49) Cf. Arthur Pope, *An Introduction to Persian Art since the Seventeenth Century,* London, 1930, passim. Roberto Marín-Guzmán, "El Islam, una religión", in *Crónica,* Number 3, 1982, pp.81-90. Marín-Guzmán, *El Islam: Ideología e Historia,* pp.107-121. Concerning the mint which struck the first Muslim dirhams in Arabic without images, in 695 or 696, see Tabari, *Ta'rikh al-Rusul wa al-Muluk,* II, p.939 (Leiden Edition). See also Baladhuri, *Futuh al-Buldan,* pp.465-466, who thinks that the first totally epigraphic Muslim coins were minted in 693 and 694 and not in 695-696. Abu al-Hasan Muhammad b. Habib al-Mawardi, *Al-Ahkam al-Sultaniyyah wa al-Wilayat al-Diniyyah,* Cairo, n.d., pp.76-77. Taha, *Al-'Iraq fi 'Ahd al-Hajjaj Ibn Yusuf al-Thaqafi,* pp.164-166, especially p.165. For the Islamic mint see Morony, *Iraq after the Muslim Conquest,* pp.38-51. Taha, *Al-'Iraq fi 'Ahd al-Hajjaj Ibn Yusuf al-Thaqafi,* pp.160-181. Kennedy, *Prophet,* p.88.

(50) Ibn Majah, *Ta'rikh al-Khulafa',* p.29. Mas'udi, *Al-Tanbih wa al-Ishraf,* pp.282-286. Kennedy, *Prophet,* p.93.

(51) Baladhuri, *Ansab al-Ashraf,* VI, p.240 (manuscript) quoted by Hasan, *Al-Qaba'il al-'Arabiyyah,* p.138. See also Ibn Qutaybah, *Al-Ma'arif,* p.357, where he explained the appointment of al-Hajjaj as governor of Iraq by the caliph 'Abd al-Malik b. Marwan after al-Hajjaj had defeated Ibn al-Zubayr in the Hijaz and had started the reconstruction of the Ka'bah in Mecca. See also Ibn Qutaybah, *Al-Ma'arif,* pp.396-397.

(52) Tabari, *Ta'rikh al-Rusul wa al-Muluk,* II, p.1018 (Leiden Edition). Baghdadi, *Al-Farq bayna al-Firaq,* passim. Baladhuri, *Ansab al-Ashraf,* IV B, pp.90-94. Ibn al-Athir, *Al-Kamil fi al-Ta'rikh,* IV, pp.365-367 and IV, pp.437-439 (Leiden-Beirut Edition). Abu 'Ali Ahmad Ibn 'Umar Ibn Rustah, *Kitab al-A'laq al-Nafisah,* edited by

M.J. de Goeje, Leiden, 1892, p.217. Henri Laoust, *Les schismes dans l'Islam*, Paris, 1977, pp.40-41. Morony, *Iraq after the Muslim Conquest*, pp.473-475. Montgomery Watt, *Free Will and Predestination in Early Islam*, London, 1948, pp.36-37. Watt, *The Formative Period*, passim, especially pp.20-21. 'Amad, *Al-Hajjaj Ibn Yusuf al-Thaqafi*, passim, especially pp.229-249. About the *Azariqah Khawarij* group see pp.232-239. About the *Shabibiyyah* see pp.240-249. See also Ruwayhah, *Jabbar Thaqif: Al-Hajjaj Ibn Yusuf*, pp.154-156. Taha, *Al-'Iraq fi 'Ahd al-Hajjaj Ibn Yusuf al-Thaqafi*, passim, especially pp.97-101. Kennedy, *Prophet*, p.98. Francesco Gabrieli, "Sulle origini del movimento Harigita", in *Rendiconti dell' Accademia Nazionale dei Lincei Classe di Scienze Morali e Storiche*, Vol. III, Fascicolo 6, Novembre, 1941, pp.110-117. About al-Hajjaj facing the *Azariqah* in Iraq see Ya'qubi, *Ta'rikh al-Ya'qubi*, II, pp.275-276. Crone, *Slaves on Horses*, p.39. For the study of the Syrian troops sent to fight the *Azariqah* in Tabaristan see Tabari, *Ta'rikh al-Rusul wa al- Muluk*, II, p.1018 (Leiden Edition). Baladhuri, *Ansab al-Ashraf*, XI, pp.338 ff. Against Shahib in Iraq see Tabari, *Ta'rikh al-Rusul wa al-Muluk*, II, pp.943 ff. (Leiden Edition).

(53) Brockelmann, *History*, p.89. Hawting, *The First Dynasty of Islam*, p.67. Kennedy, *Prophet*, p.102. About Wasit see Ibn al-Athir, *Al-Kamil fi al-Ta'rikh*, IV, pp.495-497 (Leiden-Beirut Edition). Hamdani, *Kitab Sifah Jazirat al-'Arab*, p.148. Morony, *Iraq after the Muslim Conquest*, pp.158-159. 'Amad, *Al-Hajjaj Ibn Yusuf al-Thaqafi*, pp.443-454. This author asserted (p.443) that the real reason behind the foundation and construction of Wasit was for al-Hajjaj to have a new capital for the administration and control of his province (*wilayah*), and to be able to control the Arab tribes as well. Yaqut (*Mu'jam al-Buldan*, V, p.348) asserted that those who populated Wasit, besides the Syrian troops, were generally Iraqi Arabs, especially people from Kufa, who supported al-Hajjaj. See also Yaqut, *Mu'jam al-Buldan*, IV, p.883, where he explained that al-Hajjaj wanted to build a new and special city for his administrative purposes as he did not wish to remain in Kufa. Tabari, *Ta'rikh al-Rusul wa al-Muluk*, VI, pp.383-384 (Egyptian Edition, 1969-1970). See also: Tabari, *Ta'rikh al-Rusul wa al-Muluk*, II, p.1125 (Leiden Edition). Ibn Qutaybah, *Al-Ma'arif*, p.357, where he explained that al-Hajjaj built Wasit in the year 83 H. Among Muslim historians and geographers there is no concensus about the reasons why the city was called Wasit. For a good discussion in this respect and for a comparison of what the various Arabic sources say, see Taha, *Al-'Iraq fi 'Ahd al-Hajjaj Ibn Yusuf al-Thaqafi*, pp.153-154. Muhammad b. Ahmad b. Abi Bakr al-Banna al-Muqaddasi, *Ahsan al-Taqasim fi Ma'rifat al-Aqalim*, Beirut, (reimpression of the 1906 Leiden Edition), n.d., p.118.

(54) See: Ibn Khallikan, *Wafayat al-A'yan*, IV, p.87. Kennedy, *Prophet*, p.103. Ibn al-Athir, *Al-Kamil fi al-Ta'rikh*, IV, pp.571-576. (Leiden-Beirut Edition). Ahmad Ibn Abi Ya'qub al- Ya'qubi, *Kitab al-Buldan*, edited by M.J. de Goeje, Leiden, 1892, pp.293-294. Dinawari, *Al-Akhbar al-Tiwal*, pp.327-328. *Al-'Uyun wa al-Hada'iq fi Akhbar al-Haqa'iq*, III, p.2. Ya'qubi, *Ta'rikh al-Ya'qubi*, II, pp.286-287.

(55) Abu Bakr Muhammad Ibn Ja'far Narshakhi, *Ta'rikh i-Bukhara, Description topographique et historique de Boukhara avant et pendant la conquête par les arabes*, Amsterdam, 1975 (1892). *History of Bukhara*, English translation by Richard Frye, Cambridge, Massachusetts, 1954, pp.47-55. Kennedy, *Prophet*, p.103. Cf. Ibn Khallikan, *Wafayat al-A'yan*, IV, pp.86-87. Ya'qubi, *Ta'rikh al-Ya'qubi*, II, pp.285-286. Ibn al-Athir, *Al-Kamil fi al-Ta'rikh*, IV, p.535 and p.542. (Leiden-Beirut Edition). Ya'qubi, *Kitab al-Buldan*, pp.292-293.. Dinawari, *Al-Akhbar al-Tiwal*, pp.327-328. Wellhausen, *The Arab Kingdom*, pp.437-438. Ruwayhah, *Jabbar Thaqif: Al-Hajjaj Ibn Yusuf*, p.192.

(56) Hamilton Gibb, *The Arab Conquests in Central Asia*, New York, 1970, pp.32-35. Richard Frye, *Bukhara, the Medieval Achievement*, Norman, Oklahoma, 1965, p.15. Ruwayhah, *Jabbar Thaqif: Al-Hajjaj Ibn Yusuf*, p.192.

(57) Ibn Khallikan, *Wafayat al-A'yan*, IV, p.87. *Al-'Uyun wa al-Hada'iq fi Akhbar al-Haqa'iq*, III, p.2. Ya'qubi, *Ta'rikh al-Ya'qubi*, II, p.286. Kennedy, *Prophet*, p.104.

(58) Ya'qubi, *Kitab al-Buldan*, p.294. 'Ali Bahjat, *Qamus al-Amkinah wa al-Biqa' al-Lati Yaridu Dhikruha fi Kutub al-Futuh*, Egypt (Cairo ?) 1906, pp.160-161. Ibn Khallikan, *Wafayat al-A'yan*, IV, pp.87-88. See also Gibb, *The Arab Conquests*, pp.52-53. M.A. Shaban, *The 'Abbasid Revolution*, Cambridge, 1970. pp.69-70. Wellhausen, *The Arab Kingdom*, p.436. Ruwayhah, *Jabbar Thaqif: Al-Hajjaj Ibn Yusuf*, p.192. For Farghana as one of the frontiers of *Dar al-Islam* see Istakhri, *Kitab Masalik al-Mamalik*, p.6 and also pp.11-12.

(59) Wellhausen, *The Arab Kingdom*, pp.434-439. Ibn Khallikan, *Wafayat al-A'yan*, IV, pp.86-91. Elton Daniel, *The Political and Social History of the Khurasan under 'Abbasid Rule, 747-820*, Minneapolis, 1979, passim. Shaban, *The 'Abbasid Revolution*, pp.69-70. Hawting, *The First Dynasty of Islam*, pp.84-85. Brockelmann, *History*, pp.82-83. Taha, *Al-'Iraq fi 'Ahd al-Hajjaj Ibn Yusuf al-Thaqafi*, pp.218-219.

About the *bay'ah* to al-Walid see Ibn al-Athir, *Al-Kamil fi al-Ta'rikh*, IV, pp.513-515 and IV, pp.522-523 (Leiden-Beirut Edition). Dinawari, *Al-Akhbar al-Tiwal*, p.326. About the careful policies of the caliph al-Walid I and Qutaybah Ibn Muslim's military campaigns in Central Asia see *Al-'Uyun wa al-Hada'iq fi Akhbar al-Haqa'iq*, III, pp.11 ff.

(60) Tabari, *Ta'rikh al-Rusul wa al-Muluk*, II, p.1181 (Leiden Edition). See also Ibn Khallikan, *Wafayat al-A'yan*, IV, pp.86-87.

(61) About the caliph Sulayman see Ibn Majah, *Ta'rikh al-Khulafa'*, pp.31-32. Dinawari, *Al-Akhbar al-Tiwal*, pp.329-330. Suyuti, *Ta'rikh al-Khulafa'*, pp.225-228. Mas'udi, *Al-Tanbih wa al-Ishraf*, p.291. Mas'udi, *Muruj al-Dhahab*, V, pp.396-415. For more details about Sulayman's *khilafah* see *Al-'Uyun wa al-Hada'iq fi Akhbar al-Haqa'iq*, III, pp.16-37. Ya'qubi, *Ta'rikh al-Ya'qubi*, II, pp.293-300. About Qutaybah Ibn Muslim's revolt see Tabari, *Ta'rikh al-Rusul wa al-Muluk*, II, p.1238 (Leiden Edition). Baladhuri, *Futuh al-Buldan*, pp.422-424.

(62) Baladhuri, *Ansab al-Ashraf*, XI, p.282.

(63) Ibn al-Athir, *Al-Kamil fi al-Ta'rikh*, IV, p.159.(Cairo Edition). For a good study of the relations between al-Muhallab and al-Hajjaj see Dinawari, *Al-Akhbar al-Tiwal*, pp.277-280. Patricia Crone in her *Slaves on Horses*, p.43 asserts that al-Hajjaj Ibn Yusuf did not favor the Qays confederation of tribes over the Yemenites. To support this idea she provides a list of the subgovernors under al-Hajjaj (Apendix III, numbers 1 to 47) in which a fair division of power and positions between the two confederations of tribes is clearly demonstrated. However it is important to keep in mind that al-Hajjaj, a brilliant leader and a very skillful politician, tried to keep a balance between the tribes, but in the long run his policies favored the Qays over the Yemenites in positions of power and in land ownership, as it is proven by the evidence in the Arabic sources. Al-Hajjaj started a school of rulers under his influence who followed his policies. Notably these rulers were mainly from the Qays group. About the replacement of of Yazid Ibn al-Muhallab by Qutaybah Ibn Muslim al-Bahali see *Al-'Uyun wa al-Hada'iq fi Akhbar al-Haqa'iq*, III, pp.2-3. See also Ya'qubi, *Ta'rikh al-Ya'qubi*, II, p.285, where he explained that al-Hajjaj removed Yazid Ibn al-Muhallab from the governorship of Khurasan and appointed al-Mufaddil and later Qutaybah Ibn Muslim al-Bahali.

(64) Hasan, *Al-Qaba'il al-'Arabiyyah*, pp.163-182. For the Arab settlements after the conquests (*futuh*) see: pp.163-179. For a study of

the tribes after Yazid Ibn Mu'awiyah's death see: pp.179-180. For the Qays settlements in Khurasan see: pp.181-182. For the Tamim: pp.183-189. For the Azd settlements and alliances with other tribes: pp.189-191. For an account of some of the struggles between Ibn al-Ash'ath and al-Hajjaj Ibn Yusuf see Mas'udi, *Al-Tanbih wa al-Ishraf*, pp.288-289. For the events taking place in Kufa and Basra see p.288. Ibn al-Athir, *Al-Kamil fi al-Ta'rikh*, IV, pp.467-469 and also IV, pp.501-502. For more details see: IV, pp.413-416 and IV, pp.461-462 (Leiden-Beirut Edition). Ibn Qutaybah, *Al-Ma'arif*, p.357. Ya'qubi, *Ta'rikh al-Ya'qubi*, II, pp.277-279. Dinawari, *Al-Akhbar al-Tiwal*, pp.316-324. Ruwayhah, *Jabbar Thaqif: Al-Hajjaj Ibn Yusuf*, pp.172-176. About the historic fact that Yazid Ibn al- Muhallab sent back to al-Hajjaj only the Qays followers of Ibn al-Ash'ath see: p.174. Kennedy, *Prophet*, p.102. Tabari, *Ta'rikh al-Rusul wa al-Muluk*, II, pp.1318 ff. (Leiden Edition).

(65) See: Hellmut von Ritter, "Studien zur Geschichte der Islamischen Frömmigkeit I -Hasan al-Basri", in *Der Islam*, XXI, 1933, pp.1-83. See especially pp.50-52. About Ibn al-Ash`ath's opposition to al-Hajjaj see Ruwayhah, *Jabbar Thaqif: Al-Hajjaj Ibn Yusuf*, pp.169-170. Taha, *Al-`Iraq fi `Ahd al-Hajjaj Ibn Yusuf al-Thaqafi*, pp.84-90. This author analyses the role of religion in this revolt, which was supported by a great number of *qurra'* and *fuqaha'* (pp.84-87). On the other hand, Taha also emphasizes the idea that al-Hajjaj appealed to Islam as well. Al-Hajjaj considered those supporting Ibn al-Ash`ath infidels (*kafir*) and enemies of Islam. (pp.85-86). About the support of the *qurra'* and the *fuqaha'* to Ibn al-Ash`ath see Baladhuri, *Ansab al-Ashraf*, XI, p.326, where he explained that the religious people gave the *bay`ah* to Ibn al-Ash`ath over the Book of God and the *Sunnah* of His Prophet. Tabari, *Ta'rikh al-Rusul wa al-Muluk*, II, p.1058 (Leiden Edition). Kennedy, *Prophet*, pp.101-102.

(66) Hans Heinrich Schaeder, "Hasan al-Basri. Studien zur Frühgeschichte des Islam", in *Der Islam*, XIV, 1925, pp.1-75. According to al-Tabari, al-Hasan al-Basri criticized al-Hajjaj with strong words. (Tabari, *Ta'rikh al-Rusul waal-Muluk*, II, p.1058, Leiden Edition). For more details about al-Hasan al-Basri see Ibn Khallikan, *Wafayat al-A`yan*, II, pp.69-73. Ibn Khallikan provided al-Hasan al-Basri's genealogy, which is important for the understanding of his *mawla* condition, since his father was a *mawla* of Ziyad b. Thabit al-Ansari. See also Ibn Qutaybah, *Al-Ma`arif*, pp.440-441, who also provided al-Hasan al-Basri's genealogy, which shows his *mawla* condition, as client of al-Ansari. Muhammad b. Sa`d b. Muni' Ibn Sa`d, *Kitab al- Tabaqat al-Kubra*, Leiden, 1905-1921, VII, p.156, quoted by Taha, *Al-`Iraq fi `Ahd al-Hajjaj Ibn Yusuf al-Thaqafi*, p.87. Wellhausen, *The Arab Kingdom*, p.286.

(67) Ritter, "Studien", pp.50-51. See also Morony, *Iraq after the Muslim Conquest*, p.479. Al-Hasan al-Basri's reputation and knowledge of Muslim traditions is reported in several matters, taxation in Islam not excepted. In this respect see Abu Yusuf, *Kitab al-Kharaj*, passim, especially pp.11, 13, 20, 53, etc. Ibn Sa`d, *Kitab al-Tabaqat al-Kabir*, VII, pp.118-119, quoted by Taha, *Al-`Iraq fi `Asr al-Hajjaj Ibn Yusuf al-Thaqafi*, p.87. Ibn Qutaybah in his *Al-Ma`arif* (p.441) preserved some of the various traditions praising al-Hasan al-Basri, his personality, knowledge and works.

(68) See: Ibn Qutaybah, *'Uyun al-Akhbar,* edited by Carl Brockelmann, Berlin, 1900-1908, (4 Vols.) II, passim. Morony, *Iraq after the Muslim Conquest*, pp.482-483. Ruwayhah, *Jabbar Thaqif: Al-Hajjaj Ibn Yusuf,* p.168. See Taha, *Al-'Iraq fi 'Ahd al-Hajjaj Ibn Yusuf al-Thaqafi*, p.87 and also p.94 where he mentioned from the manuscript of Ahmad b. 'Uthman Ibn A'tham's *Futuh* (II, p.106 b) that the instruction of the caliph 'Abd al-Malik b. Marwan to his brother Muhammad b. Marwan and his son 'Abd Allah, to whom he sent to stop this revolt, was to submit the Iraqis by expelling the Syrians from the Iraqis' houses. These instructions were influential in stopping the rebellion in hopes of ending the Syrian presence in those regions. Moreover, the offer of a general pardon by al-Hajjaj was also vital. However, the presence of Syrian troops was very important. See Tabari, *Ta'rikh al-Rusul wa al-Muluk*, II, pp.1060 ff. (Leiden Edition).

(69) Cf. Ibn Khallikan, *Wafayat al-A`yan*, VI, pp.278-309. Tabari, *Ta'rikh al-Rusul wa al-Muluk*, II, pp.1360 ff., especially p.1361. (Leiden Edition). Gabrieli, "La rivolta", passim. Shaban, *The 'Abbasid Revolution*, passim, especially pp.93-96. For an account of the support of the *mawali* to Yazid Ibn al-Muhallab's revolt see Tabari, *Ta'rikh al-Rusul wa al-Muluk*, II, p.1381 and II, p.1403 (Leiden Edition).

(70) Cf. Schaeder, "Hasan al-Basri", pp.70-71. Despite the fact that the caliph Yazid II's behavior offended religious people, al-Hasan al-Basri criticized and opposed Ibn al-Muhallab's rebellion and his calls to follow the *Qur'an* and the *Sunnah* in the resistance against the Umayyads. See also pp.68-69. See Tabari, *Ta'rikh al-Rusul wa al-Muluk*, II, pp.1400 and ff. (Leiden Edition). Ritter, "Studien zur", pp.50-52 and ff. Gabrieli, "La rivolta", p.209 and pp.219-221.

(71) Ibn Khallikan, *Wafayat al-A'yan*, VI, pp.278-309. Ibn Khallikan in this respect wrote: *Rama al-Khilafah li-nafsihi.* See also Baladhuri, *Ansab al-Ashraf*, 710 b from the Constantinople manuscript, quoted by Francesco Gabrieli, "La rivolta", p.216. Francesco

Gabrieli in this respect wrote the following lines ("La rivolta", pp.214-215): " É chiaro da questa formula un netto programma di auton-omismo 'iraqeno di fronte alla Siria, come già aveva tentato 'Abd ar-rahman ibn al-As'at; meno chiara è la questione se e quando Yazid si sia formalmente fatto riconoscere califfo; giacchè il 1 *sawwal*, come ap-prendiamo sempre da Baladuri-FHA, nel *'id al-fitr,* in una cerimonia sulla musallà di Basrah che non sembra sia da identificare con la hutbah suaccennata nella moschea maggiore all'indomani dalla vitto-ria su 'Adi, Yazid ripudiava sí solennemente il califfo Yazid b. 'Abd al-Malik e anatematizzava la dinastia omayyade, ma al tempo stesso *da'a ila r-rida min Bani Hashim,* cioè solleticava il legittimismo *'alide-'abbasidico,* e se ciò è esatto non poteva certo contemporane-amente presentare se stesso quale legittimo califfo." Gabrieli also wrote, dealing with this issue : ("La rivolta", pp.213-214) "Tra il 15 ramadan, entrata di Yazid in Basrah, e lo *'id al-fitr,* quando Yazid solennemente dichiarerà deposto il califfo." Shaban has a different opinion concerning these issues, and after dealing with only a few traditions he concluded in his *The 'Abbasid Revolution,* p.94, that: "There is no evidence at all that Yazid tried to supplant Umayyad rule by any other, and it is reported explicitly that he did not withdraw his alliance to Yazid II." Shaban's opinions should be read critically since there is evidence in other Arabic sources and in several traditions, as demonstrated by Gabrieli, that Yazid Ibn al-Muhallab declared him-self the caliph.

(72) Marín-Guzmán, *El Islam: Ideología e Historia,* passim, especially p.78, and pp.158-171. Ibn Khallikan, *Wafayat al-A'yan,* VI, pp.278-309. Kennedy, *Prophet,* p.105.

(73) Mas'udi, *Muruj al-Dhahab,* V, pp.454-455. Cf. Francesco Gabrieli, "L'eroe Omàyyade Maslamah Ibn 'Abd al-Malik", in *Rendi-conti Delle Sedute Dell' Accademia Nazionale Dei Lincei,* Vol. V, Fas-cicoli 1-2, 1950, pp.23-39, especially p.30 and p.35. Gabrieli, "La rivolta", p.227. Kennedy, *Prophet,* p.108. Concerning Maslamah Ibn 'Abd al-Malik's short governorship of Iraq see Ibn Qutaybah, *Al-Ma'arif,* p.358. See also Ibn Qutaybah, *Al-Ma'arif,* p.358 for a concise description of Maslamah Ibn 'Abd al-Malik's struggles and success against the Byzantines. See also Ya'qubi, *Ta'rikh al-Ya'qubi,* II, p.283.

(74) Cf. Ibn Qutaybah, *'Uyun al-Akhbar,* II, p.22 and pp.29-30.

# Chapter II

## Taxation, conversion and religious groups: The origins of the 'Abbasid revolution

The Umayyad administration of the Islamic Empire caused serious grievances to various political, religious, social and ethnic groups. Their monopoly of power blocked other people from important administrative positions and from the attending privileges and benefits.

The Umayyads were accused by several religious groups of having a weak commitment to Islam. The Shi'ites, the Khawarij and the Qadariyyah especially criticized their impious ways of ruling the Muslim community. These groups revolted, viewing the Umayyads as usurpers. Each one of these groups developed a particular notion of legitimacy and called all Muslims to revolt against the infidel Umayyads.

Aside from the political-religious grievances, this first dynasty of Islam also provoked serious problems for the *mawali*, the new non-Arab converts to Islam, who were discriminated against. The 'Abbasids took advantage of and capitalized on these facts. Through a very well directed and skillful propaganda and a new ideology, the 'Abbasids managed to concentrate in one big group of opposition to the ruling dynasty all those anti-Umayyads sentiments. This chapter addresses the social, ethnic and religious grievances that the Umayyads caused to various groups during their eighty-odd years in power. Besides the political reasons, it is useful to analyse the social, ethnic and religious motives in order to gain a clearer understanding of the different factions that supported the 'Abbasids, and led eventually to the popular basis of the 'Abbasid revolution.

# I- Taxation and Conversion: the origins of social, ethnic and economic grievances

In the year 700 a great number of Persian peasants from Khurasan converted to Islam. They travelled to Iraq in order to submit to Allah in front of al-Hajjaj Ibn Yusuf al-Thaqafi, then the Umayyad governor of Iraq. The new converts demanded from the Muslim authorities exemption from the poll-tax (*jizyah*) and the same treatment, privileges and equality accorded to the rest of the Muslims. Conversion to Islam was understood by many Persians as a way to be better off and be exempt from the heavy poll tax. However, al-Hajjaj Ibn Yusuf al-Thaqafi did not accept this massive Persian conversion, mainly due to the economic impact it could have upon the collection of the *jizyah* tax. He ordered them back to Khurasan and did not recognize them as Muslims.

This historical event, recorded in the major Arabic sources, raises the important question of conversion and taxation, the relation between the two, and the Islamic solution to this problem. This part will concentrate especially on the study of the taxation and conversion in Iraq and Khurasan, the provinces where the 'Abbasids started their *da'wah* (call, mission). It was in these provinces that the revolution first broke out and was popularly supported.

Before the Arab conquest of Khurasan, the major source of income to the State came from land. Farming was very important since most of the people were farmers. However, a large proportion of individual income derived from sources other than agriculture, as in any other provinces of the Sasanid Empire.[1]

The Sasanid Empire also taxed artisans and merchants for their activities in the cities. Special taxes were also levied on industry and trade. Aside from this, everybody from ages 20 to 50 (peasant, artisan or merchant) was charged the poll tax, graded according to income. Priests, soldiers, officials, and nobles were exempt.[2]

Arabs maintained this form of taxation for Khurasan in the same way it had been during the Sasanid period.[3] In the Persian Empire the individual was obliged to pay the land tax or the trade tax, according to occupation, as well as the poll tax. However, the Arabs referred to the taxation system as *kharaj* and *jizyah*, from whence the confusion of these technical terms, which were later differentiated: land or trade tax as *kharaj* and poll tax as *jizyah*.[4] The major Arabic sources mentioned the difficulties in differentiating *kharaj* and *jizyah* taxes in Khurasan, and other areas of the Muslim Empire. Abu Yusuf in his *Kitab al-Kharaj* clearly explained these facts.[5] However, according to the Muslim legislation, no *jizyah* tax could be levied on Muslims. The problem was that at the time of the Islamic conquests of Iraq and Khurasan, there was not a clear-cut distinction between *kharaj* (land tax) and *jizyah* (poll-tax). Furthermore, Muslims at that early stage of the *Dar al-Islam* also did not differentiate between *fay'* and *ghanimah*. These different types of taxes and booties developed only later as distinct institutions following the Islamic traditions, especially during the last Umayyads.

Undoubtedly, there was no uniformity of taxation in the early times of the Islamic expansion.[6] It varied from province to province in the Muslim Empire. The same tax had different names in different regions, and different taxes had sometimes the same name.[7] Because of this confusion, many attempts were made by several caliphs to establish uniformity. However, it took many years, and even important sources like al-Tabari's *Ta'rikh al-Rusul wa al-Muluk* still used *kharaj* and *jizyah* indistinctly on various occasions.[8] Related to these attempts for order, a different tax was imposed on the various territories according to their status when they entered Islam, either by force or voluntarily. Thus, *'ahd* was the term used when a city or a territory surrendered to Islam without fighting and agreed to pay a fixed amount never to increase or decrease.[9] *Sulh*, on the other hand, was the term applied to a place which surrendered to Islam after fighting; i.e., after it was conquered. Arabs took possession of all lands and properties whose owners had fled or died in the conquest. Shortly afterwards, some land was divided among those who participated in the wars of expansion. New problems arose about the ways to tax the lands conquered and appropriated by Muslims as spoils (*anfal*) of war. The Islamic system taxed all those lands with the *kharaj* (land tax). However, Muslims complained about these practices and sought to keep those territories tax free.

Although the Marwanids had a clear control and a strong centralized administration, which also meant a more efficient tax collection system, it was not until the end of the Marwaniyyah period when the differentiation between the various taxes was established. Hence, *kharaj* was used from that time on to refer to land tax and other taxes (industry and trade), but never to poll tax. *Jizyah* was the term for poll tax, understood as a protection tax for *dhimmis*. During the Marwaniyyah rule a clear difference between *ghanimah* and *fay'* was also established, as explained by Yahya Ibn Adam al-Qurashi in his *Kitab al-Kharaj*.[10]

Keeping in mind what has been already explained about *'ahd* and *sulh*, Daniel C. Dennett established, following al-Baladhuri, a comparative table of the amounts fixed at the time of the conquest for different cities of Khurasan, which is important for the understanding of the Arab policies towards those who accepted Islam before a war. It is important to remember that for different places -- Hira (al-Hirah) in Mesopotamia, for example -- which capitulated before conquest, the agreement was to pay a fixed sum of 60.000 dirhems. Arabs promised never to increase it, which was also the promise for other regions submitting voluntarily to Islam.[11]

In Khurasan, as in many other regions, the *'ahd* was established for those places that submitted voluntarily to Islam; i.e., surrendered without fighting. In these cases of *'ahd,* the inhabitants paid a fixed tribute, collected by themselves and given to the Arabs. Their land was not considered *kharaj* land (taxable land).

After the Umayyads consolidated control of Khurasan, conversion to Islam began, although at that time it was still very slow. Conversion was, indeed, closely related to taxation. Daniel C. Dennett's idea that conversion was encouraged by the very close and permanent contact of the conquerors and the conquered, is true only in part. Arabs did not force non-Arabs to convert to Islam, but many years of taxation and the promises of exemption from the *jizyah* persuaded many to convert to Islam.[12] It is important to bear in mind that conversion to Islam in Khurasan, as in many other parts of the Muslim Empire -- al-Andalus, for example -- was the only way for non-Muslims to avoid paying the *jizyah*, and contribute, instead, to the Muslim state with the pious *zakah*. It was clear for many that conversion would free the new Muslim from the *jizyah* tax, but not from the *kharaj* tax, then understood as a land or industry tax. This is one of the reasons why many Persians intended to convert to Islam in order to be granted the exemption from the poll tax. For this reason conversion grew quickly in Khurasan, and Muslim rulers had no choice but to recognize the new converts. The attitude of al-Hajjaj in the year 700 was not always the rule,but it shows the worry the Arab governors had about the quick conversions and their desire to stop them. They also wanted to send the peasants back to their lands, as it is described by the Arabic sources. However, the governors then ordered their ministers and associates to spy on those neo-Muslims and find out if those conversions were real. Therefore, circumcision, prayer, fasting and other religious practices and beliefs were carefully watched.[13] If their conversions were weak or specious, the governors recommended reinstating the poll tax and treating them as non-Muslims.

Although the new converts were supposedly exempted from the poll tax, and the collection of taxes in

Khurasan was left by the Arabs to the local Persian *dahaqin*, who had autonomy in the countryside, and because supervision was difficult and poor; the *dahaqin* found ways to increase the person's taxes to compensate for the loss of the poll taxes due to conversion. Some *dahaqin* of Bukhara, for example, complained that they could not raise the fixed quota (*kharaj*) because of conversion. Thus, the governor ordered taxes be collected in the old way (land, or trade and poll tax), resulting in a serious revolt. Once it was suppressed, the *dahaqin* were humiliated and asked to raise the fixed tribute from *kharaj*, while poll tax (*jizyah*) was taken only from those "weak converts".[14]

Conversion was first discouraged by Arabs. Later, however, the *dahaqin*, the Persian aristocracy, also discouraged conversion, because they did not benefit from the new converts as much as they did from the non-Muslims. Non-Muslims were forced to pay the land or trade taxes, as well as the poll tax, following the old Sasanid tradition. The *dahaqin* kept part of those taxes they levied as payment for their services.

The confusion in the technical terms of taxation caused serious abuses. A careful reading of the Arabic sources reveals that many Muslims were taxed with the *jizyah*. Although many Persians converted to Islam, not all were granted immediate exemption from the *jizyah*, which continued to be levied from them for a time. The Arabic sources describe the *mawali*'s complaints at being charged the *jizyah* even after conversion. These economic abuses can also be understood as part of the discrimination practiced against the *mawali* by the Umayyad system as well as the *dahaqin*'s exploitation of their own people. There were many instances in which Muslims in Khurasan were asked to pay the *jizyah*. It is possible to speculate that there were also Arabs besides the *mawali*. When Muslims complained, the Umayyad governors promised to remedy this situation and to apply the Islamic tradition of exempting Muslims from the *jizyah*. A good example of this situation is provided by al-Tabari, when Nasr Ibn Sayyar, the last Umayyad governor of Khurasan, affirmed in a speech:

> *Shall I accept anything except full payment of the* kharaj *according to what has been written and made known? Therefore I have appointed as overseer Mansur Ibn 'Umar Ibn Abi'l-Kharqa', and I have ordered him to act with justice to you. If there is a single Muslim from whom the* jizya *on his head has been taken, or on whom the* kharaj *is a heavy burden, while it is correspondingly lightened for the unbelievers, let him report the matter to Mansur who will transfer the burden from the Muslim to the unbeliever.* [15]

This action liberated 30,000 Muslims from the poll tax, while 80,000 non-Muslims (called unbelievers in the Arabic sources) were ordered to pay it. [16] That the Umayyads as late as their last governorship of Khurasan were still trying to remedy the tax problem -- the Muslims paying the *jizyah* -- proves that such abuses took place frequently during the whole Umayyad period. Muslims raised voices of complaint and opposition to the Umayyad authorities who allowed that situation to occur.

The Iranian population was heavily taxed by the *dahaqin* and by the Umayyads. However, Dennett's idea that taxation was not a reason for their revolt in the time of the 'Abbasid revolution or their opposition to the Umayyads, appears weak; while Gerlof van Vloten's opposite idea seems more reasonable and convincing. [17]

The local Persian population in Khurasan and Eastern Iraq, converted or not, was asked to pay heavy taxes. A way to liberate themselves from that burden was also through revolt. No wonder that they supported several of the Arab rebellions in Iraq (al-Mukhtar and Ibn al-Muhallab both had important *mawali* support) and the revolt of Ibn al-Ash'ath in Khurasan. [18] The grievances the *mawali* faced during almost the whole Umayyad period, the discrimination, and the heavy taxation, even the payment of *jizyah* after conversion to Islam, were capitalized on by the 'Abbasids. The 'Abbasid propaganda harped on the idea of liberation from heavy Umayyad taxation. The 'Abbasids were quite aware that the promise of stopping heavy taxation could lead to popular support. The taxation issue became an important appeal to the local Iranian population to revolt against the Umayyads and to support the 'Abbasid movement. In this respect al-Tabari is quite clear and probably the major source. However, some later works, like Abu al-'Abbas Ahmad b. 'Ali al-Maqrizi's *Kitab al-Niza' wa al-Takhasum fima bayna Bani Umayyah wa Bani Hashim* are also important, especially because they gathered most of the available information and described the major traditions about the rivalries between the Banu Umayyah and the Banu Hashim. Al-Maqrizi, for example, precisely pointed out the role taxes played in the 'Abbasid propaganda and ideology, which appealed to the liberation from a heavy taxation.[19]

## II- The religious groups

There is no clear separation between religion and politics in Islam, since the Prophet Muhammad was both religious leader and founder of a state. During the Umayyad period there were numerous religious protests, upheavals and revolts of various groups against those in power, each with its political connotations. The final goal of every political-religious movement was to oust the Umayyads from the caliphate and follow Islam in the way each understood it and believed it should be.

During the whole history of Islam the religious movements and the appeals to Islam have been characteristic of this culture, from Muhammad to Khumayni. The Umayyad period was no exception. Several groups appealed to Islam to revolt and oust them. No wonder that the 'Abbasids also sought religious support. They considered the Umayyads usurpers of the important office of *Amir al-Mu'minin* and skillfully spread this idea among the people. The 'Abbasids also criticized the Umayyads' weak commitment to Islam, and they called people to support their movement against that first dynasty in order to return Islam to its pristine beliefs and practices. Various groups responded actively to the 'Abbasids' *da'wah* (call) and supported their claims to the caliphate. These groups also accepted and trusted the 'Abbasids' promises.

Instead of detailing each of the numerous sects and subsects of Islam, which has been done in various Arabic sources such as al-Baghdadi's *Al-Farq bayna al-Firaq* and 'Ali Ibn Ahmad Ibn Hazm's *Al-Fasl fi al-Milal wa al-Ahwa' wa al-Nihal* [20] the major objective of this part is to identify the various religious groups, their grievances and the reasons for their support of the 'Abbasid revolution. It is also important to speculate about other possible religious groups which could have participated in the 'Abbasid revolution, although there is no clear evidence in the Arabic sources of their enrollment in the 'Abbasid movement. This speculation is not implausible, since there is evidence that these other groups were very active politically in the years previous to the 'Abbasid revolution. So, it seems reasonable to believe that if they were active before, they could have also revolted against the Umayyads when the 'Abbasids called for an armed rebellion. The difficult issue to identify, because of the lack of evidence, is whether these other religious groups (mainly the Khawarij and the *Qadariyyah*) fought against the Umayyads as members of the 'Abbasid army.

### 1- The Shi'ah

Early in the history of Islam some groups split from the community (*al-Ummah al-Islamiyyah*). The major reasons for these divisions seem to have been political, since religious differences at that early time of Islam were minimal. However, religious issues were raised as a banner to oppose those in power. Arabic chronicles, the various *Ta'rikh al-Khulafa'*, the Arabic general history books, the religious histories, and the histories of the Islamic sects, all describe in detail the origins and development of the Shi'ah as the party of 'Ali, the fourth and last of the *Rashidun* caliphs.[21]

The Shi'ah (party)[22] of 'Ali Ibn Abi Talib[23] started as a group to support him against his enemies, especially the Umayyads, after the battle of Siffin.[24] After 'Ali's death and the Umayyad takeover, the Shi'ites started facing the Umayyad persecution and the strong opposition of the Khawarij.[25] Their most tragic event (still remembered in the practice of *ta'zieh* in Iran) was the killing of the *imam* Husayn Ibn 'Ali Ibn Abi Talib in Karbala in 680.[26] The Shi'ites also became a strong opposition to the Umayyads. Throughout the Umayyad period they led several revolts all over the Empire, most frequently in the Eastern provinces. At this point one has to see the relation between the Persians, once they became *mawali*, and Shi'ism. Many Persian converts joined the Shi'ite sect also as a way to oppose the Arab rulers; i.e., the Umayyads. The *Tawwabun* (Penitents) then grew into a political-religious group to oppose the Umayyads and avenge Husayn's murder.[27]

Several of these political-religious revolts led by Shi'ite Muslims had a great impact on the Umayyad period as well as on the origins of the 'Abbasid revolution. One of the most important Shi'ite revolts in Iraq, led by al-Mukhtar Ibn Abi 'Ubayd on behalf of Muhammad Ibn al-Hanafiyyah,[28] needs to be analysed, for its impact on the origins of the 'Abbasid revolution, as well as for the various subdivisions spawned by it, some of which were either taken over by the 'Abbasids or became supporters of the 'Abbasids' aspiration.

In the previous chapter the second *fitnah* (civil war) led by 'Abd Allah Ibn al-Zubayr was analysed as one of the major political-religious and tribal challenges faced by the

Umayyads. Simultaneously with this *fitnah*, al-Mukhtar directed a Shi'ite rebellion in Kufa from 685 to 687 in favor of Muhammad Ibn al-Hanafiyyah. This rebellion also challenged the Umayyad authority. Muhammad Ibn al-Hanafiyyah was a son of 'Ali, not with Fatimah, but with al-Hanifah.[29] Al-Mukhtar had the support of the people of Kufa,[30] and after addressing Muhammad Ibn al-Hanafiyyah as *al-Mahdi* (messiah) he claimed the caliphate for this son of 'Ali.[31] At the beginning this revolt was directed against Ibn al-Zubayr, who had a strong influence in Iraq and controlled some parts of this province. Later the revolt turned against the Umayyads.[32] This war between the two movements *(al-Harakah al-Mukhtariyyah* and *al-Harakah al-Zubayriyyah)* weakened them in Iraq.[33] Probably for this reason the caliph 'Abd al-Malik was able to defeat Ibn al-Zubayr's governor of Iraq, his brother Mus'ab Ibn al-Zubayr.

Kaisan Abu 'Amra represented a group of Shi'ite *mawali* in Kufa, whose interests were defended by al-Mukhtar. This group of followers were called the *Kaisaniyyah*.[34] When al-Mukhtar started his revolt, the *Kaisaniyyah* followed this leader and supported his claims in favor of Muhammad Ibn al-Hanafiyyah. Shortly afterwards, the name was transformed to *al-Mukhtariyyah*. After al-Mukhtar's death in 687 and Muhammad Ibn al-Hanafiyyah's death in 701, (several traditions place his death variously from 700 to 705) their supporters followed Abu Hashim, Muhammad Ibn al-Hanafiyyah's son, whose father, they believed, had transmitted all his knowledge and the claims and rights to the caliphate. In a short period of time the name of the *Hashimiyyah* was popularized and almost completly replaced the names of *Kaisaniyyah* and *Mukhtariyyah*.

From the *Hashimiyyah* sect the 'Abbasids obtained their claims and pretensions to the caliphate. They spread the idea that Abu Hashim before dying transmitted the claims and rights of the caliphate to Muhammad Ibn 'Ali 'Abd Allah Ibn 'Abbas; i.e., the *imamah* (authority)

and the *'ilm* (esoteric knowledge), which developed the idea of *wasiyyah* (testament) related to *wirathah* (heir, inheritance), later capitalized on by the 'Abbasids.[35]
Wilferd Madelung has demonstrated in a recent book the relation between the *Khurramiyyah* (the Persian sect that tried to end the antagonisms between Zoroastrianism and Islam and led towards the understanding of these two faiths) and the *Kaisaniyyah*. The close ties between the *Khurramiyyah* and the *Kaisaniyyah* in fact started at the time of Abu Hashim.[36] Abu Hashim had a secret missionary organization which spread his beliefs and his claims, especially in Iraq and Iran, and later on organized itself into a sect with the name of *Hashimiyyah*. Abu Hashim was accused of supporting extremist Shi'ite doctrines. This issue is also revealed in the accusations of supporting *zindiq* ideas; i.e., dualistic beliefs levied against 'Abd Allah b. al-Harb, the leader of one of the two groups in which the *Hashimiyyah* split.[37] The other group supported the rights and the *imamate* of the 'Abbasid Muhammad b.'Ali.

It was Abu Muslim al-Khurasani who brought the support of the *Khurramiyyah* all over Iran to the 'Abbasid cause. This support was essential for the triumph of the 'Abbasids against the Umayyads. The relation between the followers of the *Khurramiyyah* and Abu Muslim was very close, to the point that the Khurramites considered Abu Muslim their *imam*, their prophet and the incarnation of the divine spirit.[38] They would carry out whatever instructions he asked of them. Their support of the 'Abbasid cause is unquestionable. Most remained faithful to the 'Abbasids, although some revolted against the new rulers of Islam when the 'Abbasid caliph al-Mansur put Abu Muslim to death in 753, since Abu Muslim by that time had become a symbol of Persian nationality and identity against the Arab domination.[39]

What is extremely important to notice is that the Shi'ite revolt of al-Mukhtar, although brief and limited in scope, incorporated for the first time a considerable group of *mawali*, who also revolted in hope of better conditions.[40]

In these events it is possible to see the *mawali*, who had serious grievances against the Umayyad administration, united with another enemy group of the Umayyads, the also persecuted and humbled Shi'ites. The 'Abbasids were very skillful with their propaganda and ideology in gaining the support of the Shi'ites and the *mawali*. First of all, they supported and sustained the ideas of the *Hashimiyyah* and made political promises to the Shi'ites. However, the 'Abbasids did not keep their word to the Shi'ites, and they used the aspirations, claims and organization of the *Hashimiyyah* to their own benefit. The 'Abbasids also accepted and encouraged the *mawali* in their claims and opposition against the Umayyads, and they gained their support for the 'Abbasid revolution by joining and helping the *Shu'ubiyyah* movement. Both groups, the Shi'ites and the *mawali*, along with the Southern Arab tribes, became the major supporters of the 'Abbasid revolution against the Umayyads.

There are two important hypotheses to raise here, both dealing with social and religious issues. The first, that the *dahaqin* supported the 'Abbasid revolution. There is no evidence of this in the Arabic sources; however, it seems possible that for various reasons, since they supported previous revolts against the Umayyads, they could have also done it when the 'Abbasids called for revolt in hope of regaining what had been lost under the Umayyad rule.

The second hypothesis is that most of the Shi'ites were of Southern tribal origin or, if they were non-Arab new converts, they became *mawali* (clients) of the Southern Arab tribes. This hypothesis needs further research. If a detailed genealogical work supports this hypothesis, there was a double reason for the Shi'ites to revolt against the Umayyads: the political-religious opposition, and the tribal dimension, which was also an important element in the 'Abbasid revolution against the first dynasty of Islam.

## 2- The Khawarij and the call for a community of saints

It seems quite possible that some other religious groups, besides the Shi'ah and its subdivisions, could have also participated in the 'Abbasid revolution. However, there is no evidence in the Arabic sources that the other religious groups, such as the Khawarij and the *Qadariyyah*, joined the 'Abbasid army led by Abu Muslim or that they supported the revolution in any other way, with the single exception of the accounts contained in the *Akhbar al-Dawlah al-'Abbasiyyah*. According to this important Arabic source, after Abu Salamah, one of the leaders of the 'Abbasid *da'wah*, liberated Bukayr b. Mahan from prison and paid his debts; Bukayr, who was also an important leader of the 'Abbasid *da'wah*, became ill. On his death-bed he prophesied that the caliph al-Walid II would die very soon and that that death would mark the beginning of the end of the Umayyads: the tribes will fight again in Khurasan; the Khawarij will revolt; and the earthquake will take place.[41]

To prophesy and thus to give religious and eschatological import to political-religious movements has been, throughout the centuries, a characteristic of this region. However, even if true that he made those prophecies it is difficult to determine if Bukayr b. Mahan really delivered those ideas. The anonymous *Akhbar al-Dawlah al-'Abbasiyyah* was written long after these events, and such ideas were likely incorporated into the book to emphasize the religious and eschatological doctrines and give more legitimacy to the 'Abbasids in power, and to the leaders of the *da'wah*.

Whether or not the prophecies were true, the important point to bring up here is mention of the Khawarij, because it is the only time that an 'Abbasid leader talked about the Kharijites. Did he simply name the Khawarij as truly a group of opposition to the Umayyads, or was he subtly suggesting they favored the 'Abbasid revolution?

This is an important question to raise. This reference can be understood as weak evidence, and the only one in the Arabic sources, of the mention of the Khawarij, or a possible alliance between the Khawarij and the 'Abbasids.

Arabic sources, like al-Tabari's *Ta'rikh al-Rusul wa al-Muluk,* describe in detail the numerous Khawarij revolts in the years previous to the 'Abbasid revolution and their stubborn opposition to the Umayyads.[42] But, of that armed revolt, there is no information available about their possible alliance with the 'Abbasids in the struggles against the Umayyads. However, it is plausible to speculate that since they were politically active before, the Khawarij could also have been during the 'Abbasid revolution.

The Khawarij declared that the judgment belongs exclusively to God *(al-Hukmah illa li-Allah)* due to the events of Siffin.[43] For this, they opposed the Umayyads and the Shi'ites. They considered the Umayyads usurpers and sinners. Because of this it was not only a right, but a duty of all Muslims, to oust from power those who have sinned. They understood the *imamah* (authority) and the charisma to be a privilege belonging exclusively to the community *(al-ummah),* and not exclusively to one person, the *imam,* as the Shi'ites believed. The Khawarij were aware, however, of the need of an *imam* to guide the *ummah.* They preached a community of saints, with all sinners excluded from the *ummah.* It was at this time when the theological argument that actions affect the faith was raised.[44]

Politically the Khawarij were very active against the Shi'ites and the Umayyads. Throughout the period of this study they revolted against the Umayyads who tried violently to stop them. The Khawarij suffered political repression and persecutions and faced unmerciful Umayyad armies. These events increased their grievances and their desires to depose the "sinful" rulers.

After what has been said, it is possible, then, to speculate that they fought against the Umayyads at the time of the 'Abbasid revolution, whether or not they had ties with the movement. The general 'Abbasid fighting, supported by the Southern tribes, the Shi'ites, the *mawali*, and probably also the *dahaqin* and the Khawarij, who all of them had strong anti-Umayyad feelings, contributed to the popular dimensions of the 'Abbasid revolution. The 'Abbasid movement was seen, then, as a strong revolt supported by various groups.

### 3- The Qadariyyah and the notion of Free Will

Most of what has been explained about the Khawarij is to a certain extent also applicable to the *Qadariyyah*. There is no evidence in the Arabic sources that this group participated in the 'Abbasid revolution. It is also difficult to determine if their followers had any kind of ties or alliances with the 'Abbasids. However, it is possible to speculate that if they were politically active in the years before the 'Abbasids started their movement, and that they fought the Umayyads in various occasions, then they could have also participated in the 'Abbasid revolution.

The Umayyads, who forwarded the idea of Predestination, which at the political level was understood as submission to the rulers, opposed at the same time very strongly the believers in Free Will, since politically it meant to fight the usurpers (i.e., the Umayyads) and to provide the *ummah* with true Muslim rulers. Al-Tabari describes how the caliph Hisham, for example, put Ghailan al-Damashqi (who was one of the leaders of the *Mu'tazilah*) to death in Damascus for defending the doctrine of Free Will. The death of Ghailan has also been interpreted as a result of his ideas of giving the *mawali* equality with Arab Muslims and the suspicions of the Umayyad authorities that Ghailan was connected to the revolt of al-Harith b. Surayj in Transoxiana.[45]

The anti-Umayyad feelings of the *Qadariyyah* were also strong. This theological school forwarded the Free

Will doctrine which also had specific political connotations. The followers of the *Qadariyyah* also suffered persecution, imprisonment and exile. Because of these grievances, they had ample reasons for opposing the Umayyads. If they also revolted against the first dynasty of Islam at the time of the 'Abbasid *da'wah*, whether or not allied with the 'Abbasids, their fighting also contributed to the impression of the 'Abbasids as rulers of a popularly supported movement.

An important issue to bring up when dealing with the *Qadariyyah* is that this theological school, as we know, was totally immersed in the *Mu'tazilah* after the 'Abbasids took power. The *Mu'tazilah* was also an important theological school that believed in the Free Will doctrine, God's unicity (*tawhid*), God's justice, God's creation of the Qur'an, and finally the practice of free thinking.[46] There is little evidence, however, that the *Mu'tazilah* had any connections with the 'Abbasid revolution. At the time of the 'Abbasid *da'wah* and the revolution, the *Mu'tazilah* was a very new school still getting organized. Aside from this, little is known about the political involvement of its followers. However, later evidence, such as the caliph al-Mansur's (754-775) contact with the *Mu'tazilah* and the caliph al-Ma'mun's (813-833) support of this school to the point of making official its doctrines in the *Dar al-Islam*, raises new questions.[47] It is possible, then, to speculate that through the *Mu'tazilah* the 'Abbasids had some contact with the *Qadariyyah*. However, the question could also be posed in terms of the 'Abbasid contact with the *Mu'tazilah* itself, suggesting the possible support of the *Mu'tazilah* and the *Qadariyyah* in the 'Abbasid revolution.

H. Nyberg believes that the 'Abbasids had good relations with the *Mu'tazilah*, even asserting that the *Mu'tazilah*'s philosophy became the doctrinal aspect of the 'Abbasids, while the *da'wah* was their political organization.[48] Nyberg affirms that the *Mu'tazilah* was almost totally devoted to the 'Abbasids at the beginning of the 'Abbasid period.[49] These ideas appear more hypothetical due to the lack of evidence. Claude Cahen has analysed Nyberg's theories and criticized them, pointing out the lack of evidence in the Arabic sources, and the limited relation between a single theologian (Wasil Ibn 'Ata al-Ghazza) and the 'Abbasids. These contacts were the main elements for Nyberg's hypotheses.[50]

The speculation that the *Qadariyyah* and the *Mu'tazilah* could have had ties with the 'Abbasids and that they might have participated in the revolution against the Umayyads is, obviously, extremely important, but before any final lines are written it needs, evidently, further research.

## Endnotes to Chapter II

(1) Daniel C. Dennett, *Conversion and Poll Tax in Early Islam,* Cambridge, 1950, p.116.

(2) Arthur Christensen, *L'Iran sous les Sassanides,* Paris, 1936, p.362.

(3) Hasan, *Al-Qaba'il al-'Arabiyyah,* p.163. Reuben Levy, "Persia and the Arabs", in John Arberry, *The Legacy of Persia,* Oxford, 1953, pp.60-88. Cf. Morony, *Iraq after the Muslim Conquest ,* pp.68-79.

(4) Dennett, *Conversion,* p.118. Wellhausen also discussed this confusion of terms in *The Arab Kingdom,* passim. Caetani, *Annali* V, pp.287-465. Cahen, *Les peuples musulmans,* pp.232-233.

(5) Cf. Abu Yusuf, *Kitab al-Kharaj,* p.30. For a detailed description of the *dhimmah* and the payment of the *jizyah* see Qurashi, *Kitab al-Kharaj,* pp.77-83. For *kharaj* from the land and *zakah* from agriculture see Qurashi, *Kitab al-Kharaj,* pp.190-194. Baladhuri, *Futuh al-Buldan,* passim, especially pp.272-273.

(6) Cf. Abu Yusuf, *Kitab al-Kharaj,* passim. About *jizyah* and *kharaj* see pp.30-31. Qurashi, *Kitab al-Kharaj,* pp.15-20 and also pp.41-50. See also Marín-Guzmán, "Las causas", pp.39-67. Marín-Guzmán, *El Islam: Ideología e Historia,* pp.151-158. About *zakat* and the Islamic fiscal institutions see Caetani, *Annali,* V, pp.287-465.

(7) A.N. Poliak, "Classification of Lands in the Islamic Law and its Technical Terms", in *The American Journal of Semitic Languages and Literatures,* Vol. LVII, Number 1, 1940, pp.50-62. See also Marín-Guzmán, "Las causas", passim. Caetani, *Annali,* V, pp.287 ff.

(8) Tabari, *Ta'rikh al-Rusul wa al-Muluk,* II, pp.1507-1510 (Leiden Edition).

(9) Sa'ih, *Ahammiyyat al-Quds,* pp.5-8. For a detailed account of *'ahd* and *sulh* for Iraq (Ahwaz and Sawad) see Abu Yusuf, *Kitab al-Kharaj,* pp.30-31. Qurashi, *Kitab al-Kharaj,* pp.51-57. For a different application of those terms during the Muslim conquests see Ibn Qutaybah, *Al-Ma'arif,* pp.568-570.

(10) Cf. Abu Yusuf, *Kitab al-Kharaj,* pp.129-131. For more details about the *jizyah* see pp.131-137, and for the *dhimmah* see pp.137-138. Qurashi, *Kitab al-Kharaj,* pp.57-67.

(11) See Dennett, *Conversion*, p.117.

(12) Dennett, *Conversion*, p.118. About the Muslim pious *zakah* see Qurashi, *Kitab al-Kharaj*, pp.135-137.

(13) Hawting, *The First Dynasty of Islam*, p.80. Crone, *Slaves on Horses*, p.52. For the Arabic sources describing the governors' worries concerning the conversion process and their desire to send the peasants back to their lands in order to preserve the taxation system see Tabari, *Ta'rikh al-Rusul wa al- Muluk*, II, pp.1122 ff., II, pp.1354 ff. (Leiden Edition). Baladhuri, *Ansab al-Ashraf*, XI, pp.336 ff.

(14) Dennett, *Conversion*, p.123. See also Crone, *Slaves on Horses*, p.52.

(15) Tabari, *Ta'rikh al-Rusul wa al-Muluk*, II, p.1688, (Leiden Edition) quoted and translated by Dennett, *Conversion*, p.124.

(16) Dennett, *Conversion*, p.124.

(17) Gerlof van Vloten, *Recherches sur la domination arabe, le Chiitisme, et les croyances messianiques sous le khalifat Omayedes*, Amsterdam, 1894, pp.20 ff.

(18) About al-Mukhtar see Baladhuri, *Ansab al-Ashraf*, V, pp.214-273. Ibn al-Athir, *Al-Kamil fi al-Ta'rikh*, edited by C.J. Tornberg, Leiden, 1869, Beirut, 1965, reimpression of the Leiden Edition (Leiden-Beirut Edition) IV, pp.228-244. See also IV, pp.267-278. (Leiden-Beirut Edition). See also the anonymous *Akhbar al-Dawlah al-'Abbasiyyah*, pp.100 ff. Dinawari, *Al-Akhbar al-Tiwal*, pp.306-308. Rayyis, *'Abd al-Malik b. Marwan*, pp.114-119. Brockelmann, *History*, pp.78-80. Kharbutli, *'Abd Allah Ibn al-Zubayr*, pp.193-197. Laoust, *Les schismes dans l'Islam*, pp.29-31. Sharon, *Black Banners*, p.81 and p.85. See also 'Arafah, *Al-Khurasaniyun wa Dawruhum*, passim, especially pp.42-43. For more details about Ibn al-Ash'ath see Hasan, *Al-Qaba'il al-'Arabiyyah*, pp.143-149. Cahen, *Les peuples musulmans*, pp.115 ff. Kennedy, *Prophet*, p.124. Crone, *Slaves on Horses*, p.51. For more details about Ibn al-Muhallab see Gabrieli, "La rivolta dei Muhallabati nel 'Iraq e il nuovo Baladuri", in *Rendiconti della R. Accademia Nazionale dei Lincei*, Vol. XIV, Serie Sesta, Fascicoli 3-4, 1938, pp.199-236. Laoust, *Les schismes dans l'Islam*, p.41. Watt, *Formative Period*, pp.44-47. Crone, *Slaves on Horses*, p.53. For the study of the whole process of conversion as a way to escape the taxes see Tabari, *Ta'rikh al-Rusul wa al-Muluk*, II, pp.1122 ff. II, pp.1354

ff., II, p.1435, II, p.1507 (Leiden Edition).

(19) Abu al-'Abbas Ahmad b. 'Ali al-Maqrizi, *Kitab al-Niza' wa al-Takhasum fima bayna Bani Umayyah wa Bani Hashim,* edited by Von Geerhardus Vos, Leiden, 1888. *Book on Contention and Strife Concerning the Relations between the Banu Umayya and the Banu Hashim,* English translation by Clifford E. Bosworth, Manchester, 1980, passim.

(20) 'Abd al-Qahir Ibn Tahir al-Baghdadi, *Al-Farq bayna al-Firaq,* Beirut, 1973, passim. 'Ali Ibn Ahmad Ibn Hazm al-Andalusi, *Al-Fasl fi al-Milal wa al-Ahwa' wa al-Nihal,* Cairo, 1964, (5 Vols). This edition also includes Muhammad b. Abi al-Qasim 'Abd al-Karim b. Abi Bakr Ahmad al-Shahrastani, *Al-Milal al-Nihal.* For secondary works about the Islamic sects see 'Abd Allah Sallum al-Samarra'i, *Al-Ghuluw wa al-Firaq al-Ghaliyah fi al-Hadarah al-Islamiyyah,* Baghdad, 1982. Muhammad al-Tahir al-Nayfar, *Ahamm al-Firaq al-Islamiyyah,* Tunisia, 1974. Wilferd Madelung, *Religious Schools and Sects in Medieval Islam,* London, 1985. Albert Nasri Nadir, *Ahamm al-Firaq al-Islamiyyah,* Beirut, n.d.

(21) See for example the Arabic sources already mentioned in this essay: Tabari, *Ta'rikh al-Rusul wa al-Muluk,* passim, especially I, pp.3340-3359. (Leiden Edition). Ibn al-Athir, *Al-Kamil fi al-Ta'rikh,* III, pp.387-391. (Leiden-Beirut Edition). Mas'udi, *Muruj al-Dhahab,* IV, pp.288-304. Suyuti, *Ta'rikh al-Khulafa',* pp.166-187. Dinawari, *Al-Akhbar al-Tiwal,* pp.140-143, pp.144-178 and also pp.211-213. In the Islamic history several scholars considered and called 'Umar Ibn 'Abd al-'Aziz ('Umar II) the Fifth of the *Rashidun* Caliphs (*Khamis al-Khulafa' al-Rashidin*). One of them was al-Suyuti who quoted the authority of Sufyan al-Thawri. See Suyuti, *Ta'rikh al-Khulafa',* p.228. According to Mas'udi, *Muruj al-Dhahab,* V, pp.422-423, the *Amir al-Mu'minin* 'Umar Ibn 'Abd al-'Aziz was very much lamented by the Byzantine Emperor who wanted to deal with him and settle peace between the two Empires. The caliph 'Umar Ibn 'Abd al-'Aziz was very popular during his short *khilafah.* The main reason for that was probably because of his famous Fiscal Rescript. About it see 'Abd al-Rahman Ibn 'Abd al-Hakam, *Sirat 'Umar Ibn 'Abd al-'Aziz,* Cairo, 1927, pp.93-100. See also Dinawari, *Al-Akhbar al-Tiwal,* p.331. See also Hamilton Gibb, "The Fiscal Rescript of 'Umar II", in *Revue de études arabes,* Tome II, Fascicule 1, 1955, pp.1-16.

(22) Much has been written about the early developments of Islam both in the Arabic sources as well as in the secondary works. Among the major secondary works are: Nayfar, *Ahamm al-Firaq al-Islamiyyah,* passim, especially pp.70-75. Samarra'i, *Al-Ghuluw wa al-Firaq al-*

*Ghaliyah*, passim, especially pp.259-262. Watt, *Formative Period*, pp.38-62. Watt, *Islamic Philosophy*, pp.20-26. Wellhausen, *Die Religiös-Politischen Oppositionsparteien im alten Islam*, Göttingen, 1901, passim. Husayn Tabatabai, *Shi'ite Islam*, Houston, 1979, passim, especially pp.39-61. S. Husayn M. Jafri, *The Origins and Early Development of Shi'a Islam*, London, 1979, passim. Sabatino Moscati, "Per una storia dell'antica Si'a", in *Rivista degli Studi Orientali*, Vol. XXX, 1955, pp.251-267. See also Manuel Ruiz Figueroa, "Imamah o autoridad en los primeros tiempos del Islam", pp.61-82. Pareja, *Islamología*, II, pp.722-723. Marín-Guzmán, "El Islam Shi'ita", in Marín-Guzmán, *Introducción a los Estudios Islámicos*, pp.173-183.Marín-Guzmán, *El Islam: Religión y Política*, pp.58-69. Marín-Guzmán, *El Islam: Ideología e Historia*, pp.167-180. Cahen, *El Islam*, pp.22-25.

(23) Some sources are in favor of the Shi'ah, while others are against it, and strongly criticize some of the Shi'ite doctrines. Shaykh al-Mufid, *Kitab al-Irshad, The Book of Guidance into the Lives of the Twelve Imams*, English translation by I.K.A. Howard, New York, 1981, seems to be one of the main apologetic works for the Shi'ah. About Shaykh al-Mufid see Domique Sourdel, "L'Imamisme vu par le Cheikh al-Mufid", in *Revue des études islamiques*, XL, Fascicule 2, 1972, pp.217-296.

(24) About Siffin see Dinawari, *Al-Akhbar al-Tiwal*, pp.155-178. Tabari, *Ta'rikh al-Rusul wa al-Muluk*, I, pp.3256-3283 (Leiden Edition). About the separation of the Khawarij from the Shi'ah see Tabari, *Ta'rik al-Rusul wa al-Muluk*, I, p.3353 (Leiden Edition). Mufid, *Kitab al-Irshad*, pp.193-196. Ibn Khallikan, *Wafayat al-A'yan*, VI, pp.357-361. Ya'qubi, *Ta'rikh al-Ya'qubi*, II, p.218. Al-Ya'qubi asserted that great numbers of Thaglib and Namir joined 'Ali in the battle of Siffin. See also Mas'udi, *Muruj al-Dhahab*, IV, pp.343-382, and IV, pp.293-294. Morony, *Iraq after the Muslim Conquest*, p.230. Marín-Guzmán, *Introducción a los Estudios Islámicos*, passim. Marín-Guzmán, *El Islam: Ideología e Historia*, pp.72-74. Marín-Guzmán, "El Islam Shi'ita", pp.173-183. Caetani, *Annali*, X, pp.30-34. Jafri, *Origins and Early Development*, pp.90-93. For the theological discussions concerning the arbitration in Siffin and the opinions of the various religious groups see Baghdadi, *Al-Farq bayna al-Firaq*, passim, especially pp.122-123 of the English translation.

(25) In order to defend themselves, some Shi'ites developed extremist ideas like the *Isma'iliyyah* and the *Ghulat*. About the *Isma'iliyyah* and its subdivisions see: H. Corbin, "La Filosofía Islámica desde sus orgenes hasta la muerte de Averroes", in Brice Parain, *Historia de la Filosofía. Del Mundo Romano al Islam Medieval*, México, 1978,

pp.267-272. Madelung, *Religious Schools and Sects*, passim. Pareja, *Islamología*, II, pp.736-745. Grunebaum, *Medieval Islam*, pp.196-197. Bernard Lewis, *The Origins of Isma'ilism. A Study of Historical Background of the Fatimid Caliphate*, Cambridge, 1940, passim. Marín-Guzmán, *El Islam: Ideología e Historia*, pp.187-188. Marín-Guzmán, "Razón y Revelación en el Islam", in *Revista de Filosofía*, Vol. XXII, Numbers 55-56, 1984, pp.133-150. About the *Ghulat* see Samarra'i, *Al-Ghuluw wa al-Firaq al-Ghaliyah*, pp.303-305. Matti Moosa, *Extremist Shiites. The Ghulat sects*, Syracuse, 1988, passim. Marín-Guzmán, "El Islam Shi'ita", pp.173-183. Marín-Guzmán, *El Islam: Ideología e Historia*, pp.173-174. M.G.S. Hodgson, "Ghulat", in *Encyclopaedia of Islam* (2), Vol. II, Leiden, 1965, pp.1093-1095. See also Baghdadi, *Al-Farq bayna al-Firaq*, passim, especially pp.34-36 of the English translation. Al-Baghdadi mentioned that the *Ghulat* group comprised twenty-two sects. (p.116) Some of the Shi'ite doctrines, especially the concepts of *imam* (leader, guide) and *imamah* (authority) were criticized evenby Muslim historians and scholars, like Ibn Khaldun, who thought that it was wrong to believe, like Shi'ites do, that the *imamate* constitutes a pillar of the religion. He said that if that were the case, the Prophet would have instituted it. In this respect see Ibn Khaldun, *Al-Muqaddimah*, Book III, Chapter XXX, p.411 (of the Spanish translation). For a general account of the Shi'ite doctrine (*imamah, nass, taqiyyah,* etc.) see Marín-Guzmán, "El Islam Shi'ita", pp.175-178. Marín-Guzmán *El Islam: Ideología e Historia*, pp.175-176. Ruiz Figueroa, "Imamah o autoridad en los primeros tiempos del Islam", pp.61-82. Tabatabai, *Shi'ite Islam*, pp.9-16. Pareja, *Islamología*, II, pp.721-727. Cahen, *Les peuples musulmans*, p.113.

(26) About the killing of the *imam* Husayn and the shi'ite traditions see Baladhuri, *Ansab al-Ashraf*, IV B, pp.12-16. Mufid, *Kitab al-Irshad*, pp.299-372. Rayyis, *'Abd al-Malik b. Marwan*, pp.102-108. This author provides a very interesting discussion about the person who was responsible for Husayn's death. Husayn had, obviously, very few supporters, in comparison with the 4,000 soldiers that the caliph Yazid's army had, according to the sources. Cf. p.104. For more details see Ibn al-Athir, *Al-Kamil fi al-Ta'rikh,* IV, pp.241-244. Ya'qubi, *Ta'rikh al-Ya'qubi*, II, pp.243-253 (Beirut Edition). Dinawari, *Al-Akhbar al-Tiwal*, pp.251-262. Tabatabai, *Shi'ite Islam*, pp.196-201. Marín-Guzmán, "El Islam Shi'ita", pp.173-183. Marín-Guzmán, *El Islam: Ideología e Historia*, pp.167-180, especially pp.178-180. Brockelmann, *History*, p.76. Jafri, *Origins and Early Development*, pp.174-221. Lassner, *Islamic Revolution*, p.124. Cahen, *Les peuples musulmans*, pp.114-115. Kennedy, *Prophet*, p.89. Sharon, *Black Banners*, p.103. 'Arafah, *Al-Khurasaniyun wa Dawruhum*, p.42.

(27) See Tabari, *Ta'rikh al-Rusul wa al-Muluk*, II, p.538 (Leiden Edition). Baladhuri, *Ansab al-Ashraf*, V, p.208. About their political activity see Tabari, *Ta'rikh al-Rusul wa al-Muluk*, II, p.545 (Leiden Edition). Hawting, *The First Dynasty of Islam*, p.51. About the Persian converts adopting the Shi'ah sect see Frye, *The Golden Age of Persia*, passim. Watt, *Islamic Philosophy*, p.21.

(28) For more details about al-Mukhtar and Muhammad Ibn al-Hanafiyyah see the references in footnote 18.

(29) Marín-Guzmán, "La Escatología Musulmana", passim. Marín-Guzmán, *El Islam: Ideología e Historia*, pp.284-285. D.B. MacDonald, "Al-Mahdi", in *Shorter Encyclopaedia of Islam*, Leiden, 1974, pp.310-313. D.S. Margoliouth, "On Mahdis and Mahdiism", in *Proceedings of the British Academy*, 1915-1916, pp.213-223. D.S. Margoliouth, "Mahdi", in *Encyclopaedia of Religion and Ethics*, Volume III, 1964, pp.336-340. Watt, *Formative Period*, pp.44-45. Cahen, *Les peuples musulmans*, p.118. Kennedy, *Prophet*, p.124. For a description of al-Mukhtar's army in his revolt see: Baladhuri, *Ansab al-Ashraf*, V, pp.261-273.

(30) Baladhuri, *Ansab al-Ashraf*, V, pp.217-218, and pp.248-251. About al-Mukhtar in Kufa and his 'amil in Iraq see Ya'qubi, *Ta'rikh al-Ya'qubi*, II, pp.258-259. See also Ibn Qutaybah, *Al-Ma'arif*, pp.400-401. About the role and position of Basra during al-Mukhtar's revolt see Baladhuri, *Ansab al-Ashraf*, V, pp.244-246. Kharbutli, *'Abd Allah Ibn al-Zubayr*, p.193.

(31) Baladhuri, *Ansab al-Ashraf*, V, pp.217-218. Cf. Rayyis, *'Abd al-Malik b. Marwan*, pp.114-119. Cf. Wellhausen, *Religiös-Politischen*, p.78. Marín-Guzmán, *El Islam: Ideología e Historia*, pp.282-285. Marín-Guzmán, "La Escatología Musulmana", passim. Kennedy, *Prophet*, pp.94-95. 'Arafah, *Al-Khurasaniyun wa Dawruhum*, p.42.

(32) Cf. Baladhuri, *Ansab al-Ashraf*, V, pp.214-256, especially p.256 for a detailed description of the struggles between al-Mukhtar and Mus'ab Ibn al-Zubayr, 'Abd Allah Ibn al-Zubayr's 'amil for Kufa and Basra. See also Baladhuri, *Ansab al-Ashraf*, V, pp.273-278. Tabari, *Ta'rikh al-Rusul wa al-Muluk*, II, pp.693-695 (Leiden Edition). *Akhbar al-Dawlah al-'Abbasiyyah*, pp.102 ff. Dinawari, *Al-Akhbar al-Tiwal*, pp.206-208. Ibn Qutaybah, *Al-Ma'arif*, pp.356 ff. See also Ya'qubi, *Ta'rikh al-Ya'qubi*, II, pp.258 ff. Kharbutli, *'Abd Allah Ibn al-Zubayr*, pp.192-197. Morony, *Iraq after the Muslim Conquest*, p.95. Morony in this respect wrote :" He sent [al-Mukhtar] eight hundred of them to Madina to protect Muhammad Ibn al-Hanafiyyah from Ibn al-Zubayr in 685" (p.95) See also Watt, *Formative Period*, p.45. Kennedy,

*Prophet*, p.96. Cahen, *Les peuples musulmans*, pp.118-119 and also p.121. For a good description of this period and the fighting between Ibn al-Zubayr and al-Mukhtar see Ya'qubi, *Ta'rikh al-Ya'qubi*, II, pp.255-267, especially p.263. (Beirut Edition). See also Sharon, *Black Banners*, pp.114-115. 'Arafah, *Al-Khurasaniyun wa Dawruhum*, p.42.

(33) Ibn al-Athir, *Al-Kamil fi al-Ta'rikh*, IV, pp.246-249. (Leiden-Beirut Edition). Kharbutli, *'Abd Allah Ibn al-Zubayr*, p.192. Brockelmann, *History*, pp.76-79. Kennedy, *Prophet*, pp.94-95. Sharon, *Black Banners*, pp.115 ff. Ya'qubi, *Ta'rikh al-Ya'qubi*, II, p.263 (Beirut Edition).

(34) Marín-Guzmán, *El Islam: Ideología e Historia*, pp.284-285. Marín-Guzmán, "La Escatología Musulmana", passim .Marín-Guzmán, *El Islam: Religión y Política*, pp.62-65. Watt, *Formative Period*, p.45, and also pp.47-49. See also A.S. Tritton, *Muslim Theology*, London, 1974, p.24. Samarra'i, *Al-Ghuluw wa al-Firaq al-Ghaliyah*, pp.294-296. Cahen, *Les peuples musulmans*, p.117. Kennedy, *Prophet*, p.96. Mas'udi, *Muruj al-Dhahab*, V, p.241. Sharon, *Black Banners*, pp.84-86 and p.117, where he discusses the controversial origins of the name *Kaisaniyyah*. See also about the origins of the *Kaisaniyyah* Baladhuri, *Ansab al-Ashraf*, V, p.229. *Akhbar al-Dawlah al-'Abbasiyyah*, pp.165-166. There are several traditions about Kaisan. The anonymous *Akhbar al-Dawlah al-'Abbasiyyah* mentioned (p.165) that the *Kaisaniyyah* was associated with al-Mukhtar, known as Kaisan, who was the first to believe in the *imamah* of Muhammad Ibn al-Hanafiyyah. In this respect Ibn Rustah's opinion was very similar. He asserted that the *Kaisaniyyah* was the group of followers of al-Mukhtar b. Abi 'Ubayd, who believed that al-Mukhtar's *laqab* was Kaisan. Ibn Rustah wrote in his *Kitab al-A'laq al-Nafisah*, (p.218) the following lines: *"Hum ashab al-Mukhtar b. Abi 'Ubayd wa yadhkuruna anna laqab al-Mukhtar Kaisan"*. Very similar lines wrote Ibn Qutaybah in his *Al-Ma'arif* (p.622): *"Hum ashab al-Mukhtar b. Abi 'Ubayd wa yadhkuruna anna laqabahu Kaisan."* See also Sharon, *Black Banners*, p.86. 'Arafah, *Al-Khurasaniyun wa Dawruhum*, p.43. Hawting, *The First Dynasty of Islam*, p.51.

(35) Sabatino Moscati, "Il testamento di Abu Hashim", in *Rivista degli Studi Orientali*, Vol. XXVII, Fasc. 1-4, 1952, pp.28-46. Marín-Guzmán, *El Islam: Religión y Política*, pp.63-64. Marín-Guzmán, *El Islam: Ideología e Historia*, p.285. About the *Hashimiyyah* see Samarra'i, *Al-Ghuluw wa al-Firaq al-Ghaliyah*, p.297. Samarra'i explains the relation between the *Kaisaniyyah*, the *Mukhtariyyah* and the *Hashimiyyah*. See also Cahen, *Les peuples musulmans*, pp.123-125, for the study of the relation and continuity of those three groups.

Cahen pointed out that these three sects were considered extremists (pp.123-124). Abu Hashim had his own *shi`ah* (party). See Cahen, *Les peuples musulmans,* p.123. Cahen discusses the reasons why Abu Hashim could have chosen Muhammad b. `Ali b. `Abd Allah Ibn `Abbas as his successor (pp.128-129). Kennedy, *Prophet,* pp.124-125. Sharon, *Black Banners,* pp.84-85, and also for more details pp.103-151, where there is a detailed analysis of the *Hashimiyyah* and the ways how the `Abbasids took it over. `Arafah, *Al-Khurasaniyun wa Dawruhum,* pp.43-44. See also *Akhbar al-Dawlah al-`Abbasiyyah,* p.177. Ibn Khaldun *Kitab al-`Ibar,* III, p.214, quoted by `Arafah, *Al-Khurasaniyun wa Dawruhum,* p.44. For more details see Mas`udi, *Al-Tanbih wa al-Ishraf,* pp.308-309.

(36) Madelung, *Religious Trends in Early Islamic Iran,* Albany, 1988, p.7. This author believes that the *Khurramiyyah* "represented Persian national sentiments looking forward to a restoration of Persian sovereign rule in contrast to the universalist religious tendencies of Manicheism" (p.2)

(37) Madelung, *Religious Trends,* p.7. Georges Vajda, "Les zindiqs en pays d'Islam au début de la période `Abbaside", in *Rivista degli Studi Orientali,* Vol. XVII, 1938, pp.173-229.

(38) Madelung, *Religious Trends,* p.8.

(39) Madelung, *Religious Trends,* p.8. See also Maqrizi, *Kitab al-Niza`,* p.99. For more details about the `Abbasids adopting the *adab* of the Persians see Maqrizi, *Kitab al-Niza`,* p.95.

(40) About the *mawali* support to al-Mukhtar's revolt see Tabari, *Ta'rikh al-Rusul wa al-Muluk,* II, pp.619-620 (Leiden Edition). Baladhuri, *Ansab al-Ashraf,* V, p.263. Ya'qubi, *Ta'rikh al-Ya'qubi,* II, p.263. Sharon, *Black Banners,* p.108. Kennedy, *Prophet,* p.96-97. Hawting, *The First Dynasty of Islam,* pp.51-52. `Arafah, *Al-Khurasaniyun wa Dawruhum,* p.42. Cahen, *Les peuples musulmans,* p.116.

(41) *Akhbar al-Dawlah al-`Abbasiyyah,* pp.249-250, in Lassner, *Islamic Revolution,* p.93. See also Marín-Guzmán, *El Islam: Ideología e Historia,* pp.267-272. Marín-Guzmán, *El Islam: Religión y Política,* pp.53-58. Marín-Guzmán, "La Escatología", passim.

(42) Cf. Tabari, *Ta'rikh al-Rusul wa al-Muluk,* passim, especially, II, pp.1898-1909, II, pp.1916-1917, II, pp. 1939-1942, II, pp.1943-1950, II, pp.1996-1997, II, pp.2007-2018, III, pp.78-81 (Leiden Edition). See also Ibn al-Athir, *Al-Kamil fi al-Ta'rikh,* IV, pp.281-286, IV, pp.342-

345 and IV, pp.388-391. (Leiden-Beirut Edition).

(43) Tabari, *Ta'rikh al-Rusul wa al-Muluk*, I, p.3339. (Leiden Edition). Cahen, *Les peuples musulmans*, p.112.

(44) For a good discussion of these theological controversies, and the theological schools see: Ralph Stehly, "Un problème de théologie islamique: la définition des fautes graves (*Kaba'ir*)," in *Revue des études islamiques*, LXV, Fascicule 2, 1977, pp.165-181. Josef van Ess, "Disputationspraxis in der Islamischen Theologie. Eine Vorlaufige Skizze", in *Revue des études islamiques*, XLIV, 1976, pp.23-60. Montgomery Watt, "The Beginnings of the Islamic Theological Schools", in *Revue des études islamiques*, XLIV, 1976, pp.15-21. Marín-Guzmán, *El Islam: Ideología e Historia*, pp.172-173. Marín-Guzmán, "Razón y revelación en el Islam", pp.133-136. Cahen, *Les peuples musulmans*, p.112. Madelung, *Religious Trends*, pp.54-76. For these theological discussions and the different points of view between the *Qadariyyah* and the *Khawarij* see Baghdadi, *Al-Farq bayna al-Firaq*, passim, especially pp.121-122 of the English translation. See also Ibn Qutaybah, *Al-Ma'arif*, pp.624-625. For the different divisions of the Khawarij and their various opinions on this matter of deeds and faith see Baghdadi, *Al-Farq bayna al-Firaq*, pp.91-92 of the English translation.

(45) Tabari, *Ta'rikh al-Rusul wa al-Muluk*, III, p.1733 (Leiden Edition). See also Baghdadi, *Al-Farq bayna al-Firaq*, p.119 of the English translation. See also Hawting, *The First Dynasty of Islam*, pp.92-93. Watt, *Formative Period*, pp.85-88.

(46) For the study of the *Qadariyyah* and its connection with the *Mu'tazilah* see Ibn Rustah, *Kitab al-A'laq al-Nafisah*, pp.220-221. See Carlo A. Nallino, "Di una strana opinione attribuita ad al-Gahiz in torno al corano", in *Rivista degli Studi Orientali*, Vol. VII, Fascicolo 2, 1916, pp.421-428. Al-Baghdadi in his *Al-Farq bayna al-Firaq* (pp.180-183 of the English translation) explained these opinions of al-Jahiz, and classified them under the section of *Jahiziyyah*, in the part of his book dealing with the interesting schools of the *Mu'tazilah* and the *Qadariyyah*. See also Carlo A. Nallino, "Sull' origine del nome dei Mu'taziliti", in *Rivista degli Studi Orientali*, Vol. VII, Fascicolo 2, 1916, pp.429-454. Carlo A. Nallino, "Rapporti fra la dogmatica Mu'tazilita e quella degli Ibaditi dell'Africa Settentrionale", in *Rivista degli Studi Orientali*, Vol. VII, Fascicolo 2, 1916, pp.455-460. Carlo A. Nallino, "Sul nome di Qadariti", in *Rivista degli Studi Orientali*, Vol.VII, Fascicolo 2, 1916, pp.461-466. See also Ibn Qutaybah, *Al-Ma'arif*, p.622. Marín-Guzmán, "Razón y Revelación en el Islam", pp.135-136. Marín-Guzmán, *El Islam: Ideología e Historia*, pp.185-

187. Marín-Guzmán, *Introducción a los Estudios Islámicos,* passim. Watt, *Islamic Philosophy,* pp.58-72. Philip Hitti, *Islam, Modo de Vida,* Madrid, 1973, pp.88-89. Cahen, *El Islam,* p.85. Samarra'i, *Al-Ghuluw wa al-Firaq al-Ghaliyah,* pp.273-276. About the *Qadariyyah* see pp.272-273. About *al-Mu'tazilah's* idea of *tawhid* see p.274. Nadir, *Ahamm al-Firaq al-Islamiyyah,* pp.48-64.

(47) For more details about al-Mansur see Ya'qubi, *Ta'rikh al-Ya'qubi,* II, pp.364-380 (Beirut Edition). About al-Ma'mun see Ya'qubi, *Ta'rikh al-Ya'qubi,* II, pp.444-453 (Beirut Edition).

(48) H. Nyberg, "Al-Mu`tazila", in *Encyclopaedia of Islam* (1), Vol. III, Leyden, 1928, pp.787-793, especially pp.788-789. Nyberg explained the relation between Wasil Ibn `Ata, the Mu`tazili philosopher and leader, with the `Abbasids, which led him to the conclusion that "In a general way the teaching of Wasil on *al-manzila* can only be perfectly understood if we see in it the theoretical crystallisation of the political programme of the `Abbasids before their accession to power. Everything leads us to believe that the theology of Wasil and the early Mu`tazila represents the official theology of the `Abbasid movement. This gives an unforced explanation of the fact that it was the official doctrine of the `Abbasid court for at least a century." (pp.788-789)

(49) Nyberg, "Mu`tazila", p.789.

(50) Cahen, *Les peuples musulmans,* pp.140-142. For more details about the school of the *Wasiliyyah,* one of the most important of the *Mu'tazilah* see Baghdadi, *Al-Farq bayna al-Firaq,* pp.119-123 of the English translation. Al-Baghdadi considered that the twenty schools in which the *Mu'tazilah* divided were real sects and that each one condemned the other as unorthodox. (p.116) The *Mu'tazilah* had also several rival schools which contradicted their beliefs and practices. Among them one of the most important was the *Karramiyyah.* About it see Clifford E. Bosworth, "Karramiyya", in *Encyclopaedia of Islam* (2), Vol. IV, Leiden, 1976, pp.667-669, see especially p.668.

# Chapter III

## Popular dimensions of the 'Abbasid Revolution

### I- Introduction

The Shi'ite experience in organizing intellectual and armed opposition to the Umayyads served well the 'Abbasid cause. Although very constant, the Shi'ite armed revolts against the first dynasty of Islam had only occasional and temporary success. All these rebellions were violently suppressed. Taking these facts into consideration, mainly the reasons for the failure of the previous rebellions, but keeping in mind their revolutionary potential as well, the 'Abbasids appealed to the Shi'ites to lead and organize a well prepared and well equipped revolution against the Umayyads. The 'Abbasid revolution in its first stages appeared as a Shi'ite movement, but better organized, more patient and more careful in all the moves.

The *Hashimiyyah*, a purely Shi'ite group, organized a secret propaganda of opposition to the Umayyads. The *Hashimiyyah* called the people of Khurasan and Iraq to oppose the rulers and secretly spread the revolution and the new ideology. This Shi'ite group was later hijacked by the 'Abbasids who then led the opposition to the Umayyads and led the *Hashimiyyah* by spreadingthe idea of Abu Hashim's testament favoring the 'Abbasids. The 'Abbasids, descendants of the Family of the Prophet, claimed legitimacy and made political promises to the Shi'ites to gain their support.

The 'Abbasids organized strong armies, especially of Khurasanis, in which all discontented elements (*mawali*, religious groups, and Southern tribes) were included and promised a share after taking power. These armies were capable of defeating the Umayyads. After a series of wars, starting in Khurasan in 747, and moving west towards Iraq and Syria, the 'Abbasid armies defeated the Umayyads in Merv, Nishapur, and other major cities in Khurasan. In Iraq, in the city of Kufa, in November 749, the 'Abbasid Abu al-'Abbas was proclaimed caliph. This proclamation became an important challenge to the Umayyad authority. The wars continued in Iraq and Syria. Wasit and all the Umayydad strongholds in Iraq fell under 'Abbasid control. In Zab, in 750, the last Umayyad caliph, Marwan Ibn Muhammad, was definitively defeated, and at that point, he lost his real power, but he saved his life for few more months. Shortly afterwards Damascus, the capital of the Empire, was captured by the revolutionary armies.

The proclamation and recognition by the Khurasani armies of an 'Abbasid as the new caliph did not satisfy the Shi'ites, who felt deceived. Some opposition was rapidly repressed, and those pro-'Alids and critical of the 'Abbasids, like Abu Salamah, were killed. Those who obtained considerable power, to the point that they could defy the new dynasty, like Abu Muslim, were killed as well, although success in the armed revolution was due to them. The new rulers were determined to keep control of the Empire through any means, even using the same ones which brought them to power.

The revolutionary changes which took place as soon as the 'Abbasids were in power, such as the new administration of the *Dar al-Islam,* the preference for the Khurasanis in the army and in the court over the Arab element, the redistribution of land for Khurasanis and members of the Southern tribes, as well as the equality to the *mawali* with the Arabs, -- these all ignored the Shi'ites, who mainly wanted leadership of the community. The Shi'ites felt left out and immediately went back to their traditional opposition, both intellectual as well as armed, against the new *dawlah*.

## II- The means of the 'Abbasid revolution: propaganda and ideology

The claim of descent from the Prophet (*Ahl al-Bayt, Ahl al-Nabi, Ahl Muhammad*) was an extremely important claim of legitimacy for the government of *al-Ummah al-Islamiyyah.*[1] This claim was taken seriously by many Muslims at the time of the 'Abbasid revolution, which lasted several years. Many Muslims accepted the claim of belonging to Muhammad's family as a strong argument of legitimacy; however, for others that was not enough.

For some Muslims, like the Shi'ites, the concept of *Ahl al-Bayt* was limited to the descendants of 'Ali and Fatimah. Other Shi'ites expanded this notion to the cousins, other descendants of 'Ali Ibn Abi Talib through his son Muhammad Ibn al-Hanafiyyah. That was the case of the *Kaisaniyyah*, the *Mukhtariyyah* and the early *Hashimiyyah*. Following those practices, the 'Abbasids extended that notion of *Ahl al-Bayt* not only to the cousins, but to all other relatives of 'Ali and Muhammad, especially to those of the Prophet's uncle al-'Abbas. For some other Muslims, like the Khawarij, the argument of descent from the Prophet meant nothing in terms of legitimacy in power, since they preached that the leader (*imam*) of the Muslim community should be the best Muslim, without consideration of his family, origin, tribe or ethnic group. Piety was for them the major argument for becoming the *Amir al-Mu'minin*. Even a freeman Muslim could become thecaliph if he was the best in the Muslim community.[2]

The 'Abbasids, true descendants of the Family of the Prophet through Muhammad's uncle al-'Abbas, claimed legitimacy and all rights to the caliphate. However, that argument was not enough for everyone. Moreover, there were many other descendants of Muhammad who, under those circumstances, could also claim the rights to the caliphate. The ʻAbbasids were clearly aware of this situation. They posed new arguments in their propaganda and their ideology to convince people to support their aspirations as the true rulers, and also to gain the help of other descendants of the Family, mainly the Shiʻites, who at that time were developing their own ideology against the Umayyads and claiming leadership of the Muslim community. The ʻAbbasids recognized the strong Shiʻite opposition, their claims to the caliphate, and their relationship to the Prophet.

Far from willing to fight the Shiʻites, they tried to gain their support. The ʻAbbasids needed all the available support to fight the Umayyads in power, and to gain the help of other religious, political, tribal, and ethnic groups, they appealed to the various grievances held against the impious, tyrannical and unjust Umayyad rule. The support of all these groups was absolutely esential for the triumph of the ʻAbbasids.

However, the ʻAbbasid revolution was not only the result of a popular upheaval. It also came from a planned and well organized propaganda (*daʻwah*) that promised help and changes favoring each group. It also had a clear ideology that comprised the various claims for power and offered to stop the heavy taxation and to give, at the same time, equality to the *mawali* with the Arab Muslims. The ʻAbbasids were able to defeat the Umayyads because they gained popular support and had established a powerful army. The ʻAbbasids were cynical enough to believe that Allah is most of the time on the side of strong armies.

The *daʻwah* was kept secret for almost 30 years (718-747). The ʻAbbasids started spreading their own ideas of revolt against the Umayyads in Kufa in Iraq, and in Khurasan mainly in Merv. The ʻAbbasids had the two major elements of any revolution: a clandestine and efficient propaganda organization for spreading their ideology; and a well equipped army for facing the Umayyads with some chance of success. This is why the ʻAbbasids used two important terms: the *daʻwah,* the call, the mis-

sion (i.e., the clandestine propaganda); and *dawlah*, the
new government, the end of the Umayyad dynasty and the
establishment of the 'Abbasids.[3] The 'Abbasid *dawlah*
meant the return to pristine Islam, to that of the time of
the Prophet; and because of this situation their whole
mission had a messianic meaning. The relation *da'wah-
dawlah* had very clear political connotations for the 'Abbasids, who were the first to start the idea of revolution in
Islam.[4]

In the early stages, the 'Abbasid propaganda appeared as a Shi'ite or 'Alid group through the *Hashimiyyah*,
claiming leadership and the caliphate for the family of the
Prophet.[5] The argument convincing the Shi'ites and their
supporters (Arabs, clients, and religious followers) that
the 'Abbasids had legitimate claims for the caliphate was
their kinship to the Family of the Prophet. The argument
used that they were pro-'Alid was Abu Hashim's testament in favor of the 'Abbasids, then his closest relatives.
The 'Abbasids spread the idea that Abu Hashim had
transmitted to them all his esoteric and exoteric knowledge. The fact that Abu Hashim, the son of Muhammad
Ibn al-Hanafiyyah, died in Humaymah, in Syria (in to-
day's Southern Jordan), in the 'Abbasids' property, was a
strong argument.

It is still possible to doubt the authenticity of the
tradition spread by the 'Abbasids that Abu Hashim in his
testament appointed Muhammad Ibn 'Abd Allah b. al-
'Abbas as his successor, despite the research that has been
done about these events in the last years.[6] It could have
been a later invention of the 'Abbasids as "proof" of their
authenticity and legitimacy in claiming rights for the
Shi'ites. The truth is that Abu Hashim died in Humaymah, the place that the 'Abbasid leaders had chosen for
their own activities due to its excellent location for secret
contacts with the Eastern parts of the Empire. However,
Abu Hashim's testament is still doubtful due to the lack of
evidence in reliable sources.[7]

Whether true or not, Abu Hashim's testament was a major argument used by the 'Abbasids in their secret propaganda. It was also enough for many to accept the 'Abbasid leadership of the *Hashimiyyah*. However, some other Shi'ites refused for some time to accept the 'Abbasid leadership and continued their own movements. In the year 740 occurred a tragic event: Zayd b. 'Ali, grandson of Husayn Ibn 'Ali Ibn Abi Talib, who believed the Imamate belonged to the member of the Family who took up arms against the Umayyads, revolted, but after defeat he was crucified in Kufa. His son Yahya b. Zayd also revolted and was killed as well, but in Khurasan. As a result, the Shi'ites lost their leaders, the direct descendants of 'Ali and Fatimah.

This event did not mean that the Shi'ites disappeared. The *Zaydiyyah* as a sect was then developed. According to al-Baghdadi the *Zaydiyyah* was one of the groups derived from the *Rawafid* (*Zaydiyyah, Imamiyyah, Kaisaniyyah* and *Ghulat*), and through its relation with the *Kaisaniyyah*, one can also easily see its connection with the *Hashimiyyah*, the Shi'ite sect of which the 'Abbasids became the leaders.[8] Keeping in mind these issues, the 'Abbasid propaganda was skillful enough to gain support of the majority of the Shi'ites, to be accepted as a pro-'Alid movement, and to inherit the leadership of *Ahl al-Bayt*. The 'Abbasids asserted commonality with the Shi'ites' anti-Umayyad feelings, and if obtaining power with the support of the Shi'ites, they would have together regained the important office of *Amir al-Mu'minin* for the House of the Prophet. The 'Abbasids promised the Shi'ites participation in appointing a descendant of the Prophet Muhammad, suitable to all Muslims, as the *Imam-Amir al-Mu'minin,* as soon as the Umayyads had been ousted. Later this pro-'Alid 'Abbasid propaganda was changed by an absolutely 'Abbasid aspiration. This was the mission of the 'Abbasid secret missionaries *(du'at)* in Iraq and Khurasan, next to the call *(da'wah),* who planned to support the 'Abbasid movement against the Umayyads.

One of the main issues in the propaganda was to keep secret their mission and the anonymity of the 'Abbasid *Imam*. Contrary to al-Mukhtar's revolt in which the leader of the movement, the Mahdi Muhammad Ibn al-Hanafiyyah, was clearly mentioned and recognized, the 'Abbasids, leading a very careful and patient propaganda for their revolution, kept the leadership hidden even from some of their own followers. There is a tradition preserved in the *Akhbar al-Dawlah al-'Abbasiyyah* in which the instruction to the propagandists was to keep the secret of the identity of the *imam* by claiming the state of *taqiyyah*.[9] In this way they could hide from the Umayyad authorities, who might stop and even kill the 'Abbasid leaders. The missionaries were told to avoid any direct contact with the *imam*. Only in case of extreme necessity could they contact him and then only during the *Hajj* (Pilgrimage) to Mecca. During the Pilgrimage the *imam* would be among thousands of people, and any contact with his followers would not be suspicious.[10]

Why was the 'Abbasid propaganda so rapidly spread and accepted? Why did the 'Abbasids choose Khurasan as their propaganda center and place to look for popular support? What were the major issues raised in the 'Abbasid propaganda?

The 'Abbasid propaganda was rapidly spread and popularly accepted because the 'Abbasids appealed to important issues. Moreover, the Umayyad authorities hardly noticed the propagandists, who disguised themselves as merchants, giving them the opportunity to travel anywhere in the Empire without suspicion. This fact made things easier for the spread of the 'Abbasid propaganda and the search for followers.[11] First of all the 'Abbasids appealed to Islam, calling for reestablishment of its purity. They accused the Umayyads of impiety. The black flags against the Umayyads' white banners became a messianic symbol for the restoration of justice and the end of tyranny. However, Muslims knew that al-'Abbas, the Prophet's uncle, was a late convert to Islam. According to some sources he became Muslim after Muhammad's conquest of Mecca to avoid being included in the group of the *tulaqa'*, the reluctant converts.[12]

These issues were used against them, and the Umayyads also had an effective propaganda. The Umayyads claimed kinship (*qaraba*) to the Prophet Muhammad through a common tribal ancestor, 'Abd al-Manaf. The Umayyads even convinced many Muslims that there were no other Prophet's relatives than the Umayyads, even before the 'Abbasids started their own propaganda. There are several traditions, especially preserved by the later source al-Maqrizi's *Kitab al-Niza'*, in which the Umayyads claimed superiority to the Banu Hashim and also to the Prophet himself, a claim much criticized by several Muslims that tainted the Umayyads' commitment to Islam. In this respect the tradition preserved by al-Maqrizi says:

> [This deception on the part of the Umayyads and their partisans reached the point] that one day, al-Hajjaj b. Yusuf ascended the wooden stairway of the pulpit and proclaimed over the heads of those present, "Is your messenger more precious to you or your caliph?" He meant that `Abd al-Malik b. Marwan b. al-Hakam was superior to the messenger of God. When Jabala b. [Zahr] heard him, he exclaimed: "By God, I swear that I will never pray behind him again! Moreover, if ever I see anybody taking up arms against al-Hajjaj, I will certainly take up arms myself and join him.[13]

Some poets of the Umayyad period praised these rulers beyond what is even allowed by Islam. Some people even believed that the *khilafah* of the Umayyads was superior to the *nubuwwah*, the prophecy of Muhammad.[14]

These traditions were skillfully used by the 'Abbasids to spread the idea that the Umayyads had a weak commitment to Islam, and that they should not be the rulers of *al-Ummah al-Islamiyyah*. Moreover, they suggested that, as Jabala b.

Zuhr mentioned, Muslims should take up arms to oust the impious Umayyads. Concerning the tradition that the Umayyads considered the *khilafah* superior to the *nubuwwah*, the famous scholar al-Jahiz in the time of the 'Abbasid caliph al-Muta-wakkil criticized these ideas, and to legitimize the 'Abbasid *dawlah* he wrote:

*They used to assert that a man's successor* (khalifa) *in his family is higher in his estimation than his messenger* (rasul) *sent to them.*[15]

Al-Tabari quoted the long and detailed speech of Abu al-'Abbas, given when he was proclaimed and recognized by a large group of followers as the new caliph in Kufa in the year 132/749, shortly after Muhammad b. Khalid al-Qasri, with strong Yemenite support, occupied that city. This proclamation of an 'Abbasid as caliph was a threat to the leadership of the Umayyads since their legitimacy was challenged by this acceptance of another leader as the legitimate *Amir al-Mu'minin*.

However, not everything was easy for the 'Abbasids, since the Shi'ites and some pro-'Alid leaders, like Abu Salamah and Sulayman, wanted to enthrone a Shi'ite; and they were extremely surprised when Abu al-'Abbas was proclaimed the new caliph. These opposition leaders to the 'Abbasids had no other choice but to comply, since the major Khurasani armies followed Abu Muslim, a loyal warrior for the 'Abbasid house. Later these pro-'Alid leaders had a tragic end when the 'Abbasids killed them, as stated in the Arabic sources.[16]

In his speech Abu al-'Abbas summarized the whole 'Abbasid ideology. First, he appealed to Islam and praised God, a balanced and skillful way to claim legitimacy and popular support with religious arguments. Then he talked about his own family, its piety and close kinship to the Prophet Muhammad.[17] These arguments were also extremely important for gaining popular support and legitimacy. Another relevant issue used in their propaganda

concerned the just distribution of wealth in the time of the
*Rashidun* caliphs, until the Umayyads took most of it for
themselves. The 'Abbasids accused the Umayyads of
appropriating the wealth and of oppressing those entitled
to it.[18]    They promised to restore the practices of the
*Rashidun*.

In his speech Abu al-'Abbas mentioned that Allah
took revenge on the Umayyads at the hands of the 'Abbasids. Through the 'Abbasids God had restored the unity of
the *Ummah* (Community), and He had given back the
leadership to the House of the Prophet.[19] All these issues
were important to the 'Abbasid propaganda. They offered
an equal distribution of that wealth, a promise that drew
many people to the 'Abbasid revolution, hoping for a share
in the Muslim wealth. Abu al-'Abbas's speech also reveals
the 'Abbasid promises used in the propaganda to restore
the unity of *al-Ummah al-Islamiyyah* and the leadership
of the House of the Prophet, two important issues taken
seriously by the majority of the Muslims at that time.
Bringing peace, ending tyranny, giving equal opportunities to all Muslims, and offering a just distribution of the
wealth were all important promises included in the 'Abbasid ideology and propaganda. These offers brought as a
result the popular support for the 'Abbasids.

Abu al-'Abbas's speech was continued by Dawud
Ibn 'Ali  in the same mosque of Kufa; in it the 'Abbasid
ideology is revealed with some more details.[20]   Moreover,
this other speech contains additional elements of the 'Abbasids' promises, since he said that the new government
will rule people according to the Book of Allah, and that the
rulers will act according to the conduct of God's Messenger.[21] He also cursed the Umayyads and criticized their
impious behavior because, in his opinion, they had preferred the worldly pleasures to the everlasting abode.[22]

In these speeches, which contain the general ideology and propaganda of the 'Abbasids, fighting the Umayyads
is justified because of their weak commitment to Islam.
The 'Abbasids asserted that the Umayyads did not rule the

*ummah* according to Allah's Book and the teachings of the Prophet Muhammad. The rebellion against the Umayyads was deemed not only a right, but also a duty of all Muslims. The 'Abbasid propaganda affirmed, then, the need to return power to the family of the Prophet.

The 'Abbasids gained popular support through their own propaganda, by calling for a member of the House of the Prophet to be *Amir al-Mu'minin,* one acceptable to all Muslims. This was a shrewd way to approach and gain support of the Shi'ites. The 'Abbasid promise of equality (*musawah*) to all Muslims also contributed to their popular support and to the rapid spread of their ideology. This promise made the *mawali* support the 'Abbasid aspirations. The 'Abbasids were then considered supporters of the *Shu'ubiyyah* movement.[23]

The 'Abbasids also had other religious arguments for gaining popular support in their struggles against the Umayyads. The term *da'wah,* coined in the time of the Prophet Muhammad, and meaning the call to Islam, was used successfully by the 'Abbasids, as those who call for the restoration of Islam. Muhammad's supporters were called *du'at.* The 'Abbasids used the same name for their supporters to give their mission a sacred connotation, which could easily attract more followers.[24] The 'Abbasids had 12 *nuqaba'* (missionaries, sing. *naqib*) in Khurasan and 70 more in other places, the same number that the Prophet Muhammad had as followers at the beginning of his mission: 12 to represent him in Medina before the *hijrah*, the same number representing the 'Abbasids in Khurasan. These issues were carefully developed by the 'Abbasids to give a more religious dimension to their aspirations. This religious propaganda had a more effective impact upon the people who could see the relations between the Prophet Muhammad and the 'Abbasids.

The 'Abbasids were always careful in all their moves. They were clearly aware that no matter how popular their movement, it meant nothing without a strong and well equipped army. They were also very well informed about the Khurasanis, excellent warriors with much military experience, who formed the major bases for the Muslim armies defending the Eastern provinces of the *Dar al-Islam*.[25] It was no coincidence that the 'Abbasids chose to spread their propaganda in Khurasan and to gain the support of the Khurasanis, guaranteeing them good soldiers for defeating the Umayyad armies.

There is a tradition, although written after the 'Abbasids took power, which explains that the 'Abbasids chose Khurasan for their propaganda because people in that province already accepted and supported them; but the people in Kufa leaned towards the children of 'Ali Ibn Abi Talib, the people of Basra were loyal to the memory of 'Uthman, the Syrians supported the Umayyads, and the people of Jazirah (Iraq) were Khawarij.[26] However, one can also see that the 'Abbasids wanted to capitalize on the *mawali* opposition to the Umayyads because of heavy taxation and the various grievances caused by discrimination, especially in Khurasan. The Umayyads caused economic problems to several groups with heavy taxation and the uneven distribution of wealth. The 'Abbasid ideology and propaganda appealed to all these issues, and gained supporters by promising to remedy these serious problems.[27]

In the antagonism and rivalry between Syria and Iraq the 'Abbasids chose the Iraqi cause and exploited in their propaganda the anti-Syrian sentiments and the strong opposition to the presence of Syrian armies in Iraq and Khurasan.

The disputes between Northern and Southern confederations of Arab tribes were also exploited by the 'Abbasids with great benefit. The 'Abbasids were aware of the power of the Yemenites in Khurasan, their enmity against the Mudar and the Umayyads. By supporting the Qahtan in their struggles against their traditional enemies the Qays, the 'Abbasids also gained their support in the war against the ruling dynasty. It has been demonstrated that the 'Abbasid army through Abu Muslim al-

Khurasani recruited a large percentage of Yemenites, also good and experienced fighters. The major Arabic sources have preserved various traditions dealing with the secret 'Abbasid propaganda in which the inter-tribal rivalry can be seen as a main issue in the 'Abbasid revolution. The revolution was popularly supported, among other reasons, because they managed to gain the Qahtan's help in ousting the Umayyads.

In this secret propaganda various Arabic sources explain that one of the first missions of the 'Abbasid emissaries was to approach and gain the support of the Yemenites in Khurasan, and not the Mudar. However, other sources offer contradictory traditions. Thus when working with the Arabic sources one has to weigh the contradictions, the reliability of the various traditions, and the reliability of the sources themselves.

The *Akhbar al-Dawlah al-'Abbasiyyah* preserved a tradition in which the instruction to Abu 'Ikrimah, concerning the Arab tribes was:

> *When you comest to Marw, dwell in the midst of the tribes of Yaman, draw near unto Rabi'ah and beware of Mudar; but draw unto thyself whomsoever thou canst of the faithful ones among them.*[28]

These instructions were clearly directed to obtain the support of the Yemenites; however, the possibility of gaining the help of other groups, Arab or *mawali*, was kept open.

A late source, but extremely important for the information and different traditions cited, is al-Maqrizi's *Kitab al-Niza'* which preserved a similar sort of instructions, but from the 'Abbasid *imam* Ibrahim to Abu Muslim. Abu Muslim was supposed to look for the Yemenites' support, to live among them, probably in order to gain their trust, and at the same time to beware of the Mudar, then considered the enemies.[29]

On the other hand, al-Tabari's *Ta'rikh al-Rusul wa al-Muluk* preserved various traditions in this respect in which the mission was to approach the Yemenites, but, contrary to the other traditions, to be gentle to the Mudar *(ud' al-nas ilaina wa anzil fi al-Yaman wa altif bi-Mudar)*.[30]

It has been demonstrated that several members of the Mudar confederation of tribes were also enrolled in the 'Abbasid army.[31] How can this apparent contradiction be solved? One explanation is that the list of Arab soldiers in the 'Abbasid army, which included some Qays elements, belong to the last period of the 'Abbasid revolution, when it broke out openly. The traditions concerning the approach to the Yemenites and the rejection of the Mudar belong to the first period of the 'Abbasid revolution, when the propaganda was still secret.

The problem could also be solved by one of two other explanations. The first is that the mission of the *nuqaba'* was to attract the Qahtan to the 'Abbasid cause, but to be gentle at the same time to the Qays. They were to gain the Yemenite support first, but be open to obtaining the Mudar's help as well, since all help was important and necessary. The second is that in the early stages of the 'Abbasid propaganda the mission of the *nuqaba'* was to gain the Yemenites' support to the 'Abbasid cause. Once obtained, the secret missionaries very carefully contacted the Mudar and obtained the help of some of them, which is evident by their enrollment in the 'Abbasid army. This second idea is more reasonable since, according to some traditions, in the early stages of the 'Abbasid *da'wah* religion *(din)* was the strongest call to support the movement, even stronger, in certain ways, than tribal solidarity *('asabiyyah)*.[32]

Who were these secret missionaries and what was their real impact upon the Khurasani society? How did they succeed in organizing the pro-'Alid and later on the pro-'Abbasid opposition to the Umayyads? What was their role in organizing an armed revolution?

Although recent research has brought new conclusions about the early stages of the *da'wah,* there is still much that remains unknown.[33] The different traditions preserved in various sources lead to different conclusions, often contradictory ones. One of the major research problems of the 'Abbasid revolution concerns the propagandists, their origins, religious beliefs, ethnicity, and mission. Much about the leaders of the 'Abbasid *da'wah* remains obscure because their identity was kept secret for a long time. Al-Tabari's suggestion that there were *mawali* and Arabs among the first propagandists seems quite reasonable, since the'Abbasids wanted to reach all elements of the Khurasani society, and by using them as missionaries, things could lean in their favor.[34] The *Akhbar al-Dawlah al-'Abbasiyyah* also preserved a tradition in which after Bukayr b. Mahan was kept in Kufa and Abu 'Ikrimah was sent to Khurasan, one of Abu 'Ikrimah's goals was to "Attract as many Persians as possible because they are the upholders of our *da'wah* and through them God will support it."[35] These two men about whom several traditions were developed, and the sources provide some information, were not the first people to be sent to Khurasan. However, they were two of the major actors when the *da'wah* was still secret. The sources mentioned a number of *nuqaba'* who were sent to organize the *da'wah* in Merv and in the whole region of Khurasan.[36] The mission was kept secret, as was the identity of the 'Abbasid *imam*, who was also the leader of the *Hashimiyyah.* The 'Abbasid relations with the *Hashimiyyah* gave the movement a pro-'Alid connotation. The 'Abbasid *da'wah* was well organized. The'Abbasids very carefully made the important decisions and waited patiently for several years until the pro-'Alid *da'wah* was transformed into a pro-'Abbasid one.[37]

According to various Arabic sources and the different traditions, it was Muhammad b. 'Ali, who had become the leader of the *Hashimiyyah* and the *imam* of the 'Abbasids, who organized the secret *da'wah* and sent missionaries to Khurasan to call people on behalf of the *Hashimiyyah* to revolt against the Umayyad dynasty and to fight for the restoration of the leadership of the House of the Prophet for *al-Ummah al-Islamiyyah*. As the movement spread and more emissaries became necessary, Bukayr b. Mahan, who led the Kufan organization, was sent to Merv as emissary of Muhammad b. 'Ali to supervise the organization of this secret society in Khurasan.[38] After Bukayr b. Mahan's death in 743, Abu Salamah al-Khallal, then leader of the group in Kufa, was sent to Merv.[39] He was accompanied by a young follower named Abu Muslim, who had been sent along by the new 'Abbasid *imam* and new leader of the *Hashimiyyah*, the *imam* Ibrahim Ibn Muhammad. After a short period of time, Abu Muslim became leader of the 'Abbasid *da'wah* in Khurasan and started the open revolution against the Umayyads. What made the 'Abbasids successful in defeating those in power? How was the 'Abbasid army organized? Who were the leaders of the armed revolution?

### III- The armed revolution: the role of Abu Muslim

The 'Abbasids were perfectly aware that the revolution could be aborted and would mean nothing without a well equipped and well organized army. After the secret propaganda and clandestine approach to the various discontented elements, the 'Abbasids gained popular support and the will of many Arabs and *mawali* to join the army and fight the Umayyads. It was Abu Muslim who had the difficult mission of organizing the army.

Undoubtedly Abu Muslim became one of the major figures of the 'Abbasid cause and one of the major leaders of the armed revolution. It was he who declared open revolt in 747 against the Umayyads after it had been kept secret for nearly thirty years. Despite his importance in the 'Abbasids' successful revolution, still his origin, his ethnic group and some of his religious beliefs puzzle the historian, due to the existence of various and contradictory traditions.[40] Some claimed he was Arabic; others, that he was Persian.[41]

At this point it is impossible, and may remain so, to determine if he was Arabic or Persian. Another major problem about Abu Muslim was that he fell from grace with the 'Abbasids, and the caliph al-Mansur killed him.[42] This fact spawned different traditions, some in favor and some others against him. Some traditions, preserved by al-Shahrastani and Ibn Hazm al-Andalusi, call him a heretic.[43] The religious group of the *Khurramiyyah* in Iran considered him its lord. This fact suggests that he was Persian. Moreover, he was the one who could lead the Khurasanis in a great army for the 'Abbasids against the Umayyads.[44]

Several researchers have concluded that Abu Muslim was a *mawla*.[45] His full name was Abu Muslim 'Abd al-Rahman Ibn Muslim al-Khurasani. Whether true or not, he was considered a *mawla* by many of his followers in Khurasan. That fact was important to the local people who favored the assimilation programs; i.e. favored the *Shu'ubiyyah* aspirations. Undoubtedly this appointment was extremely important since the *mawali* gave their popular support to the 'Abbasid revolution in the hope of fulfilling the 'Abbasid promise of equality (*musawah*) to the *mawali* with the Arab Muslims.

Abu Muslim organized an efficient army in which Arabs and *mawali* were combined and, for the first time, treated equally. He also followed the 'Abbasid *imam*'s orders to revolt at the appropriate time against Marwan b. Muhammad, the Umayyad caliph.[46] Along with Abu Muslim, Abu Salamah, Qahtabah b. Shabib and 'Abd Allah b. 'Ali were undoubtedly the major military leaders of the 'Abbasid forces in Khurasan, Iraq, Mesopotamia and Syria against the Umayyads.[47]

Marwan II had achieved power after a war between members of his own family. He was an experienced warrior who had defended the Muslim frontiers in Armenia and Azerbaijan. His strength and stubbornness had given him the nickname of *al-Himar* (the Ass).[48] He was determined to give all power to the Qays in the inter-tribal feuds and expel the Yemenites from Syria. These actions caused him serious political problems and opposition to his leadership. Revolts in Iraq broke out almost immediately. Marwan's lieutenants, the Qaysite Ishaq b. Muslim al-'Uqayli and Yazid b. 'Umar b. Hubayrah, controlled the situation in the various areas of conflict, especially in Kufa and Wasit. Yazid b. 'Umar b. Hubayrah was then appointed governor for the East, stationed in Wasit. However, this peace was temporary because economic problems in Syria, aggravated by plagues and famine after the wars, worsened the political situation of Marwan II. New discontent broke out. Abu Muslim, advantageously for the 'Abbasids, declared the open revolution against the Umayyads in Khurasan (*Shawwal* 1, 129, June 15, 747).

There is evidence in the Arabic sources that when Abu Muslim called for this revolt, tribal outbreaks took place again in Khurasan. The wars between Nasr Ibn Sayyar, the last Umayyad governor of Khurasan, and Juday' Ibn al-Kirmani, whom he had removed from office, undoubtedly had tribal connotations.[49] The Mudar accused Ibn al-Kirmani of agitation and of calling the Yemenites to revolt, to the *fitnah*. Nasr Ibn Sayyar fought them to stop a new *fitnah*.

What was the role of the 'Abbasid emissaries in these new inter-tribal wars in Khurasan? Were these new tribal outbreaks caused by the 'Abbasid propaganda and Abu Muslim's support of the Yemenites? Did the Mudar feel left out of the 'Abbasid outbreak? Did they with the help of the Umayyad governor of Khurasan fight one more time the Qahtan, their traditional enemies? Did most of the Mudar in Khurasan remain loyal to the Umayyads? Was the new tribal fighting the result of a Yemenite opposition to their enemies? Was it because the 'Abbasids were trying to approach the Mudar after gaining the Qahtan's help?

The answers to all these questions remain speculations. However, further research could bring new results and lead to a better understanding of these problems and the 'Abbasid support of the Yemenites. The Qahtan became one of the major forces in the 'Abbasid cause against the Umayyads, which is proven by the evidence in the Arabic sources.[50]

There were some Northerners in Khurasan who had various grievances against the Umayyad administration and openly opposed the dynasty in power. The 'Abbasids were aware of these grievances and took advantage of them by appealing to the discontented elements of the Mudar. Abu Muslim capitalized on the struggles between Nasr Ibn Sayyar and Ibn al-Kirmani.[51] He also approved the various victories of Ibn al-Kirmani against Nasr Ibn Sayyar. Abu Muslim capitalized on these events and sent an army against the Umayyad governor of Khurasan under the command of Qahtabah b. Shabib. This army was at first successful and defeated Nasr Ibn Sayyar. With the capture of Merv and Nishapur in Khurasan, and after getting rid of Ibn al-Kirmani and his sons, Abu Muslim became the supreme leader and major support for the 'Abbasids in Khurasan.

The 'Abbasid armies then moved against the Umayyads in other parts of Khurasan. In a short period of time, but after furious wars, the 'Abbasids controlled Herat and Balkh, and in Central Asia Tukharistan, Tirmidh, Samarqand and Bukhara. Many other wars took place in Iran against the Umayyads. The 'Abbasids attacked and conquered Yazd, Jurjan, Rayy (October 748), Hamadan, Qum and the villages near Isfahan, and finally Nahawand, which marked the real 'Abbasid control of Central and Northern Iran. The 'Abbasids moved successfully southwest and gained dominion over Sistan and Sind.

The 'Abbasid forces were later directed to the West, and once again Qahtabah b. Shabib in many wars in Iraq defeated the Umayyads. In Iraq the resentment the Southern tribes held against the Qays predominance caused new inter-tribal wars that were capitalized on by the

'Abbasids. In Basra, for example, the Muhallabis failed to take the city from the Umayyads. But in Kufa the South-erner Muhammad b. Khalid al-Qasri took the city of Kufa, (September 2, 749) where Abu al-'Abbas was proclaimed and recognized as the new caliph by a large group of followers and loyal forces.[52]

After these events, Ibn Hubayrah was still holding the Umayyad control of Wasit. However, he was defeated by the 'Abbasids, led first by Hasan b. Qahtabah, the son of Qahtabah b. Shabib, and later by the caliph's brother al-Mansur, who directed the 'Abbasid army to stop the new inter-tribal disputes and rivalries between Arabs and Khurasanis. This important battle marked the end of Umayyad control of Iraq and tipped the balance to the revolutionary group. The battle of Wasit was undoubtedly one of the major 'Abbasid triumphs and also one of the major examples of military participation of the Shi'ites, whether or not they opposed and betrayed the 'Abbasids. It also exemplifies the role of the Southern tribes against the Umayyads in the 'Abbasid revolution.[53]

Marwan II organized a large army of loyal Qaysite to face the 'Abbasid challenge and the advance towards Syria. In the battle of the river Zab (*Jumada* II, 132, February 750), the 'Abbasids defeated the Umayyad ca-liph Marwan b. Muhammad.[54] The deposed caliph fled to Egypt, probably trying to move to North Africa (*Ifriqiyyah*). He was persecuted by the revolutionary forces, and in *Dhu al-Hijjah* 132 (August 750) he courageously faced the 'Abbasid armies in the village of Busir, where he was killed. The 'Abbasids took power and almost immediately launched important reforms and radical changes in the structure and institutions of the Empire. Their hatred of the Umayyads, their persecution and extermination of almost all the members of this family, and their violation of the Umayyad rulers' tombs (excepting only 'Umar Ibn 'Abd al-'Aziz) proves that the new leaders were also ruth-less and determined to erase the Umayyad past.

The persecution and almost total extermination of the Umayyads was one of the more radical actions of the 'Abbasids. The 'Abbasids in some instances admired several Umayyad caliphs and even considered a few of them brave, intelligent and skillful rulers, such as Mu'awiyah, 'Abd al-Malik b. Marwan, 'Umar Ibn 'Abd al-'Aziz and Hisham.[55] They even followed some of their ways of ruling. But that admiration was temporary. They started important changes in land distribution, in the army, and in the administration and institutions of the Empire. This 'Abbasid hatred of the Umayyads eventually led the 'Abbasid caliph al-Ma'mun to replace the inscription of the Umayyad 'Abd al-Malik as builder of the mosque *Qubbat al-Sakhra* in Jerusalem with his own inscription in an attempt to rout the Umayyad past and replace it by the new *dawlah,* the 'Abbasid dynasty.[56] History, as an important discipline of cultural dimensions, was then directed to reinterpret and rewrite the Umayyad period, and to praise and elevate the 'Abbasid dynasty, its actions and its revolution.[57]

## IV- Change or Revolution?

The 'Abbasids directed the first revolution in Islamic history. There were several earlier attempts at change, but they did not become true revolutions in the sense of rapid changes of the major structures. Even the meaning of the terms *da'wah-dawlah* of the 'Abbasids was that of revolution.

The 'Abbasids revolutionized the whole structure of the Empire. They gave the *mawali* equality with the rest of the Arab Muslims and allowed them to share with Islam all their experience, knowledge and sciences. After the 'Abbasids took over, the Islamic Empire experienced an Iranian conquest of Islam in its cultural aspects.[58] The predominance of Arabs in the Muslim Empire was finished. A combination of the Arab and the *mawali* elements

was then developed under the major aspirations of the
*Shu'ubiyyah* movement.

Important and radical changes in the political and
cultural spheres took place in the *Dar al-Islam* with the
'Abbasids; however, they are beyond the scope of this
research. But there were also important changes in other
respects, which are necessary to analyse in this essay, at
least under the early 'Abbasid caliphs. After the third
'Abbasid caliph many changes occurred, especially at the
religious, political and ethnic levels, mainly because of the
incorporation of Turks in the army, and also because of the
Arab tribal rivalries.[59]

Some of these changes can be seen as fulfillment of
the 'Abbasid promises to the various groups, mainly the
Khurasanis (obviously the *mawali*) and the Southern
tribes. Through an analysis of what was done by the
'Abbasids it is possible to draw a clear idea of what they
had promised their supporters. The 'Abbasids' promises in
their propaganda of justly dividing the wealth that the
Umayyads had appropriated was clearly manifested in
the land distribution in Syria for Khurasanis and Yemenites.
This process was obviously under the Islamic conditions of
revivification of the dead land *(ihya' al-ard al-mayyitah)*.[60]
Apparently in this way the 'Abbasids paid them for their
services.

Among those changes were the new administration of
Syria and the confiscation of the Umayyad properties,
especially those belonging to Maslamah Ibn 'Abd al-Malik
and his family, one of the major landowners of the Umayyad
dynasty.[61] These properties became 'Abbasid territories
after 'Abd Allah b. 'Ali, uncle of the caliph Abu al-'Abbas,
and one of the main military leaders in the struggle
against the Umayyads, confiscated those properties.[62]

The 'Abbasids started new villages and improved the
existing fortresses *(misr*, pl. *amsar)* in Syria along the
frontier bordering the Byzantine Empire. Those fortresses,
as well as the new villages, were given to the Khurasani
military chiefs, who had supported the 'Abbasid revolu-

tion. These chiefs, therefore, became *junds*.[63] New problems with the Byzantine Empire led the 'Abbasids to make considerable changes in the frontier zones to defend the *Dar al-Islam*. However, the military divisions established during the conquest were maintained by the 'Abbasids with few military changes because of the new challenges. The Khurasani military chiefs were given the mission to defend those territories. They had the trust of the 'Abbasids, and they replaced the Syrian *junds* of the Umayyad period.

With the 'Abbasid changes in the land distribution it is reasonable to conclude that they took seriously their position in favor of Iraq over Syria; e.g., the 'Abbasids founded Baghdad as the new capital of the Empire,[64] moving the orientation of the *Dar al-Islam* from the Mediterranean to Central Asia and the Eastern provinces, along with changing the balance of political power. The new capital also caused a serious decrease in commerce and agricultural production in Syria, in comparison with the same activities in Iraq.[65] Baghdad also became the major intellectual center of the *Dar al-Islam*. Literature, philosophy and the various sciences developed on a major scale. The school of translators in Baghdad shaped the greatness of Islam, in turn preserving for posterity the ancient Greek scientific knowledge, around which Muslims shaped the great Islamic Empire of the Middle Ages.[66]

This change of capital exemplifies the 'Abbasids' policies focusing on the *mawali* rather than on the Arabs. The *Shu'ubiyyah* movement had a great impact on this process. It is possible to infer from the change of capital that the 'Abbasids were more interested in the Iraqis than in the Syrians. The 'Abbasids also helped the Iraqis more than the Syrians in the army, giving them special privileges and even offering them an increase in the *'ata'*, which was one of the major promises of Abu al-'Abbas in his inaugural speech in the great mosque of Kufa.[67]

The 'Abbasids had the help of the Yemenite tribes, which held them to their promises of land ownership and

power. Although there is no evidence in the Arabic sources
that the *da'wah* promised the Yemenites land ownership,
it is implied since the 'Abbasids did give some land they
had confiscated in Syria from the Umayyads to the Khurasani military chiefs and also to some Yemenites. The
Qahtan managed to control Northern Syria after the
'Abbasids took over because they had a share of the
confiscated lands.[68] They controlled mainly the territories
from Hims to Tadmur (Palmyra). The Qays, on the other
hand, controlled and owned land in Central and Southern
Syria, those same territories that the Umayyads had
always controlled even during the second *fitnah*, the one
led by 'Abd Allah Ibn al-Zubayr, until they were expelled
by the 'Abbasids.[69]

Again land ownership was not the only privilege
granted. Just as the Umayyads had granted positions in
the army and administration of provinces and cities, the
'Abbasids also granted those same privileges to members
of the Southern tribes who had supported the revolution.
The Muhallabi family, who had survived despite the fall
of Yazid Ibn al-Muhallab, was rewarded with governorships, mainly in Basra, but also in other areas, especially
in Ifriqiyyah.[70] The Yemenite family of Khalid b. al-Qasri,
whose son Muhammad conquered Kufa for the 'Abbasids,
was also rewarded with governorships.[71]

Also, when 'Abd Allah b. 'Ali fought against al-Mansur in the succession after Abu al-'Abbas's death, Abu
Muslim, who was probably a Khurasani, was appointed
governor of Syria by al-Mansur, who had control of the
Empire -- further evidence of the fulfillment of the 'Abbasid promises to the Khurasanis. Al-Mansur needed Abu
Muslim's help to keep his power, another reason for al-
Mansur's appointment of Abu Muslim in Syria, although
for only a short period, after which he was replaced by
another caliph's uncle, Salih b. 'Ali.[72] In this fighting for
power between Abu Ja'far al-Mansur and 'Abd Allah b.
'Ali, the tribal rivalries between Northern and Southern
confederations were also present.

The first 'Abbasid caliph Abu al-'Abbas al-Saffah and his successors tried to win support of the Qays by granting privileges, although never matched by those rewarded to the Yemenites. The 'Abbasids in fact won support of many Qaysite warriors on the frontier of Armenia and the Byzantine Empire. The sources mentioned especially Ishaq b. Muslim al-'Uqayli. The 'Abbasids were also successful in gaining support of the descendants of Qutaybah Ibn Muslim, the famous conqueror of the great cities of Bukhara, Samarqand, Khwarizm and Farghana.[73]

In these armed conflicts between members of the same 'Abbasid family, one finds not only the inter-tribal rivalries, but also the problems and hatred between Arabs and *mawali*, since the 'Abbasids relied on and supported more the *mawali* than the Arabs. The support of Abu Muslim and his famous army of Khurasanis tilted the balance toward al-Mansur and away from 'Abd Allah b. 'Ali, which gave predominance to the *mawali* over the Arab in the 'Abbasid court, army and society.[74] This process became more evident in the next few years. The replacement of the Syrian *junds* by Khurasanis were to provoke several serious rivalries and wars between the Syrian Arab tribes and the Khurasanis. Both groups claimed the same privileges from the 'Abbasid caliphs, especially in the time of Harun al-Rashid. These groups took different positions in the wars between the two brothers al-Amin and al-Ma'mun for the succession of Harun al-Rashid.[75]

By the time of Harun al-Rashid and his descendants, the tensions between Arabs and *mawali* (mainly Persians or Khurasanis), had become commonplace with the 'Abbasids preferring and relying on their loyal soldiers the Khurasanis. This situation angered the Arabs in general against the *mawali* and made them complain constantly to the *Amir al-Mu'minin* who, according to various sources, favored the Khurasanis.[76] At this point several traditions developed in which Arabs complained about the caliphs' preference for the Khurasanis and other traditions were

against the Arabs.[77] Celebrated Muslim writers and scholars of the 'Abbasid period, notably Ibn al-Muqaffa' and al-
Jahiz, wrote about this phenomenon.[78]

According to the sources, the 'Abbasids promised the
Shi'ites a share in power and in the choice of the *Imam-
Amir al-Mu'minin*. Having a caliph suitable to all Muslims was one of the major 'Abbasid promises in their
propaganda. However, the fact that the Shi'ites revolted
against the 'Abbasids almost as soon as they took power
proves several things. First, it shows that the 'Abbasids
did not keep their promise to the Shi'ites. An intellectual
dispute for legitimacy broke out almost immediately. Second,
the Shi'ites, who had been politically active against the
Umayyads, remained active and fought for their rights.
Third, the 'Abbasids took advantage of the Shi'ites' enmity against the Umayyads and led them to fight the first
dynasty of Islam.

Social problems also developed between Muslims
and the religious minorities. That some Christians and
Jews also revolted against the payment of the *jizyah*
proves these social tensions.[79] From these revolts it is
possible to infer several things. First of all, the 'Abbasids
retained some of the Umayyad ways of discrimination
against the *Ahl al-Dhimmah*, including a heavy taxation
on the protected people. No matter how hard the 'Abbasids
tried to establish a more equitable society, the discrimination against the religious minorities, although not a rule,
was kept as part of the Islamic tradition of giving social
inferiority to the *Ahl al-Dhimmah*. Second, these Christian and Jewish revolts in Hims also brought as a conse-
quence new conversions to Islam as a way to escape the
*jizyah* tax and be treated as Muslims.[80]

What is still difficult to determine is the impact that
the mobilization of Khurasanis and Yemenites had upon
this conversion process, in which it is possible to notice, one
more time, its increase as a result of the taxation.

This reactivation of tensions between Arabs and *mawali* after the 'Abbasids took power was caused by the changes the 'Abbasids effected in the army and the way soldiers were conscripted. These changes constituted a complete revolution. In fact, conscription in the new army (the 'Abbasid *diwan* or the *Diwan al-'Abbasi)* was totally different after the 'Abbasid revolution.

During the Umayyad period, the army was almost absolutely a privilege of the Arab tribes, and they were drafted according to their tribal *nasab* (pl. *ansab* = origin, kin, pedigree). During the 'Abbasid period the *mawali* were incorporated into the Muslim army, and they were paid the *'ata'* equally with the Arab Muslims, which meant a major transformation of the Muslim society, opening the doors for the equality of the *mawali*, and later on for their predominance in the community.

Abu Muslim in his military reforms incorporated *mawali* in his army, under equal treatment and equal pay (*'ata'*) with the Arabs. This made a very loyal army that was tied to the 'Abbasids by religious motives as well. There were *mawali* before in the Umayyad army, but they had not been treated equally. Several of the Muslim armies drafted local populations for the expansion wars.[81]

The major 'Abbasid change in classifying people for drafting was that the *nasab* would be the village, or the place of origin, not the Arab tribe. This was one of the main reforms of Abu Muslim. This practice, undoubtedly, opened the door for other groups to be incorporated into the army, first Persians and later on Turks. Both ethnic groups were renowned as excellent soldiers. The Persianization of the Empire under the 'Abbasids, as well as the presence of Turks in the army, was often criticized by Muslim scholars, among them al-Maqrizi.[82]

From the time of the 'Abbasid takeover to al-Ma'mun (b.786-d.833), the Muslim army had Arab elements and Khurasanis (and the *abna')* as well. From the caliphate of

al-Ma'mun to the time of al-Mu'tasim (b.794-d.842) the
non-Arab element became the major characteristic of the
Muslim army.[83] From the *khilafah* of al-Mu'tasim onward,
Arabs were eliminated from the army and Turks gradu-
ally replaced them, to the point that they became the new
leaders of the *Dar al-Islam*, through the Ottoman and the
Mamluk reigns.[84]

### V- The 'Abbasids in power: the problem of legitimacy

*Yours is the inheritance of Muhammad, and*
  *through your justice is injustice swept aside.*
*The daughter's children desire the caliphate*
  *inheritance, yet their rights to it do not even*
  *amount to the equivalent of a nailparing!*
*The daughter's husband is not to be accounted*
  *an heir, and the daughter cannot inherit*
  *the imamate.*[85]

Those verses, written for the 'Abbasid caliph al-
Mutawakkil (b.822-d.861), summarized the whole discussion of legitimacy that the 'Abbasids had to face as one of
the major problems almost as soon as they took over. Many
poets, writers, religious authorities and philosophers wrote
their opinions, in many occasions supported by the 'Abbasids, favoring the new *dawlah*. However, the enemies of
the 'Abbasids, and those who rejected their legitimacy,
also developed doctrines of legitimacy to oppose the new
dynasty.

One of the major arguments at that time was that the
caliphate belonged exclusively to the Prophet Muhammad's descendants. But who, among all his descendants,
had the major arguments and the rights for the important
position of *Amir al-Mu'minin*? According to the Arab
custom and the Islamic tradition, who was first in claiming
legitimacy, a descendant from an uncle or the offspring of

a daughter? In order to claim legitimacy many doctrines were developed, some appealing even to the most unusual issues, by the 'Abbasids and the Shi'ites, both claiming rights to the caliphate, and both descendants of the Prophet Muhammad.

As soon as the 'Abbasids took over, and almost for as long as they remained in power, many discussions and controversies took place, and many groups questioned their legitimacy through several new doctrines. The 'Abbasids also created doctrines to claim legitimacy. Again the Shi'ites were the major competitors for power and the important office of *Amir al-Mu'minin*. The Shi'tes spread new ideas, because they had been deprived of power by the 'Abbasids, whom they had helped gain the caliphate. Their first idea opposing the 'Abbasids was the doctrine of *Nur Muhammad* (The Light of Muhammad), which they claimed was passed from the Prophet Muhammad to 'Ali. That meant that the light went directly from the Prophet Muhammad to the line of Abu Talib, one of Muhammad's uncles.

The idea of the light has been extremely important in the history of Islam. In the Qur'an God is described as the Light.[86] Knowledge and in general all the sciences have been described as light in Islam. No wonder that the Shi'ites used it to claim legitimacy for the *imamate* and the caliphate, since they claimed that *Nur Muhammad* was transmitted only to the descendants of Abu Talib. The 'Abbasids were forced to respond to the Shi'ites with equally valid arguments, using also the powerful doctrine and understanding of the Light.

The 'Abbasids developed, in clear opposition to the doctrine of *Nur Muhammad,* the doctrine of the Divine Light, *Nur al- Khilafah*, which claimed that the light had been transmitted to the Banu Hashim, from Hashim Ibn 'Abd Manaf to al-'Abbas. *Nur al-Khilafah* was also understood by the 'Abbasids as the light of authority, in clear opposition to those who claimed to have the *Nur Muhammad*. The 'Abbasids also used this doctrine as a powerful

argument to stop the Umayyads' claim on the title of
*Khalifat Allah.*

The meaning of *Khalifat Allah,* as explained by the
*'ulama',* was that of deputies of Allah, since nobody can be
a successor of God. This explanation occurred during the
caliphate of 'Umar, when serious discussions about the
role of the caliph and the separation between religious and
political authority took place. The *'ulama'* wanted to
monopolize and control the religious authority, leaving to
the caliph the political administration. These controversies occurred throughout the *Rashidun* and the Umayyad
periods. During their reign, and even after they were
expelled, the Umayyads regarded themselves as the successors of Allah at the head of the Community. Recent
research has proven the Umayyads calling themselves
*Khalifat Allah,* literally meaning successor of Allah. Arabic sources show this practice in speeches, in special
documents and on coins. Arabic literature in both prose
and poetry has countless examples of this term refering to
the Umayyad caliphs. The same is also true for the 'Abbasid caliphs and for many other rulers of Muslim communi-
ties in various parts of the world, and in different periods
of history.[87]

The 'Abbasids rejected  the Umayyad use of the
doctrine of *Khalifat Allah* and claimed  closer kinship to
the Prophet than the Umayyads, thus the authority should
belong to the Banu Hashim and not to the Banu Umayyad.
The argument of kinship, or *qaraba,* to the Prophet was
then extremely important. Several Arabic sources indi-
cate that the 'Abbasids were not chosen by the Prophet
Muhammad as members of the administrative positions
for *al-Ummah al-Islamiyyah*, arguments that were raised
on various occasions against them  by their enemies.[88]
However, the 'Abbasids justified this situation by explain-
ing that the Prophet purposefully did not appoint members of the Banu Hashim as tax collectors (*musaddiq*)
because this position had traditionally been considered
non-prestigious. Muhammad did not want his *qaraba* in a

position so frequently associated with rude behavior and violence. That was the reason, according to the explanations of the 'Abbasid ideology, why the Prophet did not appoint his cousins al-Fadl Ibn al-'Abbas and 'Abd Allah Ibn 'Abd Allah of the Banu al-Muttalib, as collectors of *sadaqah*. The 'Abbasids avoided the responsibility of those secular positions. They elaborated on these ideas and asserted that those transitory positions meant nothing in comparison with God's choice of the Prophet Muhammad from the Banu Hashim, and not from other groups of the Quraysh tribe.

According to the 'Abbasids' ideology, the Hashimites were the most noble and held the highest status, as explained by the Arabic sources, especially by the later source al-Maqrizi's *Kitab al-Niza'*.[89] Al-Maqrizi asserted that the Prophet's appointment of members of the Banu Umayyad to important administrative positions was a premonitory indication that power would later pass to them.[90]

The doctrine of *Nur Muhammad* was not successful for the Shi'ites. Despite their doctrinal opposition, the 'Abbasids gained more supporters, who entrusted them with the legitimacy of true rulers and heirs of the authority (*Nur al-Khilafah*). The Shi'ites noted the failure of their doctrine of *Nur Muhammad* and forwarded a new one demonstrating that they were the closest relatives (*qaraba*) of the Prophet Muhammad. The Shi'ites spread the claim of authority, since they were the descendants of 'Ali and Fatimah. They developed the notion of *aqraba*, related to *qaraba*, the descendants of 'Ali and Fatimah, which had a great impact upon the theological discussions in Islam. The Shi'ites also spread the doctrine of *Mulk Mutawarith*; i.e., authority should be hereditary. They also claimed closest kinship to the Prophet through his daughter Fatimah.

However, the 'Abbasids in their own claim for legitimacy minimized inheritance through a daughter, following the ancient ways the Arabs had used for centuries, coming from the times of the *Jahiliyyah*. Through the years, the 'Abbasids gave more importance to this doctrine and even favored the poets *(shu'ara')*, jurists *('ulama')*, and historians *(mu'arrikhun)*, who imbued their works with belief in the 'Abbasid legitimacy. The 'Abbasids also favored those who discounted inheritance following the matrilinear and supported the sole claim of patrilinear inheritance.

Marwan Ibn Sulayman Ibn Yahya Ibn Abi Hafsa wrote a poem for the caliph al-Mahdi (b.743/745-d.785) in which he denied inheritance through a daughter and placed it in the 'Abbasids' power. The argument used during the time of al-Mahdi was that the 'Abbasids were chosen by God to be in power because of their condition of *qaraba* (kinship) to the Prophet Muhammad, through a paternal uncle, al-'Abbas, for whom his nephew Muhammad had a special respect. The poet wrote:

> *How can the inheritance of the paternal uncles*
> *pass to the daughters' children?*
> *Such a thing is impossible.*
> *God has diverted away from them*
> *(sc. from the House of 'Ali and Fatima)*
> *shares [in the inheritance], but then*
> *they have tried to get hold of it*
> *without being entitled to shares.*[91]

The idea that the 'Abbasids were the only legitimate rulers and heirs of the Prophet's caliphate, through the notion of the *Nur al-Khilafah,* was overemphasized in subsequent years of 'Abbasid rule. In the time of the caliph al-Mutawakkil the doctrine that the 'Abbasids were the legitimate heirs of the caliphate was further developed, again claiming patrilinear legitimacy and discounting matrilinear claims.[92]

An important writer favoring the 'Abbasids in the time of al-Mutawakkil was Abu 'Uthman 'Amr Ibn Bahr al-Jahiz, who asserted that the Banu Hashim was superior to the Banu 'Abd Shams and the Banu Umayyad. He affirmed that the superiority went back to pre-Islamic times, emphasizing the uninterrupted claim to nobility of Hashim from the founder 'Amr Ibn 'Abd Manaf, while exposing the interrupted claims of the Umayyads.[93]

Al-Jahiz also developed the doctrine of *qaraba* as a major defense of the 'Abbasids' legitimacy. He concluded that the Banu Hashim were closer relatives to the Prophet than the Umayyads or the 'Abd Shams, since a paternal uncle has more importance than a female relative, as in the concrete case of 'Abbas Ibn 'Abd al-Muttalib, Muhammad's uncle, and Fatimah, Muhammad's daughter.[94]

Related to these doctrines is the notion of *nass* (designation) as one of the major principles of Shi'ah Islam.[95] The Shi'ites also responded to the 'Abbasids' doctrine of inheritance. As an answer to the 'Abbasid understanding of *Nur al-Khilafah,* the Shi'ites created the notion of a divine light, *Nur Allah*, which came directly to the Prophet Muhammad from Adam, following the chain of Prophets.[96] This light of God (*Nur Allah*), according to the Shi'ites, was transmitted by the Prophet Muhammad to 'Ali, his cousin, as a testamentary disposition. In this way the Shi'ah developed the notion of *wasiyyah* (inheritance), which meant the esoteric divine knowledge in 'Ali and his descendants the *imams*. The esoteric knowledge came from the Prophets and was an exclusive privilege of the Shi'ite *imams*.[97]

Although the Shi'ites fought with intellectual arguments and armed revolts, the 'Abbasids controlled the Empire and responded effectively to any new ideological arguments or any Shi'ite rebellion. Furthermore, the 'Abbasid ideology was more nearly universal for facing the daily life and the problems of Islam, than the Shi'ite doctrine. The 'Abbasids were capable of keeping Muslims together, both Arabs and *mawali*, while the Shi'ites were divisive, incapable of keeping even themselves together under one leader.

In all these discussions regarding legitimacy, the 'Abbasids were associated with *Sunnah* Islam. In fact, they were also the champions of *Sunnism*. Their popular support came from their relation with and their defense of *Sunnah* Islam, while the Shi'ites remained a minority sect of the *al-Ummah al-Islamiyyah.*

# Endnotes to Chapter III

(1) Sharon, *Black Banners,* pp.37-38. Anwar Chejne, *Succession to the Rule in Islam, with Special Reference to the Early 'Abbasid Period,* Lahore, 1960, passim, especially pp.37-57. See also pp.63-76. For a more detailed description see Kennedy, *Prophet,* pp.124-125. Moshe Sharon, "The Military Reforms of Abu Muslim, their Background and Consequences", in Moshe Sharon, *Studies in Islamic History and Civilization in Honour of Professor David Ayalon,* Jerusalem and Leiden, 1986, pp.105-143, especially p.105. Moshe Sharon, "The Development of the Debate around the Legitimacy of Authority in Early Islam", in *Jerusalem Studies in Arabic and Islam,* 1984, 5, pp.121-142. Cahen, *Les peuples musulmans,* p.106 and also pp.158-159. Crone, *Slaves on Horses,* p.65. See also pp.66-67 for a good discussion of the terms *Abna', Ahl al-Bayt, Abna' al-Dawlah, Abna' al-Shi'ah,* and *Abna' al-Da'wah.* For a good account of *Ahl al-Bayt* see Moshe Sharon, "Ahl al-Bayt -- People of the House", in *Jerusalem Studies in Arabic and Islam,* 8, 1986, pp.169-184.

(2) Sharon, *Black Banners,* p.44. Cf. Nadir, *Ahamm al-Firaq al-Islamiyyah,* pp.10-11. Nayfar, *Ahamm al-Firaq al-Islamiyyah,* pp.57-59.

(3) Sharon, *Black Banners,* p.20.

(4) Sharon, *Black Banners,* p.22 and also pp.26-27. F. Rosenthal, "Dawlah", in *Encyclopaedia of Islam* (2), Vol. II, Leiden, 1965, pp.177-178.

(5) *Akhbar al-Dawlah al-'Abbasiyyah,* pp.202-204. See also Sharon, *Black Banners,* p.159. For more details about the *da'wah* see Tabari, *Ta'rikh al-Rusul wa al-Muluk,* II, pp.1358 ff. (Leiden Edition). *Al-'Uyun wa al-Hada'iq fi Akhbar al-Haqa'iq,* III, pp.179 ff. See also 'Arafah, *Al-Khurasaniyun wa Dawruhum,* pp.47-48. Faruq 'Omar, *Al-'Abbasiyun al-Awa'il,* Baghdad, 1977, pp.7-27, especially pp.13-17. Faruq 'Omar, *Al-Khilafah al-'Abbassiyah fi 'Asr al-Fawda al-'Askariyyah,* Baghdad, 1977, pp.8-14.

(6) Moscati, "Il Testamento di Abu Hashim", pp.28-46. Lassner, *Islamic Revolution,* pp.55-62, and also p.76. Sharon, *Black Banners,* pp.121 ff. `Arafah, *Al-Khurasaniyun wa Dawruhum,* p.43. Kennedy, *Prophet,* pp.125-126. Cahen, *Les peuples musulmans,* pp.124-125.

(7) About al-Humaymah becoming an 'Abbasid place see Ya'qubi,

*Ta'rikh al-Ya'qubi,* II, pp.290 ff. Mas'udi, *Al-Tanbih wa al-Ishraf,* Cairo, 1938, p.292, quoted by 'Arafah, *Al-Khurasaniyun wa Dawruhum,* pp.43 ff.

(8) Baghdadi, *Al-Farq bayna al-Firaq,* pp.34-35. About the *Zaydiyyah* being a subdivision of the *Rawafid,* al-Baghdadi wrote: "Then the Rawafid, after the time of `Ali separated into four classes, the Zaydiyah, the Imamiyah, the Kaisaniyah, and the Ghulat" (p.34) Al-Baghdadi asserted that the subdivisions of the *Ghulat* were out of Islam, but the *Zaydiyyah* and the *Imamiyyah* were considered among the sects of the *Ummah.* See also Tabari, *Ta'rikh al-Rusul wa al-Muluk,* II, pp.1820 ff. (Leiden Edition) Ibn Rustah, *Kitab al-A`laq al-Nafisah,* p.219, where he described them as those who follow Zayd b. `Ali, the assassinated one (*"Hum yansabuna ila Zayd b. `Ali al-Maqtul).* For a similar account of this see Ibn Qutaybah, *Al-Ma`arif,* p.623. Cf. R. Strothman,"Al-Zaidiya", in *Shorter Encyclopaedia of Islam,* Ithaca, New York, 1961, pp.651-652. See also Kennedy, *Prophet,* p.125, where this author explains that the *Zaydiyyah* spread the idea that the *imamate* belonged to a member of the Family who had the courage to take up arms. Cf. `Allamah Tabataba'i, "Shi`ism, Zaydism, Isma`ilism and Shaykhism", in Seyyed Hossein Nasr, *Shi`ism, Doctrines, Thought, and Spirituality,* Albany, 1988, pp.85-86. Madelung, *Religious Trends in Iran,* pp.77-92, especially p.86. See also Hodgson, *The Venture of Islam,* p.372. Brockelmann, *History,* p.142. Muhammad Ibn `Abd al-Karim al-Shahrastani, "Zaydism", in Nasr, *Shi`ism,* pp.86-88. About the basic ideology of the Zaydiyyah al-Shahrastani wrote: " These are the followers of Zayd Ibn `Ali al-Husayn Ibn `Ali Ibn Abu Talib. They hold that the imamate belongs to the offspring of Fatimah, and cannot legitimately be held by others. However, they recognize as imam any Fatimid who is learned, pious, brave, generous, and who declares his Imamate: allegiance they maintain, must be given to such a one whether he is a descendant of Hasan or a descendant of Husayn ... They also admit the possibility of two imams in different regions; provided they are both endowed with the above qualities, each has a right to allegiance" (p.86) About the crucifixion of Zayd Ibn `Ali see al-Shahrastani, "Zaydism", p.87. *Akhbar al-Dawlah al-`Abbasiyyah,* p.167. Margoliouth, "On Mahdis and Mahdiism", p.218. Margoliouth, "Mahdi", p.337. Marín-Guzmán, *El Islam: Ideología e Historia,* pp.285-286. Marín-Guzmán, *El Islam: Política y Religión,* pp.64-65. Hodgson, *The Venture of Islam,* p.274. Lassner, *Islamic Revolution,* passim, pp.91-92. Cahen, *Les peuples musulmans,* p.119 and also p.131.

(9) *Akhbar al-Dawlah al-'Abbasiyyah,* pp.202-204. For more details about the Shi'ite practice of *taqiyyah* see Marín-Guzmán, "El

Islam Shi'ita", pp.173-183. Marín-Guzmán, *El Islam: Ideología e Historia*, p.175. 'Allamah Tabataba'i", "Taqiyyah", in Nasr, *Shi'ism*, pp.204-205.

(10) *Akhbar al-Dawlah al-'Abbasiyyah*, pp.240-241. See also Sharon, *Black Banners*, p.161.

(11) Tabari, *Ta'rikh al-Rusul wa al-Muluk*, II, p.1434. (Leiden Edition) See also Ya'qubi, *Ta'rikh al-Ya'qubi*, II, pp.338-348. For more details of the religious dimensions of the 'Abbasid propaganda see Cahen, *Les peuples musulmans*, p.134 and pp.137 ff.

(12) Cf. Majid al-Din Ibn al-Athir, *Al-Nihayah fi Gharib al-Hadith wa al-Athar*, Edited by Tahir Ahmad al-Zawi and Mahmud Muhammad al-Tannahi, Vol. III, Cairo, 1963, p.136.

(13) Maqrizi, *Kitab al-Niza'*, p.68.

(14) The different theological problems have been understood in various ways in Islam, according to the school or the religious sect. The Shi'ite theologians (*mutakallimun*) have explained that there are two levels of the *nubuwwah* (prophecy). The *muqayyadah*, the restricted or particular prophecy, and the *mutlaqah*, the absolute prophecy. The absolute prophecy is the absolute Muhammadan reality. The particular prophecy (*muqayyadah*) is the result of the partial realities of the absolute prophecy (*al-Nubuwwah al-Mutlaqah*). These partial realities were the various prophets that God sent before Muhammad, the Seal of the Prophets (*Khatam al-Nabiyyin*). The Shi'ite theologians believed that in the same way that the particular prophecy of each of the prophets was a partial reality of the absolute prophecy, the *walayah* of all the Messengers of God is only one part of the absolute *walayah* that was sealed by the first Shi'ite *imam* ('Ali Ibn Abi Talib). Likewise, the twelfth *imam* sealed the Muhammadan *walayah*. As a result of those explanations, the Shi'ites understood that the end of the cycle of the prophecy, meant the beginning of the cycle of the *walayah*, the spiritual initiation. For more details see: Marín-Guzmán, "Razón y Revelación en el Islam", p.136. Marín-Guzmán, *El Islam: Ideología e Historia*, pp.189-191. Fazlur Rahman, *Prophecy in Islam. Philosophy and Orthodoxy*, London, 1958, passim. Corbin, "La Filosofía Islámica", passim. 'Allamah Tabataba'i, "The Shi'i View of Revelation and Prophecy", in Nasr, *Shi'ism*, pp.127-137. H. Corbin, "The Meaning of the Imam for Shi'i Spirituality", in Nasr, *Shi'ism*, pp.167-187, especially pp.172-174. Watt, *Islamic Philosophy and Theology*, pp.20-26. Moscati, "Per una storia dell'antica Si'a", pp.251-267.

(15) Abu 'Uthman 'Amr Ibn Bahr al-Jahiz, "Risala fi al-Nabita", in *Rasa'il al-Jahiz,* edited by 'Abd al-Salam Muhammad Harun, Cairo, Baghdad, 1965, II, pp.16-17. French translation by Ch. Pellat, "Un document important pour l'histoire religieuse de l'Islam. "La Nabita" de Djahiz", AIEO, Alger, X, 1952, pp.319-320, quoted by Clifford Bosworth, "Introduction" to the translation of Maqrizi, *Kitab al-Niza',* p.18.

(16) See Tabari, *Ta'rikh al-Rusul wa al-Muluk,* III, pp.19-23 (Leiden Edition), for a good description of Muhammad b. Khalid al-Qasri's revolt on behalf of the 'Abbasids in Kufa and Basra. Ibn al-Athir, *Al-Kamil fi al-Ta'rikh,* V, pp.404-407. (Leiden-Beirut Edition) For Abu al-'Abbas's speech in Kufa see Tabari, *Ta'rikh al-Rusul wa al-Muluk,* III, pp.29-30. (Leiden Edition) About the *bay'ah* to Abu al-'Abbas in Kufa see Ibn Qutaybah, *Al-Imamah wa al-Siyasah,* II, p.118. Ibn Qutaybah explained Abu Salamah's claims for the caliphate to be given to a Shi'ite, to a descendant of 'Ali Ibn Abi Talib. Abu Salamah did not have any other choice than to comply. See Tabari, *Ta'rikh al-Rusul wa al-Muluk,* III, pp.28 ff. Ibn al-Athir, *Al-Kamil fi al-Ta'rikh,* V, pp.408-417. (Leiden-Beirut Edition) Ya'qubi, *Ta'rikh al-Ya'qubi,* II, p.345. 'Arafah, *Al-Khurasaniyun wa Dawruhum,* pp.78-82, especially p.80. Cahen, *Les peuples musulmans,* pp.150-151, asserted that Abu Salamah pointed out that the caliph should be elected by a *shurah* of the *Hashimiyyah,* but Cahen does not mention that for Abu Salamah, at that time, the caliph should be a descendant of 'Ali Ibn Abi Talib, and the *Hashimiyyah* was, by then, almost absolutely controlled by the 'Abbasids. See also Crone, *Slaves on Horses,* p.65. Wellhausen, *The Arab Kingdom,* p.544. About the appointment of Muhammad b. Khalid b. 'Abd Allah al-Qasri as governor of Kufa see Tabari, *Ta'rikh al-Rusul wa al-Muluk,* III, p.22. (Leiden Edition) See also Kennedy, *Prophet,* p.128. The 'Abbasids were skillful in taking power and obtaining the support and *bay'ah* of the people of Kufa for themselves and not for the 'Alids. It is important to bear in mind that the city of Kufa had traditionally been one of the major places for the Shi'ites. See Dinawari, *Al-Akhbar al-Tiwal,* p.370. 'Omar, *Al-Khilafah al-'Abbasiyyah,* p.14.

(17) Tabari, *Ta'rikh al-Rusul wa al-Muluk,* III, p.29. (Leiden Edition) Ibn Qutaybah, *Al-Imamah wa al-Siyasah,* II, p.118. See also 'Arafah, *Al-Khurasaniyun wa Dawruhum,* pp.79-80. Wellhausen, *The Arab Kingdom,* pp.544-545.

(18) Tabari, *Ta'rikh al-Rusul wa al-Muluk,* III, p.30. (Leiden Edition)

(19) Tabari, *Ta'rikh al-Rusul wa al-Muluk,* III, p.30. (Leiden Edition)

(20) Tabari, *Ta'rikh al-Rusul wa al-Muluk,* III, pp.31-33. (Leiden Edition)

(21) Tabari, *Ta'rikh al-Rusul wa al-Muluk,* III, p.31. (Leiden Edition)

(22) Tabari, *Ta'rikh al-Rusul wa al-Muluk,* III, p.31. (Leiden Edition)

(23) Dinawari, *Al-Akhbar al-Tiwal,* p.333. 'Arafah, *Al-Khurasaniyun wa Dawruhum,* p.49. This author also analysed the social situation of the *mawali* in Khurasan before the triumph of the 'Abbasid revolution, and their economic grievances due to the predominant role of the *dahaqin,* the landowners.

(24) *Akhbar al-Dawlah al-'Abbasiyyah,* p.221. Tabari, *Ta'rikh al-Rusul wa al-Muluk,* II, pp.1358 ff. (Leiden Edition) Ibn al-Athir, *Al-Kamil fi al-Ta'rikh,* V, pp.356-357. (Leiden-Beirut Edition) See also Sharon, *Black Banners,* pp.20-21. M. Canard, "Da'wa", in *Encyclopaedia of Islam* (2), Vol. II, Leiden, 1965, pp.168-170. Cahen, *Les peuples musulmans,* p.137.

(25) Sharon, *Black Banners,* pp.53-54. Cahen, *Les peuples musulmans,* pp.136-137.

(26) Baladhuri, *Ansab al-Ashraf,* III, p.81, quoted by Sharon, *Black Banners,* pp.51-52. See also *Akhbar al-Dawlah al-'Abbasiyyah,* pp.205-207. Muqaddasi, *Ahsan al-Taqasim Ma'rifat al-Aqalim,* pp.293-294. According to Tabari, when Abu al-'Abbas was proclaimed caliph in the great mosque of Kufa, after the 'Abbasid conquest of this city from the Umayyads, in his inaugural speech, Abu al-'Abbas appealed and praised the people of Kufa. See Tabari, *Ta'rikh al-Rusul wa al-Muluk,* III, p.30. (Leiden Edition). I quote John Alden Williams's translation of this part (*The 'Abbasid Revolution,* New York, 1985, p.154): "People of Kufah, you are the halting-place of our love, the lodging of our affections. You it is who remained steadfast, you who were not deflected from our love by the injustice of the people of tyranny against you until you reached our epoch and God brought you our revolution." See also 'Arafah, *Al-Khurasaniyun wa Dawruhum,* p.81.

(27) Tabari, *Ta'rikh al-Rusul wa al-Muluk,* II, pp.1358 ff. (Leiden Edition). See also III, pp.29-30. (Leiden Edition) Maqrizi, *Kitab al-Niza',* pp.83-84. For more details see Kennedy, *Prophet,* pp.109-110, about the military experience of the Khurasanis facing the Turgesh in Transoxiana. See also p.126. Cahen, *Les peuples musulmans,* p.138. Cahen explained that the direction of the 'Abbasid propaganda in Kufa was left to the *mawali,* while in Khurasan, it was given to the Arabs, especially Yemenites and Rabi'ah, the enemies of the Mudar. The Mudar were the major supporters of the Umayyads. In this way the 'Abbasids pursued to unite the Arabs with the *mawali* in their struggles against the Umayyads.

(28) *Akhbar al-Dawlah al-'Abbasiyyah,* pp.202-204, quoted by Sharon, *Black Banners,* p.158. For more details about Abu 'Ikrimah preaching the 'Abbasid *da'wah* in Khurasan see Dinawari, *Al-Akhbar al-Tiwal,* p.333. Ya'qubi, *Ta'rikh al-Ya'qubi,* II, p.312. 'Arafah, *Al-Khurasaniyun wa Dawruhum,* p.49.

(29) Maqrizi, *Kitab al-Niza',* p.88. The *imam* Ibrahim's instructions to Abu Muslim, as preserved by al-Maqrizi was: "You are one of us, the House of the Prophet; observe faithfully my instructions to you. Look to this group of the Yamanis; treat them with honour and dwell amongst them, for God will only bring this affair to a successful conclusion by means of their support. But be wary of how you handle Rabi'ah, and as for Mudar, they are the enemy who lurks close to your door. So kill anyone whose loyalty you are doubtful about; if you are able to clear Khurasan of every single Arabic speaker, then do it, and if there is any youth who has reached five spans in height and you are suspicious about him, then kill him." Tabari, *Ta'rikh al-Rusul wa al-Muluk,* III, pp.25-26 (Leiden Edition) also relates the letter of the *imam* Ibrahim to Abu Muslim in which the *imam* ordered him to kill all the Arabic speakers in Khurasan. What does this tradition really mean? Was it created after the 'Abbasids took power as an anti-Arab feeling? At this point it is difficult to determine using the Arabic sources. On the other hand, Tabari also preserved different traditions about these events, sometimes even in clear contradiction. For a detailed study of the various traditions see Lassner, *Islamic Revolution,* passim, especially pp.62-71. See also 'Arafah, *Al-Khurasaniyun wa Dawruhum,* p.79, where she analysed the fear of the caliph Marwan II that the 'Abbasids could spread their revolt to other parts of the Empire. For this reason the caliph decided to keep Ibrahim, the 'Abbasid *imam,* in prison. For more details about these events see Dinawari, *Al-Akhbar al-Tiwal,* p.359. Ya'qubi, *Ta'rikh al-Ya'qubi,* II, pp.342-343. *Al-'Uyun wa al-Hada'iq fi Akhbar al-Haqa'iq,* III, pp.183 ff. See also Cahen, *Les peuples musulmans,* pp.149-150. Crone, *Slaves*

*on Horses,* p.65. Crone asserted that this important leader of the 'Abbasid revolution died in Marwan II's prison. See also Tabari, *Ta'rikh al-Rusul wa al-Muluk,* III, p.42, (Leiden Edition) where Tabari explained that despite the existence of various traditions, the 'Abbasid *imam* Ibrahim died in Marwan's prison.

(30) Tabari, *Ta'rikh al-Rusul wa al-Muluk,* edited by Muhammad Abu al-Fadl Ibrahim, Cairo, 1976, VII, p.49, quoted by 'Arafah, *Al-Khurasaniyun wa Dawruhum,* p.50. See also Cahen, *Les peuples musulmans,* p.137, where he analysed the tribal rivalries between Northern and Southern confederations of tribes. Cahen also pointed out that the 'Abbasids capitalized on these rivalries. The anonymous *Kitab al-'Uyun wa al-Hada'iq fi Akhbar al-Haqa'iq,* III, pp.183-184, also preserved the various traditions about these inter-tribal rivalries and the 'Abbasid approach to the tribes.

(31) Sharon, *Black Banners,* pp.223-226.

(32) Sharon, *Black Banners,* passim, especially pp.158-159. Lassner, *Islamic Revolution,* passim, especially p.45, for a clear case study, the case of 'Ali b. 'Abd Allah al-Sajjal, according to the 'Abbasid tradition. For more details about the idea of *'asabiyyah* see Ibn Khaldun, *Al-Muqaddimah,* passim, especially pp.141 ff. 'Arafah, *Al-Khurasaniyun wa Dawruhum,* p.51. See also *Akhbar al-Dawlah al-'Abbasiyyah,* pp.144-145.

(33) Sharon, *Black Banners,* passim.

(34) Tabari, *Ta'rikh al-Rusul wa al-Muluk,* II, p.1358.(Leiden Edition)

(35) *Akhbar al-Dawlah al-'Abbasiyyah,* p.204, quoted by Sharon, *Black Banners,* p.158.

(36) Ya'qubi, *Ta'rikh al-Ya'qubi,* II, p.319. Dinawari, *Al-Akhbar al-Tiwal,* p.333. 'Arafah, *Al-Khurasaniyun wa Dawruhum,* p.46.

(37) Sharon thinks that it was in the year 125 of the *hijrah,* when the pro-'Alid *da'wah* became absolutely 'Abbasid. Sharon, *Black Banners,* p.229. However, it is important to keep in mind that the 'Abbasid *da'wah* started in the year 100 of the *hijrah.* See Mas'udi, *Al-Tanbih wa al-Ishraf,* p.308. Tabari, *Ta'rikh al-Rusul wa al-Muluk,* II, pp.1358 ff. (Leiden Edition). Ibn Qutaybah, *Al-Imamah wa al-Siyasah,* II, pp.108-109. For more details see also 'Arafah, *Al-Khurasaniyun wa Dawruhum,* p.45. Lassner, *Islamic Revolution,* passim, especially

p.64 and p.75.

(38) Cf. Ya'qubi, *Ta'rikh al-Ya'qubi*, II, p.319. Dinawari, *Al-Akhbar al-Tiwal*, pp.333-334. *Al-'Uyun wa al-Hada'iq fi Akhbar al-Haqa'iq*, III, pp.183 ff. 'Arafah, *Al-Khurasaniyun wa Dawruhum*, pp.46-47. Kennedy, *Prophet*, p.127.

(39) Cf. Tabari, *Ta'rikh al-Rusul wa al- Muluk*, III, pp.22 ff. (Leiden Edition) Dinawari, *Al-Akhbar al-Tiwal*, p.334. Ya'qubi, *Ta'rikh al-Ya'qubi*, II, p.319. 'Arafah, *Al-Khurasaniyun wa Dawruhum*, p.46.

(40) Cf. Tabari, *Ta'rikh al-Rusul wa al-Muluk*, III, pp.85 ff. (Leiden Edition). Ibn Qutaybah in his *Al-Imamah wa al-Siyasah* (II, pp.113-116) provided various traditions about the origins of Abu Muslim. See also Ibn Qutaybah, *Al-Ma'arif*, p.420. For a clear study of the various traditions  concerning Abu Muslim's ethnic origin  and religious beliefs see Sabatino Moscati, "Studi su Abu Muslim. I- Abu Muslim e gli 'Abbasidi", in *Rendiconti delle Sedute dell'Accademia Nazionale dei Lincei*, Volume IV, Fascicoli 5-6, 1949, pp.323-335. Sabatino Moscati, "Studi su Abu Muslim. II- Propaganda e politica religiosa di Abu Muslim", in *Rendiconti delle Sedute dell'Accademia Nazionale dei Lincei*, Volume IV, Fascicoli 7-10, 1949, pp.474-495. Sabatino Moscati, "Studi su Abu Muslim. III- La fine di Abu Muslim", in *Rendiconti delle Sedute  dell'Accademia Nazionale dei Lincei*, Volume V, fascicoli 1-2, 1950, pp.89-105. Lassner, *Islamic Revolution*, pp.99-126. Sharon, *Black Banners*, pp.203-208. Daniel, *The Political and Social History*, pp.100 ff. R. Frye, "The role  of Abu Muslim", pp.28-38. Shaban, *The 'Abbasid Revolution*, pp.153-158. Shaban, *El Islam*, I, pp.227 ff. 'Arafah, *Al-Khurasaniyun wa Dawruhum*, pp.91-99. See also Ibn Khallikan, *Wafayat al-A'yan*, III, pp.145-146.

(41) Ibn Qutaybah, *Al-Imamah wa al-Siyasah*, II, pp.113-116. Ibn Qutaybah, *Al-Ma'arif*, p.420. Moscati, "Studi su Abu Muslim", II, pp.474-481. Lassner, *Islamic Revolution*, p.100. Sharon, *Black Banners*, pp.203-204. Daniel, *The Political and Social History*, pp.100 ff., where he analysed the various traditions concerning Abu Muslim's origins. Shaban, *The 'Abbasid Revolution*, pp.153-154. 'Arafah, *Al-Khurasaniyun wa Dawruhum*, pp.106-112.

(42) Cf. Tabari, *Ta'rikh al-Rusul wa al-Muluk*, III, pp.108-111.(Leiden Edition) Ibn al-Athir, *Al-Kamil fi al-Ta'rikh*, V, pp.468-481. (Leiden-Beirut Edition) Dinawari, *Al-Akhbar al-Tiwal*, pp.380-383. Ibn Qutaybah, *Al-Ma'arif*, p.420. Mas'udi, *Muruj al-Dhahab*, VI, pp.180-186. Sharon, *Black Banners*, pp.203-204. Lassner, *Islamic Revolution*, pp.110-115, where he analysed in detail the various tradi-

tions concerning Abu Muslim's death by the caliph al-Mansur. See
also Moscati, "Studi su Abu Muslim", I, pp.323-335 for a detailed
analysis of the various traditions concerning the hostility between
Abu Muslim and Ja'far al-Mansur. See also Moscati, "Studi su Abu
Muslim", III, pp.101-103, for a clear description of Abu Muslim's
death. Daniel, *The Political and Social History*, pp.113-117. Maqrizi,
*Kitab al-Niza'*, p.99. Cahen, *Les peuples musulmans*, p.145. Madelung,
*Religious Trends*, pp.8-9. 'Omar, *Al-Khilafah al-'Abbasiyyah*, pp.15-
16. 'Omar, *Al-'Abbasiyun al-Awa'il*, pp.50-56.

(43) Cf. Shahrastani, *Book of Religious and Philosophical Sects*,
edited by W. Cureton, London, 1842-1846, pp.114-115, quoted, by
Moscati, "Studi su Abu Muslim", II, pp.476-477. Ibn Hazm, *Al-Fasl fi
al-Milal wa al-Ahwa' wa al-Nihal*, II, p.115, quoted by Moscati,
"Studi su Abu Muslim", II, pp.478-479. See also Ibn Khallikan,
*Wafayat al-A'yan*, III, pp.145-155. Frye, "The Role of Abu Muslim",
pp.28-38. Cahen, *Les peuples musulmans*, p.153.

(44) Madelung, *Religious Trends*, p.8. Hodgson, *The Venture of
Islam*, pp.274-275. Cahen, *Les peuples musulmans*, pp.146-149. Cahen
analysed the Khurasani revolts against the 'Abbasids after al-Mansur
killed Abu Muslim. Cf. Cahen, *Les peuples musulmans*, p.153. See also
Tabari, *Ta'rikh al-Rusul wa al-Muluk*, III, p.117. (Leiden Edition)
Crone, *Slaves on Horses*, p.56. Daniel, *The Political and Social
History*, pp.78 ff.

(45) See Shaban, *The 'Abbasid Revolution*, p.154. Shaban tends
to describe Abu Muslim as he was usually considered, as a Muslim,
more than Arab or *mawla*. See Daniel, *The Political and Social
History*, pp.100 ff., especially p.104. Brockelmann, *History*, p.103,
where he asserted that Abu Muslim was Persian by birth.

(46) About the 'Abbasid army organized by Abu Muslim see
Tabari, *Ta'rikh al-Rusul wa al-Muluk*, III, pp.51-64 (Leiden Edition).
*Akhbar al-Dawlah al-'Abbasiyyah*, p.376. See also Crone, *Slaves on
Horses*, p.61. About Marwan b. Muhammad (Marwan II), the last
Umayyad caliph, see Suyuti, *Ta'rikh al-Khulafa'*, pp.254-255. Ibn
Majah, *Ta'rikh al-Khulafa'*, pp.35-36 Mas'udi, *Al-Tanbih wa al-
Ishraf*, pp.297-300. For more details about the fate of the Umayyads
and their replacement by the 'Abbasids see pp.300-308, where al-
Mas'udi also explained how 'Abd al-Rahman b. Mu'awiyah obtained
power in al-Andalus. See also Mas'udi, *Muruj al-Dhahab*, VI, pp.46-
49. Dinawari, *Al-Akhbar al-Tiwal*, pp.351-360. Tabari, *Ta'rikh al-
Rusul wa al-Muluk*, II, pp.1890 ff. (Leiden Edition) Ibn al-Athir, *Al-
Kamil fi al-Ta'rikh*, V, pp.323-324. (Leiden-Beirut Edition) Ibn Qutay-

bah, *Al-Imamah wa al-Siyasah*, II, p.113. Ya'qubi, *Ta'rikh al-Ya'qubi*, II, pp.338-348. *Al'Uyun wa al-Hada'iq fi Akhbar al-Haqa'iq*, III, pp.154-165. See also Wellhausen, *The Arab Kingdom*, pp.370-396, and also pp.536-549. Sharon, *Black Banners*, pp.214-226. Kennedy, *Prophet*, pp.114-115. Shaban, *The 'Abbasid Revolution*, p.167. Brockelmann, *History*, pp.104-106. Hodgson, *The Venture of Islam*, pp.272-275. Hawting, *The First Dynasty of Islam*, pp.96-103.

(47) Cf. Kennedy, *Prophet*, p.115 and also pp.127-128. About Abu Salamah see Ibn Qutaybah, *Al-Imamah wa al-Siyasah*, II, p.117. *Al-'Uyun wa al-Hada'iq fi Akhbar al-Haqa'iq*, III, p.195. About Qahtabah b. Shabib see Ibn Qutaybah, *Al-Imamah wa al-Siyasah*, pp.117-118. *Al-'Uyun wa al-Hada'iq fi Akhbar al-Haqa'iq*, III, pp.194-195.

(48) Lassner, *Islamic Revolution*, p.71. Kennedy, *Prophet*, p.114. Brockelmann, *History*, p.100.

(49) Tabari, *Ta'rikh al-Rusul wa al-Muluk*, II, p.1865. (Leiden Edition) Dinawari, *Al-Akhbar al-Tiwal*, p.351; see also pp.352-355. Ya'qubi, *Ta'rikh al-Ya'qubi*, II, p.340-345, for a general explanation of these issues. Mas'udi, *Muruj al-Dhahab*, VI, pp.60-61. *Al-'Uyun wa al-Hada'iq fi Akhbar al-Haqa'iq*, III, pp.184-185. See also Ibn Qutaybah, *Al-Ma'arif*, pp.409-410, for a short biography of Nasr Ibn Sayyar. 'Arafah, *Al-Khurasaniyun wa Dawruhum*, pp.27-28. Sharon, *Black Banners*, pp.55-58.

(50) Tabari, *Ta'rikh al-Rusul wa al-Muluk*, II, pp.1965-1970 (Leiden Edition), where he also explained the opposition of some of the Northern tribes to Abu Muslim in Khurasan. Ibn al-Athir, *Al-Kamil fi al-Ta'rikh*, V, pp.347-348, (Leiden-Beirut Edition) for a clear explana- tion of Abu Muslim's mission in Khurasan, when he was sent by the *imam* Ibrahim. See also Ibn al-Athir, *Al-Kamil fi al-Ta'rikh*, V, pp.356-363, V, pp.366-370 and also V, pp.408-417. (Leiden-Beirut Edition) Maqrizi, *Kitab al-Niza'*, p.88. Wellhausen, *The Arab King- dom*, p.532. Bernard Lewis, "Abbasids", in *Encyclopaedia of Islam*, (2), Vol. I, Leiden, 1960, pp.15-23. Moscati, "Studi su Abu Muslim", II, pp.482-486. Frye, *Bukhara*, pp.20-21.

(51) Baladhuri, *Futuh al-Buldan*, p.378. Ibn Khallikan, *Wafayat al-A'yan*, III, pp.145-155. Ibn al-Athir, *Al-Kamil fi al-Ta'rikh*, V, pp.363-366.(Leiden-Beirut Edition) Tabari, *Ta'rikh al-Rusul wa al-Muluk*, II, pp.1965 ff. (Leiden Edition) Tabari explained that Ibn al-Kirmani even asked Abu Muslim for help against Nasr Ibn Sayyar. Abu Muslim then sent Shibl b. Tahman to help Ibn al-Kirmani. Tabari, *Ta'rikh al-Rusul wa al-Muluk*, II, p.1967. (Leiden Edition)

Dinawari, *Al-Akhbar al-Tiwal,* pp.366-369. Ibn Qutaybah, *Al-Ima-mah wa al-Siyasah,* II, pp.116-117. Hasan, *Al-Qaba'il al-'Arabiyyah,* pp.189-191. Shaban, *The 'Abbasid Revolution,* pp.159-163. Wellhausen, *The Arab Kingdom,* pp.488-491, and also pp.531 ff. Hawting, *The First Dynasty of Islam,* p.107 ff. Brockelmann, *History,* pp.102-106. 'Arafah, *Al-Khurasaniyun wa Dawruhum,* pp.47-57, and also pp.65-68. 'Omar, *Al-'Abbasiyun al-Awa'il,* pp.42-44. Daniel, *The Political and Social History,* pp.78-80.

(52) Tabari, *Ta'rikh al-Rusul wa al-Muluk,* III, pp.18-23. (Leiden Edition) Dinawari, *Al-Akhbar al-Tiwal,* passim, especially pp.369 ff. Ya'qubi, *Ta'rikh al-Ya'qubi,* II, p.345. Kennedy, *Prophet,* p.115. Moscati, "Studi su Abu Muslim", II, pp.486-487.

(53) The battle of Wasit, described in detail in the major Arabic sources (Tabari, *Ta'rikh al-Rusul wa al-Muluk,* III, passim, especially pp.37-38 and III, pp.61-71. (Leiden Edition) *Akhbar al-Dawlah al-'Abbasiyyah,* passim. Dinawari, *Al-Akhbar al-Tiwal,* pp.369 ff. Ya'qubi, *Ta'rikh al-Ya'qubi,* II, pp.344 ff. Ibn al-Athir, *Al-Kamil fi al-Ta'rikh,* V, pp.437-442, (Leiden-Beirut Edition). *Al-'Uyun wa al-Hada'iq fi Akhbar al-Haqa'iq,* III, pp.194 ff. was academically reexamined and reinterpreted after Wellhausen's account (*The Arab Kingdom,* pp.441-443) by Sabatino Moscati, "Il tradimento di Wasit", in *Le Museon,* LXIV, 1951, pp.177-186. More recently these events were reexamined again and reinterpreted at the light of new Arabic sources by Amikam Elad, "The Siege of al-Wasit (132/749). Some aspects of 'Abbasid and 'Ali Relations at the Beginning of the 'Abbasid Rule", in Moshe Sharon, *Studies in Islamic History and Civilization in Honour of Professor David Ayalon,* Jerusalem, Leiden, 1986, pp.59-90. For a general description of these events see 'Arafah, *Al-Khurasaniyun wa Dawruhum,* pp.77-82. Kennedy, *Prophet,* p.115. Brockelmann, *History,* pp.105-106.

(54) For Marwan b. Muhammad's army see Crone, *Slaves on Horses,* p.55. For the battle of Zab and the defeat of the Umayyads see Tabari, *Ta'rikh al-Rusul wa al-Muluk,* III, p.45. (Leiden Edition) Ibn al-Athir, *Al-Kamil fi al-Ta'rikh,* V, pp.417-421. (Leiden-Beirut Edition) Dinawari, *Al-Akhbar al-Tiwal,* pp.368-370. *Al-'Uyun wa al-Hada'iq fi Akhbar al-Haqa'iq,* III, pp.201-202, see also III, pp.203 ff. Ya'qubi, *Ta'rikh al-Ya'qubi,* II, pp.345-346. Mas'udi, *Muruj al-Dhahab,* VI, p.73. Al-Mas'udi asserted that 300 Umayyads were killed in that battle. Shaban, *The 'Abbasid Revolution,* p.167. Brockelmann, *History,* p.105. Shaban, *El Islam,* I, p.232. Cf. Wellhausen, *The Arab Kingdom,* pp.547-548. William Muir, *The Caliphate. Its Rise, Decline*

*and Fall,* London, n.d., pp.430-432. Lassner, *Islamic Revolution,* p.135. Kennedy, *Prophet,* p.116. 'Arafah, *Al-Khurasaniyun wa Dawruhum,* pp.83-88.

(55) For more details about the killing of the Umayyads in Syria, by the 'Abbasids, see Ibn Qutaybah, *Al-Imamah wa al-Siyasah,* II, pp.121-123. See also Ibn al-Athir, *Al-Kamil fi al-Ta'rikh,* V, pp.429-432. Cahen, *Les peuples musulmans,* p.159. Those actions were also criticized by Muslim writers like al-Maqrizi, *Kitab al-Niza',* p.92; see also p.102. About the 'Abbasid admiration for some Umayyad rulers see Rayyis, *'Abd al-Malik b. Marwan,* p.228. Kennedy, *Prophet,* p.120. Sabatino Moscati, "Le massacre des Umayyades dans l'histoire et dans les fragments poétiques", in *Archiv Orientální,* Vol. XVIII, Number 4, 1950, pp.88-115.

(56) Sourdel, "La Syrie", pp.168-169.

(57) For more details about the Muslim historiography and in particular the 'Abbasid historiography see F. Rosenthal, *A History of Muslim Historiography,* Leiden, 1952, passim, especially pp.114-163. See also Marín-Guzmán, *El Islam: Ideología e Historia,* pp.219-262.

(58) For a good discussion of the Persian influence on the Muslim Empire see Richard Frye, *The Heritage of Persia,* New York, 1963, pp.263-285. Maqrizi, *Kitab al-Niza',* pp.94-97 criticized the 'Abbasids for replacing the Muslim *adab* by that of the Persians *('Ajam).* In this respect al-Maqrizi wrote: "By God, the whole of *adab* is contained within the custom of the Prophet, for it comprehends the code of behaviour as laid down by the Prophet *(al-adab an-nabawi)* and the divine prescriptions. But overweening pride became general amongst the 'Abbasids, haughtiness became impressed on their characters and a despotic attitude appeared amongst them. Hence they called the usages of the Persian *adab,* and gave it a preferential position over the *sunna,* which is the fruit of prophethood." (p.95)

(59) About the incorporation of Turks in the Muslim army see Sharon, "Military Reforms", pp.137-139. 'Omar, *Al-Khilafah al-'Abbasiyyah,* pp.51-66. For more details about the inter-tribal rivalries after the 'Abbasids took over see Sourdel, "La Syrie", pp.159 ff. For a major Arabic source criticizing this process of Turks replacing Arabs in the army see Maqrizi, *Kitab al-Niza',* pp.101. 'Omar, *Al-'Abbasiyun al-Awa'il,* pp.239-250.

(60) For the confiscation of the Umayyad properties by the 'Abbasids see Baladhuri, *Futuh al-Buldan,* p.129, where he described

this process especially in Balqa'. Baladhuri explained that after the conquest of Balqa' Mu'awiyah and his sons obtained the land, but after the 'Abbasids took over, it was confiscated and it passed especially to some sons of the caliph al-Mahdi. He wrote *"Thumma qubidat fi awwal al-dawlah wa sarat li-ba'd walad Amir al-Mu'minin al-Mahdi"*. See also Ya'qubi, *Kitab al-Buldan*, p.324. Baladhuri, *Futuh al-Buldan*, p.134, for more general information about these events. See also Sharon, *Black Banners*, p.23. Sourdel "La Syrie", pp.160-161.

(61) For more information about the properties of Maslamah Ibn 'Abd al-Malik see Baladhuri, *Futuh al-Buldan*, p.148, where he explained that the land of Baghras, for example, belonged to Maslamah Ibn 'Abd al-Malik who gave it as *waqf* (inalienable property) to be used for good purposes. Al-Baladhuri wrote: *"Kanat ard Baghras li-Maslamah Ibn 'Abd al-Malik fa-waqqafaha fi sabil al-birr."* See also Kennedy, *Prophet*, p.111.

(62) Baladhuri, *Futuh al-Buldan*, p.148. For more information about the ways these properties were later distributed to other 'Abbasid leaders, and how they were tax exempt and administered by the 'Abbasids, see Sourdel "La Syrie", pp.160-161.

(63) Cf. Baladhuri, *Futuh al-Buldan*, pp.168-169 and p.179. Tabari, *Ta'rikh al-Rusul wa al-Muluk*, III, p.373 (Leiden Edition) for a detailed description of the role of the Khurasanis as *junds* in Syria. See also Sourdel, "La Syrie", pp.160-161. The division of Syria in five *junds* of the time of the Muslim conquest was kept by the `Abbasids. The five divisions were: 1) Qinnasrin in the north, including the city of Aleppo (Halab). 2) Hims in the northwest. 3) Damascus that included the cities of the coast, Beirut, Sayda, Jawlan and Hawran. 4) Al-Urdun, that included Tiberiades and the northern parts of Palestine, the village of Jarash and the ports of Acre and Tyre. 5) Palestine, included Jerusalem, al-Ramlah and `Asqalan. For more details see Sourdel, "La Syrie", pp.157-158.

(64) For more details about the founding of Baghdad by al-Mansur, as the new capital of the Muslim Empire, as well as for a good description of it before becoming the new capital see Tabari, *Ta'rikh al-Rusul wa al-Muluk*, III, pp.204 ff. (Leiden Edition) Ibn al-Athir, *Al-Kamil fi al-Ta'rikh*, V, pp.557-560 and also V, pp.573-575. (Leiden-Beirut Edition) Dinawari, *Al-Akhbar al-Tiwal*, p.383. Ibn Rustah, *Kitab al-A'laq al-Nafisah*, pp.108-109, for a good description of the founding of Baghdad, its organization, layouts, limits, the doors of the city, their names, the roads connecting Baghdad with other cities and

regions (Basra, Kufa, al-Sham and Khurasan) and also about the green domes adorning each door of the city, as well as for the founder al-Mansur's casttle in the middle of the city. See also Ya'qubi, *Kitab al-Buldan*, pp.232 ff. for a good description of the major activites of the city, mainly trade and also for its location in a very well communicated area both with Iraq and with the rest of the Muslim Empire. G. Le Strange, *Baghdad during the 'Abbasid Caliphate*, Oxford, 1900, passim, especially pp.5-29. Muir, *The Caliphate*, pp.459-462. Brockelmann, *History*, pp.109-111. Frye, *Bukhara*, pp.21-22.

(65) For further information see Ya'qubi, *Kitab al-Buldan*, passim, especially pp.325-329. Baladhuri, *Futuh al-Buldan*, p.144. Sourdel, "La Syrie", pp.162-163. Hodgson, *The Venture of Islam*, p.275. Crone, *Slaves on Horses*, p.71. Crone analysed the opposition of the Syrians to the 'Abbasids due to their preference for Iraq. Again it is possible to notice the traditional confrontation between Syria and Iraq.

(66) See Grunebaum, *Medieval Islam*, pp.258-293. Corbin, "La Filosofía Islámica", pp.236-358. Marín-Guzmán, "Razón y Revelación en el Islam", pp.133-150. Marín-Guzmán, *El Islam: Ideología e Historia*, pp.181-217. Miguel Cruz Hernández, *La Filosofía Arabe*, Madrid, 1963, passim. Brockelmann, *History*, pp.117-122.

(67) Cf. Tabari, *Ta'rikh al-Rusul wa al-Muluk*, III, p.30. (Leiden Edition). Sharon, "Military Reforms", pp.128-129.

(68) Cf. Baladhuri, *Futuh al-Buldan*, p.129 and also p.134. Ya'qubi, *Kitab al-Buldan*, p.324. Sourdel, "La Syrie", pp.160-161.

(69) Sourdel, "La Syrie", p.161. Ya'qubi, *Kitab al-Buldan*, pp.324 ff.

(70) Kennedy, *Prophet*, p.129.

(71) Kennedy, *Prophet*, p.129.

(72) Cf. Sourdel "La Syrie", p.159.

(73) Kennedy, *Prophet*, pp.129-130.

(74) About these conflicts between Abu Ja'far al-Mansur and 'Abd Allah b. 'Ali and the role of Abu Muslim see Tabari, *Ta'rikh al-Rusul wa al-Muluk*, III, pp.92-97. (Leiden Edition) Ibn al-Athir, *Al-Kamil fi al-Ta'rikh*, V, pp.464-468. (Leiden-Beirut Edition) Ya'qubi,

*Ta'rikh al-Ya'qubi,* II, pp.438-439. Mas'udi, *Muruj al-Dhahab,* VI, pp.176-178. Dinawari, *Al-Akhbar al-Tiwal,* pp.378-383 and also p.385. Crone, *Slaves on Horses,* p.71. Lassner, *Islamic Revolution,* pp.110-115. Moscati, "Studi su Abu Muslim", III, pp.95-96. 'Omar, *Al-'Abbasiyun al-Awa'il,* p.49. 'Omar, *Al-Khilafah al-'Abbasiyyah,* p.16.

(75) Cf. Dinawari, *Al-Akhbar al-Tiwal,* pp.387-401. See also Tabari, *Ta'rikh al-Rusul wa al-Muluk,* III, pp.842 ff. (Leiden Edition) Ya'qubi, *Ta'rikh al-Ya'qubi,* II, pp.438-439. Ibn Qutaybah, *Al-Imamah wa al-Siyasah,* II, pp.174-175. Sourdel, "La Syrie", p.171. For more details about these political conflicts between al-Amin and al-Ma'mun see also Brockelmann, *History,* pp.121-123. 'Omar, *Al-Khilafah al-'Abbasiyyah,* pp.26-36. Hodgson, *The Venture of Islam,* pp.299-300. Marín-Guzmán, *El Islam: Ideología e Historia,* p.79. Marín-Guzmán, *Introducción a los Estudios Islámicos,* passim. For a good discussion of the succession issue see Chejne, *Succession to the Rule in Islam,* pp.110-118. See also Francesco Gabrieli, "La successione di Harun ar-Rasid e la guerra fra al-Amin e al-Ma'mun", in *Rivista degli Studi Orientali,* Vol. XI, Fascicolo 4, 1928, pp.341-397. See also Mas'udi, *Muruj al-Dhahab,* VI, pp.326-328. About the wars between al-Amin and al-Ma'mun see Mas'udi, *Muruj al-Dhahab,* VI, pp.419-423. *Al-'Uyun wa al-Hada'iq fi Akhbar al-Haqa'iq,* III, pp.220-280.

(76) Cf. Tabari, *Ta'rikh al-Rusul wa al-Muluk,* III, passim, especially p.392, p.429, p.461 and p.1142. (Leiden Edition) For more details about the 'Abbasid policy of preferring the *mawali* (Khurasanis) over the Arabs see Hodgson, *The Venture of Islam,* pp.275 ff. Crone, *Slaves on Horses,* pp.173-196 (Appendix V), where she proves that the *mawali* were prefered by the 'Abbasids over the Arabs, and they were employed in private or semi-private functions associated with the household, the court, the postal service and the espionage system. See also pp.70-71.

(77) Sharon, "Military Reforms", pp.132-133. Sharon analysed those various traditions. The Khurasanis even boasted saying that "The Ansar are two, the tribes of Aws and Khazraj, who helped the Prophet at the beginning *(fi awwal al-zaman)* and the Khurasanis who helped him at the end *(fi akhir al-zaman)*", quoted by Sharon, "Military Reforms", p.132. See also Tabari, *Ta'rikh al-Rusul wa al-Muluk,* III, p.1142. (Leiden Edition). Tabari also preserved some traditions of the preference for khurasanis over the Arabs practiced by several 'Abbasid caliphs, among them especially al-Ma'mun. Some people asked the caliph to see the Syrians (Arabs) with the same eyes (with equality) that he saw the Khurasanis.

(78) Cf. Abu 'Uthman 'Amr Ibn Bahr al-Jahiz, *Manaqib*, in Sharon, "Military Reforms", pp.134-143. Ibn al-Muqaffa', *Risalah*, in S.D. Goitein, *Studies in Islamic History*, pp.149-167. For more details about Ibn al-Muqaffa' see Goitein, *Studies in Islamic History*, pp.158-163. Francesco Gabrieli, "L'opera di Ibn al-Muqaffa'", in *Rivista degli Studi Orientali*, Vol.XIII, Fascicolo 3, 1932, pp.197-247. See also the interesting discussion by P. Kraus, "Zu Ibn al-Muqaffa'", in *Rivista degli Studi Orientali*, Vol. XIV, Fascicolo 1, 1933, pp.1-20. For more information about Ibn al-Muqaffa' see Carlo Nallino, "Noterelle su Ibn al-Muqaffa' e suo figlio", in *Rivista degli Studi Orientali*, Vol. XIV, Fascicolo 2, 1933, pp.130-134. Sharon, "Military Reforms", pp.134-135. Ibn al-Muqaffa' described this process of the caliphs' preference for the Khursanis over the Arabs, and also how the Arabs were affected by this problem. Ibn al-Muqaffa' wrote about the Arabs losing power and administrative positions in the army and the court. As a result of this situation they lost their privileges and social status over the *mawali*. Several other Muslim writers also noticed this process and even mentioned that the Khurasanis were kept in separate military units and were separated from the Iraqis by placing them in separate localities. Among them see Ya'qubi, *Kitab al-Buldan*, p.21. Yaqut, *Mu'jam al-Buldan*, II, pp.234-235. See also Sharon, "Military Reforms", pp.128-129. The Khurasanis were kept in separate units while the Arabs were organized according to their tribes. See Sharon, "Military Reforms", p.130. Brockelmann, *History*, p.176. About these issues see also al-Jahiz's "Risalah fi Manaqib al-Turk", in *Rasa'il al-Jahiz*, edited by 'Abd al-Salam Muhammad Harun, Cairo, 1384/1964, pp.5-86. For an excellent explanation of al-Jahiz's *Risalah* see Francesco Gabrieli, "La Risala di al-Gahiz sui Turchi", in *Rivista degli Studi Orientali*, Vol. XXXII, Part II, 1957, pp.477-483. In this respect Gabrieli wrote: "Ma la Risala fi manaqib at-Turk, forse oltre le intenzioni dell'autore, è apparsa post eventum un'anticipazione e quasi un presentimento dell'avvenire; così come, su tutt'altri presupposti intellettuali e morali, il famoso trattatello di Tacito sui Germani, i futuri eversori della fortuna di Roma." (p.483).

(79) For more details about the revolts of the *Ahl al-Dhimmah* in Hims, especially against the caliph al-Mansur, the second 'Abbasid ruler, see Baladhuri, *Futuh al-Buldan*, p.162, especially for Lebanon, and also p.167. See also Sourdel, "La Syrie", pp.162-163 and also p.170.

(80) About these conversions not only for Hims, but also for other areas, like Halab (Aleppo) and Qinnasrin, in the time of the 'Abbasid caliph al-Mahdi, see Baladhuri, *Futuh al-Buldan*, p.145, where he explained that the caliph al-Mahdi wrote on their hands

Qinnasrin with green color, as a symbol of submission to Allah. Green is the color of Islam. Al-Baladhuri wrote:*"Inna jama'ah min ahl dhalika al-hadir aslamu fi khilafat Amir al-Mu'minin al-Mahdi fa-kataba 'ala aydihim bi al-Khudrah Qinnasrin".*

(81) There are several examples of Arab military leaders who drafted local people converted to Islam (*mawali*) into the armies for new campaigns. Among the major examples are Tariq b. Zyad who, for the conquest of al-Andalus, drafted Berber soldiers, and Qutaybah Ibn Muslim who enrolled Persians in his army for his campaigns in Transoxiana. For further information about these issues of *mawali* in the Muslim armies, and even the *dahaqin's* acquisition of *'ata'* in the army, see Baladhuri, *Futuh al-Buldan,* pp.457-458. See also Sharon, "Military Reforms", p.120.

(82) Maqrizi, *Kitab al-Niza',* p.92. In this respect al-Maqrizi wrote: "As for Abu Ja'far 'Abd Allah Ibn Muhammad al-Mansur, he adopted the style of dress of the ancient Persian emperors, and he made Persians, such as the Barmaki and the Nawbakhti families, the chief men of his regime. He introduced such innovations as full-length prostration and kissing the ground before the ruler (*tabqil*). He withdrew himself from all direct contact with the public and regarded them with contempt." Al-Maqrizi intended to generalize those ideas to be applied to all 'Abbasid caliphs. Several caliphs lost power or even were killed by their Turkish soldiers. A good example of this situation was al-Mutawakkil, who was murdered by his Turkish soldiers in 861 in Samarra. For more details see Suyuti, *Ta'rikh al-Khulafa',* pp.346-355. Ibn Majah, *Ta'rikh al-Khulafa',* pp.42-43. Mas'udi, *Al-Tanbih wa al-Ishraf,* pp.329-330. Mas'udi, *Muruj al-Dhahab,* VII, pp.189-290; see especially pp.267-273. Tabari, *Ta'rikh al-Rusul wa al-Muluk,* Ya'qubi, *Ta'rikh al-Ya'qubi,* II, pp.484-492, especially p.492. See also 'Omar, *Al-'Abbasiyun al-Awa'il,* pp.250-255. See also Olga Pinto, "Al-Fath b. Haqan favorito di al-Mutawakkil", in *Rivista degli Studi Orientali,* Vol. XIII, Fascicolo 2, 1931-1932, pp.133-149.

(83) Sharon has demonstrated this situation in his "Military Reforms", passim, especially pp.142-143.

(84) Al-Jahiz in his *Manaqib,* p.62 described the composition of the army in the time of al-Mu'tasim as containing three elements: Ahl Khurasan, Abna' and Turks. No Arabs were included in this army according to al-Jahiz. See also Sharon, "Military Reforms", p.143.

(85) Poem by Marwan Ibn Abi al-Janub Yahya Ibn Marwan, quoted by Tabari, *Ta'rikh al-Rusul wa al-Muluk,* III, pp.1465-1466,

quoted and translated by Bosworth, "Introduction" to the translation of Maqrizi, *Kitab al-Niza`*, p.21.

(86) See the Qur'an, *Surat al-Nur* (XXIV, 35), that says: "Allah is the Light of the heavens and the earth. The similitude of His light is as a niche wherein is a lamp. The lamp is in a glass. The glass is as it were a shining star.(This lamp is) kindled from a blessed tree, an olive neither of the East nor of the West, whose oil would almost glow forth (of itself) though no fire touched it. Light upon light. Allah guideth unto His light whom He will. And Allah speaketh to mankind in allegories, for Allah is knower of all things." The idea of God being the Light *(Al-Nur)* was also common among the sufis. For this see Marín-Guzmán, "Razón y Revelación en el Islam", pp.137-142. Marín-Guzmán, *El Islam: Ideología e Historia,* pp.191-202. Reynold Nicholson, *Los Místicos del Islam,* México, 1975, passim. Hitti, *El Islam, un Modo de Vida,* passim, especially pp.96-115. Brockelmann, *History*, pp.148-150.

(87) For more details about these important issues see Patricia Crone and Martin Hinds, *God's Caliph. Religious Authority in the First Centuries of Islam,* Cambridge, 1986, passim, especially, pp.4-23.

(88) Especially see Maqrizi, *Kitab al-Niza'*, pp.83-84 and also pp.79-80.

(89) Maqrizi, *Kitab al-Niza'*, pp.101 ff.

(90) Maqrizi, *Kitab al-Niza'*, p.86.

(91) Abu Mansur 'Abd al-Malik b. Muhammad b. Ibrahim al-Tha'alibi, *Lata'if al-Ma'rif,* edited by I. al-Abyari and H. K. al-Sayrafi, Cairo, 1960. *The Book of Curious and Entertaining Information, the Lata'if al-Ma'rif of Tha'alibi,* English translation, introduction and notes by Clifford Bosworth, Edinburgh, 1968, p.76, quoted by Bosworth, "Introduction" to the translation of Maqrizi, *Kitab al-Niza'*, p.21. About the caliph al-Mahdi see Tabari, *Ta'rikh al-Rusul wa al-Muluk,* III, pp.451-454. (Leiden Edition) Ibn al-Athir, *Al-Kamil fi al-Ta'rikh,* V, pp.577-581. (Leiden-Beirut Edition) Ya'qubi, *Ta'rikh al-Ya'qubi,* II, pp.392-403. Suyuti, *Ta'rikh al-Khulafa',* pp.271-279. Ibn Majah, *Ta'rikh al-Khulafa',* pp.37-38. Dinawari, *Al-Akhbar al-Tiwal,* p.386. Mas'udi, *Al-Tanbih wa al-Ishraf,* pp.312-313. Mas'udi, *Muruj al-Dhahab,* VI, pp.224-260. *Al-'Uyun wa al-Hada'iq fi Akhbar al-Haqa'iq,* III, pp.269-282. Sabatino Moscati,"Studi storici sul califfato di al-Mahdi", in *Orientalia,* Vol. XIV, Fasc. 3-4, 1945, pp.300-354.

Sabatino Moscati, "Nuovi studi storici sul califfato di al-Mahdi", in *Orientalia*, Vol. XV, Fasc.1-2, 1946, pp.155-179. Hugh Kennedy, "Al-Mahdi", in *Encyclopaedia of Islam*, (2) Vol.V, Leiden, 1985, pp.1238-1239. Brockelmann, *History*, pp.112-114. Cahen, *Les peuples musulmans*, p.156. Cahen asserted that at the time of al-Mahdi the 'Abbasids proclaimed legitimacy according to the Rawandite principles.

(92) Among those intellectuals was the poet Marwan Ibn Abi al-Janub Yahya Ibn Marwan, who wrote a poem to the caliph al-Mutawakkil, in which he explained that the inheritance of the Prophet Muhammad belonged to the caliph al-Mutawakkil. The poet also rejected the claims of those who believed that the inheritance belonged to the descendants of 'Ali and Fatimah. See Tabari, *Ta'rikh al-Rusul wa al-Muluk*, III, pp.1465-1466 (Leiden Edition), quoted and translated by Bosworth, "Introduction" to the translation of Maqrizi, *Kitab al-Niza'*, p.21.

(93) Abu 'Uthman 'Amr Ibn Bahr al-Jahiz, *Kitab Fadl Hashim 'ala 'Abd Shams, in Rasa'il al-Jahiz,* edited by Hasan al-Sandubi, Cairo, 1933, pp.58-62, quoted by Bosworth, "Intoduction", p.38.

(94) Al-Jahiz, *Kitab Fadl Hashim 'ala 'Abd Shams,* pp.58-62, quoted by Bosworth, "Introduction", pp.38 ff.

(95) About the Shi'ite doctrine of *nass* see Marín-Guzmán, "El Islam Shi'ita", pp.173-183. Marín-Guzmán, *El Islam: Ideología e Historia*, p.174. Ruiz Figueroa, "Imamah o autoridad en los primeros tiempos del Islam, pp.61-82. Pareja, *Islamología*, II, p.722 and p.739. Jafri, *Origins and early Development,* passim, especially pp.290-291. Watt, *Islamic Philosophy and Theology*, pp.20-25, especially p.25. Kennedy, *Prophet*, p.125.

(96) For theological and philosophical Shi'ite thought see Tabatabai, *Shi'ite Islam*, pp.106-181.

(97) Tabatabai, *Shi'ite Islam*, pp.78-79 and also p.181.

# Conclusion

During the Umayyad period, there were several revolts, rebellions, civil wars (*fitnah*, pl. *fitan*), and other outbreaks of social unrest. Some were locally organized; others, more extended into vast areas. Some rebellions against the Umayyads focused on religious issues, such as the Shi'ite, the Khawarij and the *Qadariyyah*; others were more political, such as those organized by 'Abd al-Rahman Ibn al-Ash'ath and Yazid Ibn al-Muhallab, revolts that also had socio-economic causes.

There were several reasons for the unrest during the Umayyad period. The following were the major ones:

1- Socio-economic conditions. The Umayyad government relied on certain groups and tended to favor them. When a particular caliph relied on and supported either confederation of tribes (Mudar or Qahtan) the unfavored confederation of tribes opposed and often fought their traditional enemies. In various instances they went beyond the tribal rivalries and enrolled in broader revolts against the Umayyads. The Umayyads favored and supported tribes through land ownership, administrative positions such as governors of cities and provinces, and commanders in expeditionary wars. Such privileges and patronage angered the opposition.

2- Social grievances. The major example was the Umayyad discrimination against the *mawali* (non-Arab new converts to Islam), who also revolted. The *mawali* wanted equality (*musawah*) of treatment and opportunities. To reach these goals they revolted and supported several rebellions against the Umayyads. The *mawali* joined the revolt of al-Mukhtar on behalf of Muhammad Ibn al-Hanafiyyah. The new Muslim converts also developed and joined the intellectual *Shu'ubiyyah* school which had a clear claim for equality (*musawah*) in the Muslim society.

3- Heavy taxation. During the eighty-odd years of the first dynasty of Islam, heavy taxation was one of the main reasons for revolt in some social sectors in the *Dar al-Islam* (The Muslim Empire). The heavy taxation also had a clear influence and impact upon religious conversion. Those non-Muslims payers of the *jizyah* (poll-tax), along with the other taxes, saw conversion to Islam as a fair and special way to be exempted from the *jizyah* tax and to pay the pious and smaller Muslim *zakah* instead.

4- Rivalries between Syria and Iraq. The Umayyad dynasty was based in Syria and thus relied and supported this region and its inhabitants over the people of other areas. Opposition and fighting against the Umayyads was also spurred by the rivalries between Syrians and Iraqis (the Khurasanis, obviously, were included in this last group). The caliph's troops were Syrian, and their presence in Iraq and Khurasan always brought problems since the *Amir al-Mu'minin*'s army tended to represent Syrian interest against local ones. These rivalries were intense, and the fighting became a constant of the Umayyad period.

Those were the four main reasons for revolt and social unrest during the Umayyad dynasty; however, it is important to bear in mind that none of the many rebellions before the 'Abbasids was successful. Some revolts only lasted for few months until they faced the Umayyad Syrian army. Examples include the various religious Khawarij revolts, the Shi'ite upheavals such as that of Husayn Ibn 'Ali Ibn Abi Talib, and the political revolts led by 'Abd al-Rahman Ibn al-Ash'ath and by Yazid Ibn al-Muhallab. All these revolts were explained in detail in the Arabic chronicles and histories, such as Abu Ja'far Muhammad al-Tabari's *Tarikh al-Rusul wa al-Muluk,* Abu al-'Abbas Ahmad b. Yahya al-Baladhuri's *Ansab al-Ashraf* and *Futuh al-Buldan,* Abu Muhammad 'Abd Allah b. Muslim Ibn Qutaybah's

*'Uyun al-Akhbar* and *Al-Imamah wa al-Siyasah*, and Abu al-Hasan 'Ali b. al-Husayn b. 'Ali al-Mas'udi's *Muruj al-Dhahab* and *Al-Tanbih wa al-Ishraf*, 'Izz al-Din Abu al-Hasan 'Ali b. Muhammad b. 'Abd al-Karim Ibn al-Athir's *Al-Kamil fi al-Ta'rikh*, etc.

Some rebellions lasted two or three years such as the one directed by al-Mukhtar in Kufa (spread to other places of Iraq) from 685 to 687. Some others were true civil wars (*fitnah*, pl. *fitan*), like that of 'Abd Allah Ibn al-Zubayr in the Hijaz, which also spread to Iraq (680 to 692). Other peoples and groups revolted repeatedly during the Umayyad period. Examples include uprisings of the Berbers in North Africa and al-Andalus, one of the most powerful taking place in 740. One must also count the persistent religious upheavals such as the Shi'ites and the Khawarij. However, all of these movements, religious, political and ethnic, were suppressed and in most cases came to tragic ends. The Umayyads controlled the Empire, and using their Syrian army they preserved and kept together the *Dar al-Islam*. Their brutal and ruthless ways earned them their notoriety as repressive tyrants. This political tyranny, shrewdly described in various propagandas and ideologies, cost the Umayyads their legitimacy. Various Muslim groups spread the notion that the Umayyads were usurpers and impious Muslims who should be ousted. This propaganda fueled further opposition and rebellion. In the opinion of several groups, mainly the Shi'ites, the Khawarij and the Qadariyyah, the Umayyads had no legitimacy to rule the Muslim Empire.

The 'Abbasids organized a very skillful propaganda network that secretly spread their ideology from 718 to 747. They gained popular support in the struggles against the Umayyads by promising to end grievances, the discrimination, and the heavy taxation. Although the Arabic sources are not explicit, it is plausible to infer that the 'Abbasids made those promises to attract followers in several levels.

The 'Abbasids' appeals to return Islam to its pristine form and practices after ousting the Umayyads also gave them popular support. The Umayyads were considered usurpers, an idea that attracted the Shi'ites and probably other religious groups. There is little evidence in the Arabic sources that the Khawarij and the *Qadariyyah* through the *Mu'tazilah* participated in the 'Abbasid revolution when it became open in 747. However, the fact that they had been politically active in earlier years against the Umayyads implies that they could have also been active in the 'Abbasid revolution. Their rebellion, whether or not allied with the Banu Hashim, gave the impression that the 'Abbasids were leading a major revolt, with a strong popular support, against the Umayyads.

The 'Abbasids gained support of the Shi'ites by promising to choose the *Imam-Amir al-Mu'minin* from the House of the Prophet (*Ahl al-Bayt*), a leader suitable to all Muslims. Being from the Family of the Prophet, the 'Abbasids claimed legitimacy, and in their secret propaganda they appeared as a pro-'Alid group. Using the controversial issue of Abu Hashim's testament they gained popularity and leadership in the Shi'ite group of the *Hashimiyyah*. In time the pro-'Alid 'Abbasid propaganda became absolutely pro-'Abbasid. The 'Abbasids effectively hijacked the Shi'ite opposition and used it for their own benefit. The 'Abbasids also took advantage of the Shi'ite experience and organization of opposition groups, but they were careful in all their moves and more patient in making the important decisions.

The traditional inter-tribal feuds between Qahtan and Qays were also advantageously used by the 'Abbasids, who supported the Southern tribes against the Northerners, in exchange for their help in fighting the Umayyads. The Qahtan were also against the Umayyad administration that had discriminated against them by more often helping the Qays. The Yemenites also became an important part of the 'Abbasid army.

Khurasan was chosen by the 'Abbasids for the spread of their secret propaganda, since much resentment against the Umayyads already characterized its people. The 'Abbasids wanted support of the Khurasanis, renowned as excellent soldiers. This fact assured recruitment of skillful and experienced warriors to face the Umayyad armies. To solidify support the 'Abbasids even created some traditions in which the loyalty of Khurasanis to the 'Abbasids was emphasized. This meant that the 'Abbasids were helping the *mawali* struggles against the Umayyads, asking in return support for the new *da'wah*.

After numerous and intense wars the 'Abbasid armies, led mainly by Abu Muslim al-Khurasani, Abu Salamah al-Khallal, Qahtabah b. Shabib, and 'Abd Allah b. 'Ali, defeated the Umayyads. These armies included both Arabs and *mawali*, as well as religious discontents, which reflects the broad ethnic, religious and popular dimensions of the 'Abbasid revolution.

Persecution and almost total extermination of the Umayyads were among the first steps taken by the 'Abbasids. Immediately after, other important and radical changes took place. The 'Abbasids confiscated the Umayyad properties, and those in Syria were given to Khurasani military chiefs and to members of the Southern tribes. These allotments lead us to conclude that the 'Abbasids were fulfilling promises made to the Qahtan and the Khurasanis in their propaganda. The 'Abbasids' preference for the Khurasanis in the court, the army and some administrative positions, opened the doors to other groups, especially Turks, who later took control of the Muslim Empire. With the 'Abbasids the leadership of the Arabs came to an end. The participation of other ethnic groups, mainly Persians and Turks in the leading positions in the Muslim Empire, has been the topic of much controversy, since many Muslim authors saw their participation as the beginning of the decline of the Muslim Empire. Others, however, have defended the 'Abbasid revolution for elevating the Persians to giving their knowledge and experience to the greatness of the Islamic culture.

In the controversy between Syria and Iraq the 'Abbasids chose the latter. The change of the capital of the Empire from Damascus to Baghdad reflects this preference.

The Shi'ites felt betrayed when the 'Abbasids took power and did not share it with them. Some pro-'Alid leaders in the 'Abbasid armies, such as Abu Salamah al-Khallal, were surprised that not an 'Ali, but the 'Abbasid Abu al-'Abbas, was proclaimed caliph in Kufa shortly after the capture of the city. However, the 'Abbasids were able to control power, to get rid of the major opponents like Abu Salamah and later the possible menace of Abu Muslim, and to rebut effectively any new doctrines for legitimacy that the Shi'ites developed. Because the 'Abbasids were associated with *Sunnism*, they also gained popular support once in power, and because of that, they were able to give to Islam a universal dimension and to keep Muslims together, both Arabs and *mawali*, fulfilling the major aspiration of the *Shu'ubiyyah*.

## Glossary

*Abna'* the sons, refers to the descendants of the Khurasanis who were enrolled in the 'Abbasid army after they took power.

*Ahadith* see *Hadith*.

*Ahl al-Bayt* lit. the People of the House; i.e. the descendants of the Prophet Muhammad.

*Ahl al-Dhimmah* the protected people. The minority religious groups accepted as protected people in the Muslim Empire. They were required to pay the poll tax (*jizyah*). The *Ahl al- Dhimmah* were first the Christians and the Jews, those who had a revealed religion. Later the Zoroastrians were also accepted as a minority religious group. Zarathustra was considered a prophet, and his preachings a revealed religion.

*Ahl Muhammad* the descendants of the Prophet Muhammad.

*'Alim* (pl. *'ulama'*) religious leader, Muslim intellectual.

*Amir* prince, ruler.

*Amir al-Mu'minin* Prince of the Believers, the title used by the caliphs, comprising religious, political and judicial authority.

*Amsar* see *misr*

*'Ata'* stipend, used mainly for military stipends.

*Barid* postal service. The Muslim postal service, under the direct control of the caliph, was also a very efficient espionage system, to keep control and information of any possible revolts.

*Bayt al-Mal* the Imperial Treasury.

*Dahaqin* the Persian aristocracy.

*Dar al-Harb* the territories beyond the Muslim frontiers, usually in state of war against the enemy empires.

*Dar al-Islam* the Muslim Empire; i.e., the secured frontiers of the Empire.

*Din* religion.

*Diwan al-Barid* the postal service. See *barid.*

*Diwan al-Khatam* the office of the seal, dealing with the official sealing of documents.

*Da'wah* the mission, the call.

*Dawlah* the State, the dynasty, the Empire.

*Dhimmah* see *Ahl al-Dhimmah.*

*Du'at* missionaries, preachers of the *da'wah.*

*Fay* booty. This term was used as booty in the early Islamic times. However, later its meaning changed to refer to those territories or peoples that voluntarily accepted Islam.

*Fitnah* (pl. *fitan*) civil war, mutiny, upheaval.

*Ghanimah* the booty captured in the Islamic conquests.

*Hadith* (pl. *ahadith*) the sayings of the Prophet Muhammad.

*Hajj* the Muslim Pilgrimage to Mecca.

*Imam* the leader of the Muslim prayer. Extended it refers to the Muslim leaders, mainly the Shi'ites. In Shi'ism the *imam* is infallible and characterized by sinlessness.

*Imamah* authority, leadership. The *imamah* is one of the major Shi'ite principles.

*Imamate* the political form; i.e., a state, in which the *imamah* is put into practice by the *imam..*

*Jizyah* poll tax. This tax was levied only from the *Ahl al-Dhimmah.*

*Junds* soldiers, especially a frontier soldier; the equivalent of the ancient Roman *limitanei.*

*Khalifah* (pl. *Khulafa'*) caliph, the ultimate Muslim authority in political, religious and judicial affairs.

*Khalifat Allah*   God's caliphate, used by the Umayyads as a principle for claiming legitimacy.

*Kharaj*  tax, mainly the land tax.

*Khatam al-Nabiyyin*   the Seal of the Prophets; the Prophet Muhammad who was, according to the Muslim traditions, the last Prophet.

*Khilafah*  caliphate.

*Mawla* (pl. *mawali*) a non-Arab converted to Islam, client of an Arab tribe.

*Misr* (pl. *amsar*)  Fortress.

*Mu'arrikhun*  historians.

*Mulk Mutawarith*   the hereditary authority, one of the major principles of Shi'ah Islam to claim legitimacy.

*Musaddiq*  tax collector.

*Musawah*  equality, one of the major principles spread by the *Shu'ubiyyah* for the non-Arab Muslims to obtain equality with the Arab Muslims.

*Naqib* (pl. *nuqaba'*)  propagandist, preacher.

*Nasab* (pl. *ansab*)   origin, kin, pedigree.

*Nass*  designation.

*Nubuwwah*  prophecy.

*Nubuwwah Muqayyadah*  the restricted or limited prophecy.

*Nubuwwah Mutlaqah*  the absolute prophecy.

*Nuqaba'*  see *naqib*.

*Nur al-Khilafah*   the Light of the Caliphate, used by the 'Abbasids as a principle to claim legitimacy.

*Nur Muhammad*  the Light of Muhammad, used by the Shi'ites as a principle to claim legitimacy.

*Qadi* (pl. *qudat*) Muslim Judge.

*Qaraba* (pl. *aqraba*) kin, relative. In the Muslim discussion for legitimacy this term refers to the relatives of the Prophet   Muhammad.

*Qudat* see *qadi*.

*Rashidun* the straightly guided caliphs: Abu Bakr, 'Umar, 'Uthman and 'Ali.

*Rasul* (pl. *rusul*) messenger, prophet.

*Rasul Allah* the Messenger, Prophet of God; i.e., Muhammad.

*Sadaqah* charity. The voluntary alms given to the Muslim State after the payment of the *zakah*.

*Sha'ir* see *shu'ara'*.

*Shaykh* (pl. *shuyukh*) the eldest in the Arabic culture, the leader of a *Sufi* order.

*Shu'ara'* poets.

*Sunnah* Tradition. The *sunnah* comprises the sayings and the deeds   of the Prophet Muhammad.

*Taqiyyah* simulation. The simulation became a very common Shi'ite   practice allowing a person, in case of danger, to hide his identity as a Shi'ite.

*Tulaqa'* reluctants.

*Ummah* community.

*Al-Ummah al-Islamiyyah* the Muslim Community.

*Waqf* (pl. *awqaf*) the religious endowments. The properties given   to a mosque as *waqf* became inalienable.

*Wasiyyah* inheritance.

*Zakah* the Muslim religious principle of pious and obligatory alms.

# BIBLIOGRAPHY

## Arabic Primary Sources

Abu Yusuf, Ya'qub b. Ibrahim, *Kitab al-Kharaj*, Cairo, 1392 H.

Anonymous, *Akhbar al-Dawlah al-'Abbasiyyah wa fihi Akhbar al-'Abbas wa Waladihi*, edited by 'Abd al-'Aziz al-Duri and 'Abd al-Jabbar al-Muttalibi, Beirut, 1971.

Anonymous, *Akhbar Majmu'ah*, edited and Spanish translation by Emilio Lafuente y Alcántara, Madrid, 1867.

Anonymous, *Kitab al-'Uyun wa al-Hada'iq fi Akhbar al-Haqa'iq*, edited by M.J. de Goeje and P. de Jong, Leiden, 1869, Vol. III.

Anonymous, *Kitab al-'Uyun wa al-Hada'iq fi Akhbar al-Haqa'iq*, edited by 'Umar al-Sa'idi, Damascus, 1972, Vol. IV.

Al-Azdi, Abu Zakariya Yazid, *Ta'rikh al-Mawsil*, edited by 'A. Habiba, Cairo, 1387/1967.

Al-Azdi, Muhammad b. 'Abd Allah, *Ta'rikh Futuh al-Sham*, edited by A.A. 'Amir, Cairo, 1970.

Al-Baghdadi, Abu Mansur 'Abd al-Qahir Ibn Tahir Ibn Muhammad, *Al-Farq bayna al-Firaq*, Beirut, 1973.

----, *Moslem Schisms and Sects*, English translation by Kate Chambers Seelye, New York, 1966.

Al-Baladhuri, Abu al-Hasan Ahmad b. Yahya, *Ansab al-Ashraf*, edited by M. Hamidullah, Cairo, 1959, Vol. I.

----, *Ansab al-Ashraf*, edited by Max Schloessinger, Jerusalem, 1971, Vol. IV A.

----, *Ansab al-Ashraf*, edited by Max Schloessinger, Jerusalem, 1938, Vol. IV B.

----, *Ansab al-Ashraf*, edited by S.D. Goitein, Jerusalem, 1936, Vol. V.

----, *Ansab al-Ashraf*, edited by W. Ahlwardt, Griefswald, 1883, Vol. XI.

----, *Futuh al-Buldan*, edited by M.J. de Goeje, Leiden, 1866, second edition Leiden, 1968.

Dinawari, Abu Hanifah Ahmad b. Dawd, *Al-Akhbar al-Tiwal*, edited by A.M. 'Amir and G. al-Shayyal, Cairo, 1960.

Al-Hamdani, Abu Muhammad al-Hasan Ahmad b. Ya'qub b. Yusuf b. Dawd, *Kitab Sifah Jazirat al-'Arab*, edited by David Heinrich Müller, Leiden, 1968.

Ibn 'Abd al-Hakam, Abu al-Qassim 'Abd al-Rahman b. 'Abd Allah, *Futuh Ifriqiyyah wa al-Andalus, La Conquista de Africa del Norte y de España*, Spanish translation by Eliseo Beltrán, Valencia, 1966.

----, *Futuh Misr wa Akhbaruha*, edited by Charles C. Torrey, Leiden, 1920.

----, *Sirat 'Umar Ibn 'Abd al-'Aziz*, Cairo, 1927.

Ibn 'Abd Rabbihi, Abu 'Umar Ahmad b. Muhammad, *Al'Iqd al-Farid*, Cairo, 1948.

Ibn al-Athir, 'Izz al-Din, *Al-Kamil fi al-Ta'rikh*, edited by C. J. Tornberg, Leiden, 1869, reimpression, Beirut, 1965. (Leiden-Beirut Edition)

Ibn al-Athir, Majid al-Din, *Al-Nihayah fi Gharib al-Hadith wa al-Athar*, edited by Tahir Ahmad al-Zawi and Mahmud Muhammad al-Tannahi, Cairo, 1963.

Ibn Battutah, *Rihlah*, edited by 'Ali al-Muntasir al-Kattabi, Beirut, 1975.

Ibn Hawqal, Muhammad, *Surat al-Ard*, edited by J.H. Kramers, Leiden, 1938-1939.

Ibn Hayyan, Abu Mansur, *Al-Muqtabis Balad al-Andalus. Crónica del Califa 'Abdarrahman III an-Nasir entre los años 912 y 942*, Spanish translation by Ma. Jesús Viguera and Federico Corriente, Zaragoza, 1981, Vol. V.

Ibn Hazm al-Andalusi, 'Ali Ibn Ahmad, *Al-Fasl fi al-Milal wa al-Ahwa' al-Nihal,* Cairo, 1964.

Ibn Hisham, 'Abd al-Malik, *Sirat Rasul Allah. The Life of Muhammad,* English translation by A. Guillaume, London, 1955.

Ibn al-Jawzi, Abu al-Faraj 'Abd al-Rahman Ibn 'Ali, *Manaqib Amir al-Mu'minin 'Umar Ibn al-Khattab,* edited by Zaynab Ibrahim al-Qarut, Beirut, 1982.

----, *Manaqib Baghdad,* edited by Muhammad Bahjat al-Athari, Baghdad, 1342 H.

----, *Manaqib al-Imam Ahmad Ibn Hanbal,* edited by 'Ali Muhammad 'Umar, Egypt, 1399/1979.

----, *Al-Muntazam fi Ta'rikh al-Muluk wa al-Umam,* n.p., 1357 H.

Ibn Khaldun, 'Abd al-Rahman, *Kitab al-'Ibar wa Diwan al-Mubtada wa al-Khabar,* Beirut, 1956.

----, *Al-Muqaddimah,* edited by Wafi 'Ali 'Abd al-Wahid, Cairo, 1965.

----, *Al-Muqaddimah. Intoducción a la Historia Universal,* Spanish translation by Juan Feres, México, 1977.

Ibn Khallikan, Abu al-'Abbas Shams al-Din Ahmad b. Muhammad b. 'Abu Bakr, *Wafayat al-A'yan wa Anba' Abna' al-Zaman,* edited by Ihsan 'Abbas, Beirut, 1972.

Ibn Khurdadhbih, Abu al-Qasim 'Ubayd Allah Ibn 'Abd Allah, *Kitab al-Masalik wa al-Mamalik,* edited by M.J. de Goeje, Leiden, 1889.

Ibn Majah, Abu 'Abd Allah Muhammad Ibn Yazid, *Ta'rikh al-Khulafa',* edited by Muhammad Muti' al-Hafiz, Damascus, 1979.

Ibn al-Muqaffa', *Risalah fi al-Sahabah,* edited by 'Umar Abu al-Nasr, Beirut, 1966.

Ibn Qutaybah, 'Abd Allah Ibn Muslim, *Al-Imamah wa al-Siyasah,* edited by Taha Muhammad al-Zayni, n.p., 1967.

----, *Al-Ma'arif,* edited by Tharwat 'Ukasha, Cairo, 1969.

----, *Ta'wil al-Qur'an,* Cairo, 1973.

----, *'Uyun al-Akhbar,* edited by Carl Brockelmann, Berlin, 1900-1908.

Ibn Qutiyyah al-Qurtubi, *Ta'rikh Iftitah al-Andalus,* edited and Spanish translation *(Historia de la Conquista de España)* by Julián Ribera, Madrid, 1926.

Ibn Rustah, Abu 'Ali Ahmad Ibn 'Umar, *Kitab al-A'laq al-Nafisah,* edited by M.J. de Goeje, Leiden, 1892, Vol. VII.

Ibn al-Sunni, Abu Bakr, *'Amal al-Yawm wa al-Laylah,* edited by 'Abd al-Qahir Ahmad 'Ata, Cairo, 1969.

Al-Isfahani, Abu al-Faraj, *Kitab al-Aghani,* Bulaq, Egypt, 1285/1868-1869, 20 volumes.

Istakhri, Abu Ishaq Ibrahim b. Muhammad al-Farisi, *Kitab Masalik al-Mamalik,* edited by M.J. de Goeje, Leiden, 1927.

Al-Jahiz, Abu 'Uthman 'Amr Ibn Bahr, *Al-Bukhala',* edited by Taha al-Hajiri, Cairo, n.d.

----, *Fi Mu'awiyah wa al-Umawyin,* edited by 'I.A. al-Husayni, Cairo, 1364/1946.

----, *Al-Hayawan,* edited by 'Abd al-Salam Muhammad Harun, Egypt, 1966-1969.

----, *Kitab Fadl Hashim 'ala 'Abd Shams,* in *Rasa'il al-Jahiz,* edited by Hasan al-Sandubi, Cairo, 1933.

----, *Kitab al-Taj,* edited by Ahmad Zaki Pasha, Cairo, 1914.

----, "Risala fi al-Nabita", in *Rasa'il al-Jahiz,* edited by 'Abd al-Salam Muhammad Harun, Cairo, Baghdad, 1965. French translation by Ch. Pellat, "Un document important pour l'histoire religieuse de l'Islam. "La Nabita de Djahiz", AIEO, X, Alger, 1952.

----, "Risalah ila al-Fath b. Khaqan fi Manaqib al-Turk wa 'Ammat Jund al-Khilafah", in *Rasa'il al-Jahiz*, edited by 'Abd al-Salam Muhammad Harun, Cairo, 1384/1964-1965.

Al-Khatib al-Baghdadi, Ahmad Ibn Thabit, *Ta'rikh Baghdad*, Cairo, 1931.

Al-Maqqari, Abu al-'Abbas Ahmad b. Muhammad, *Kitab Nafh al-Tibb*, edited by Reinhart Dozy and Guztave Dugat, Leiden, 1855-1861, reipression, Amsterdam, 1967.

Al-Maqrizi, Abu al-'Abbas Ahmad b. 'Ali, *Kitab al-Niza' wa al-Takhasum fima bayna Bani Umayyah wa Bani Hashim*, edited by Von Geerhardus Vos, Leiden, 1888.

----, *Book on Contention and Strife between Banu Umayya and Banu Hashim*, English translation by Clifford E. Bosworth,
          Manchester, 1980.

Al-Mas'udi, Abu al-Hasan 'Ali b. al-Husayn b. 'Ali, *Muruj al-Dhahab wa Ma'adin al-Jawhar*, edited by C. Barbier de Meynard and Pavet de Courteille, Paris, 1917.

----, *Al-Tanbih wa al-Ishraf*, Beirut, 1981.

Al-Mawardi, Abu al-Hasan Muhammad b. Habib, *Al-Ahkam al-Sultaniyyah wa al Wilayat al-Diniyyah*, Cairo, n.d.

Al-Mufid, Shaykh, *Kitab al-Irshad. The Book of Guidance into the Lives of the Twelve Imams*, English translation by I.K.A. Howard, New York, 1981.

Al-Muqaddasi, Muhammad Ibn Ahmad Ibn Abu Bakr al-Banna al-Basshari, *Ahsan al-Taqasim fi Ma'rifat al-Aqalim*, edited by M.J. de Goeje, Leiden, 1906.

Narshakhi, Abu Bakr Muhammad Ibn Ja'far, *Tarikh i-Bukhara, Description topographique et historique de Boukhara avant et pendant la conquête par les arabes*, Amsterdam, 1892 (1975). *History of Bukhara*, English translation by R. Frye, Cambridge, Massachusetts, 1954.

Al-Nawbakhti, Abu Muhammad al-Hasan b. Musa, *Kitab Firaq al-Shi'ah*, edited by Helmutt Ritter, Istanbul, 1931.

Qudamah, Ibn Ja'far, *Kitab al-Kharaj*, (selection) edited by M.J. de Goeje, Leiden, 1889.

Al-Qurashi, Yahya Ibn Adam, *Kitab al-Kharaj*, Lahore, 1395 H.

Al-Sam'ani, 'Abd al-Karim Ibn Muhammad, *Kitab al-Ansab*, edited by D.S. Margoliouth, London, 1912.

Al-Shahrastani, Muhammad b. Abu al-Qasim 'Abd al-Karim b. Abu Bakr Ahmad, *Al-Milal wa al-Nihal*, Cairo, 1964.

Al-Suyuti, al-Hafiz Jalal al-Din 'Abd al-Rahman b. Abu Bakr, *Al-Itqan fi 'Ulum al-Qur'an*, edited by Muhammad Abu Fadl Ibrahim, Cairo, 1967.

----, *Ta'rikh al-Khulafa'*, edited by Muhammad Muhyi al-Din 'Abd al-Hamid, Cairo, 1964.

Al-Tabari, Muhammad Ibn Jarir, *Ta'rikh al-Rusul wa al-Muluk*, edited by M.J. de Goeje, Leiden, 1879-1901.

----, *Ta'rikh al-Umam wa al-Muluk*, Cairo, n.d. (Egyptian Edition)

----, *Ta'rikh al-Rusul wa al-Muluk*, Cairo, 1969-1970. (Egyptian Edition 1969-1970)

Al-Tha'alibi, Abu Mansur 'Abd al-Malik b. Muhammad b. Ibrahim, *Lata'if al-Ma'arif*, edited by I. al-Abyari and H. K. al-Sayrafi, Cairo, 1960.

Al-Ya'qubi, Ahmad b. Abu Ya'qub, *Kitab al-Buldan*, edited by M.J. de Goeje, Leiden, 1892.

----, *Ta'rikh al-Ya'qubi*, edited by Th. Houtsma, Leiden, 1883, reimpression, Beirut, 1960.

Yaqut, Shihab al-Din b. 'Abd Allah al-Rumi, *Mu'jam al-Buldan*, edited by Wüstenfeld, Leipzig, 1866-1873.

**Secondary Works**

Abel, Armand, "Spain: Internal Division", in Gustav von Grunebaum, *Unity and Variety in Muslim Civilization*, Chicago,1979.

Al-'Adawi, Ibrahim Ahmad, *Ibn Battutah fi al-'Alam al-Islami*, Cairo, n.d.

'Amad, Ihsan Sidqi, *Al-Hajjaj Ibn Yusuf al-Thaqafi. Hayatuhu wa Ara'uhu al-Siyasiyah*, Beirut, 1981.

'Arafah, Thurayya Hafiz, *Al-Khurasaniyun wa Dawruhum al-Siyasi fi 'Asr al-'Abbasi al-Awwal*, Jiddah, 1982.

Arberry, John, *The Legacy of Persia*, Oxford, 1953.

'Athamina, Khalil, "Arab Settlements during the Umayyad Calipahte", in *Jerusalem Studies in Arabic and Islam*, 8, 1986, pp.185-207.

Azizi, M., *La domination arabe et l'épanouissement du sentiment national en Iran*, Paris, 1938.

Bahjat, 'Ali, *Qamus al-Amkinah wa al-Biqa' al-Lati Yaridu Dhikruha fi Kutub al-Futuh*, Egypt, 1906.

Barthold, W., *Turkestan down to the Mongol Invasion*, English translation by Hamilton Gibb, London, 1928.

Beg, Muhammad 'Abdul Jabbar, "Agricultural and Irrigation Labourers in Social and Economic Life of 'Iraq during the Umayyad and 'Abbasid Caliphates", in *Islamic Culture*, Vol. XLVII, Number 1, 1973, pp.15-30.

Boisard, Marcel A., *L'Humanisme de l'Islam*, Paris, 1979.

Bosworth, Clifford E., "Karramiyyah", in *Encyclopaedia of Islam* (2), Vol. IV, Leiden, 1976, pp.667-669.

Böwering, Gerhard, "Mi'raj", in Mircea Eliade, editor in chief, *The Encyclopaedia of Religion*, New York, Vol. IX, 1987, pp.552-556.

Brockelmann, Carl, *History of the Islamic Peoples*, English translation by Joel Carmichael and Moshe Perlman, New York, 1960.

Busse, Heribert, "'Omar b. al-Khattab in Jerusalem", in *Jerusalem Studies in Arabic and Islam*, 5, 1984, pp.73-119.

----, "'Omar's image as the Conqueror of Jerusalem", in *Jerusalem Studies in Arabic and Islam*, 8, 1986, pp.149-168.

Caetani, Leone, *Annali dell'Islam*, Milano, 1905-1926.

Cahen, Claude, "Fiscalité, proprieté, antagonismes sociaux en Haute-Mésopotamie au temps des premiers 'Abbasides", in *Arabica. Revue d'études arabes*, Vol. I, Fascicule 2, 1954, pp.136-152.

----, *El Islam*, Madrid, 1974.

----, "Notes sur l'historiographie dans la communauté musulmane Médiévale", in *Revue des études islamiques*, Vol. XLIV, 1976, pp.81-88.

----, *Les peuples musulmans dans l'histoire médiévale*, Damascus, 1977.

----, "Points de vue sur la révolution 'abbaside", in *Revue Historique*, Vol. CCXXX, 1963, pp.295-338.

Canard, M., "Da'wa", in *Encyclopaedia of Islam* (2), Vol. II, Leiden, 1965, pp.168-170.

----, *L'expansion arabo-islamique et ses répercusions*, London, 1974.

Cantarino, Vicente, *Entre Monjes y Musulmanes. El Conflicto que fue España*, Madrid, 1978.

Castro, Américo, *España en su Historia: Cristianos, Moros y Judíos*, Buenos Aires, 1948.

----, *La Realidad Histórica de España*, México, 1954.

Chejne, Anwar, *Succession to the Rule in Islam, with Special Reference to the Early 'Abbasid period*, Lahore, 1960.

----, *Muslim Spain. Its History and Culture.* Minneapolis, 1974.

Christensen, Arthur, *L'Iran sous les Sassanides,* Paris, 1936.

Corbin, H., "La filosofía islámica desde sus orígenes hasta la muerte de Averroes", in Brice Parain, *Historia de la Filosofía. Del Mundo Romano al Islam Medieval,* México, 1978, pp.267-272.

----, "The Meaning of the Imam for Shi'i Spirituality", in Seyyed Hossein Nasr, *Shi'ism, Doctrines, Thought and Spirituality,* Albany, 1988, pp.167-187.

Crone, Patricia and Martin Hinds, *God's Caliphs: Religious Authority in the First Centuries of Islam,* Cambridge, 1986.

Crone, Patricia, *Hagarism: the Making of the Islamic World,* Cambridge, 1977.

----, *Meccan Trade and the Rise of Islam,* Princeton, 1987.

----, *Slaves on Horses. The Evolution of the Islamic Polity,* Cambridge, 1980.

Cruz Hernández, Miguel, *La Filosofía Arabe,* Madrid, 1963.

----, *Historia del Pensamiento en el Mundo Islámico* Madrid, 1981.

Daniel, Elton, *The Political and Social History of Khurasan under 'Abbasid Rule. 747-820,* Minneapolis, 1979.

----, "The Anonymous 'History of the 'Abbasid Family' and its place in Islamic Historiography", in *International Journal of Middle East Studies,* Vol. XIV, Number 4, 1982, pp.419-434.

Dennett, Daniel C., *Conversion and the Poll Tax in Early Islam,* Cambridge, 1950.

----, "Marwan b. Muhammad: The Passing of the Umayyad Caliphate", Ph.D. dissertation, Harvard University, 1939.

Dixon, 'Abd al-Ameer, "A Malcontent from the Umayyad Period", in *Islamic Culture,* Vol. XLVII, Number 1, 1973, pp.31-36.

----, *The Umayyad Caliphate 65-86/684-705,* London, 1971.

Donner, Fred, *The Early Islamic Conquests,* Princeton, 1981.

Dozy, Reinhart, *Historia de los Musulmanes de España,* Buenos Aires, 1946.

Elad, Amikam, "The Siege of al-Wasit (132/749). Some Aspects of 'Abbasid and 'Alid Relations at the Beginning of 'Abbasid Rule", in Moshe Sharon, *Studies in Islamic History and Civilization in Honour of Professor David Ayalon,* Jerusalem, Leiden, 1986, pp.59-90.

Van Ess, Josef, "Disputationspraxis in der Islamischen Theology. Eine Vorlaufige Skizze", in *Revue des études islamiques,* Vol. XLIV, 1976, pp.23-60.

----, "Une lecture à rebours de l'histoire du Mu'tazilisme" (1), in *Revue des études islamiques,* Vol. XLVI, Fascicule 2, 1978, pp.163-240.

----, "Une lecture à rebours de l'histoire du Mu'tazilisme" (2), in *Revue des études islamiques,* Vol. XLVII, Fascicule 1, 1979, pp.19-69.

Fischer, A., "Kahtan", in *Encyclopaedia of Islam* (1), Vol. II, Leyden, 1927, pp.628-630.

----, "Kays 'Aylan", in *Encyclopaedia of Islam* (1), Vol. II, Leyden, 1927, pp.652-657.

Forand, Paul, "The Relation of the Slave and the Client to the Master or Patron in Medieval Islam", in *International Journal of Middle East Studies,* Vol. II, Number 1, 1971, pp.59-66.

Frye, Richard, "The 'Abbasid Conspiracy and Modern Revolutionary Theory", in *Indo-Iranica,* Vol. V, Number 3, 1952, pp.9-14.

----, *Bukhara, the Medieval Achievement,* Norman, Oklahoma, 1965.

----, *The Golden Age of Persia,* New York, 1975.

----, *The Heritage of Persia,* New York, 1963.

----, *Islamic Iran and Central Asia (7th-12th Centuries),* London, 1979.

----, "The Role of Abu Muslim in the 'Abbasid Revolt", in *Muslim World,* Vol. XXXVII, Number 1, 1947, pp.28-38.

Gabrieli, Francesco, "L'eroe Omàyyade Maslamah Ibn `Abd al-Malik", in *Rendiconti delle Sedute dell'Accademia Nazionale dei Lincei*, Vol. V, Fascicoli 1-2, 1950, pp.23-39.

----, *Mahoma y las Conquistas del Islam*, Madrid, 1967.

----, "L'opera de Ibn al-Muqaffà'", in *Rivista degli Studi Orientali*, Vol. XIII, Fascicolo 3, 1932, pp.197-247.

----, "La Risala di al-Gahiz sui Turchi", in *Rivista degli Studi Orientali*, Vol. XXXII, Part II, 1957, pp.477-483.

----, "La rivolta dei Muhallabati nel Iraq e il nuovo Baladuri", in *Rivista degli Studi Orientali*, Vol. XIV, Serie Sesta, Fascicoli 3-4, 1938, pp.199-236.

   ----, "La successione de Harun ar-Rasid e la guerra fra al-Amin e al-Ma'mun", in *Rivista degli Studi Orientali*, Vol. XI, Fascicolo 4, 1928, pp.341-397.

----, "Sulle origini del movimento Harigita", in *Rendiconti delle Sedute dell'Accademia Nazionale dei Lincei classe di Scienze Morali e Storiche*, Vol. III, Fascicolo 6, 1941, pp.110-117.

----, "Al-Walid Ibn Yazid, il califfo e il poeta", in *Rivista degli Studi Orientali*, Vol. XV, Fascicolo 1, 1934, pp.1-64.

García de Cortázar, José Angel, *La Epoca Medieval*, Madrid, 1973-1974.

Gaudefroy-Demombynes, Maurice, *Muslim Institutions*, London, 1954.

Gibb, Hamilton, *The Arab Conquests in Central Asia*, New York, 1970.

----, "The Fiscal Rescript of 'Umar II", in *Arabica. Revue d' études arabes*, Tome II, Fascicule 1, 1955, pp.1-16.

----, *El Mahometismo*, México, 1963.

Gil, Moshe, "The Medinan Opposition to the Prophet", in *Jerusalem Studies in Arabic and Islam*, 10, 1987, pp.65-96.

Glick, Thomas, *Islamic and Christian Spain in the Early Middle Ages*, Princeton, 1979.

Goitein, S.D., *Studies in Islamic History and Institutions*, Leiden, 1968.

Goldziher, Ignaz, *Muslim Studies*, English translation by S.M. Stern, 2 Vols., Chicago, 1966, London, 1971.

González Palencia, Angel, *Historia de la España Musulmana*, Barcelona, 1925.

Grunebaum, Gustav von, *Medieval Islam*, Chicago, 1953.

----, *Unity and Variety in Muslim Civilization*, Chicago, 1979.

Hasan, Naji, *Al-Qaba'il al-'Arabiyyah fi al-Mashriq, khilal al-'Asr al-Umawi*, Beirut, 1980.

Hasan, S.A., "A Survey of the Expansion of Islam into Central Asia during the Umayyad Caliphate", in *Islamic Culture*, XLVII, Number 1, 1973, pp.1-13.

----, "A Survey of the Expansion of Islam into Central Asia during the Umayyad Caliphate", in *Islamic Culture*, XLVIII, Number 3, 1974, pp.177-186.

Hawting, G.R., *The First Dynasty of Islam*, London and Sydney, 1986.

Hill, D.R. *The Termination of Hostilities in the Early Arab Conquests A.D. 634-656*, New York, 1971.

Hinds, Martin, "Kufan Political Alignments and their Backgrounds in the Mid-7th. Century A.D.", in *International Journal of Middle East Studies*, Vol. II, Number 4, 1971, pp.346-367.

Hitti, Philip, *History of the Arabs*, New York, 1951.

----, *Islam, Modo de Vida*, Madrid, 1973.

Hodgson, Marshall, "Ghulat", in *Encyclopaedia of Islam* (2), Vol. II, Leiden, 1965, pp.1093-1095.

----, "How Did the Early Shi`ah Become Sectarian?", in *Journal of the American Oriental Society*, Vol. LXXV, Number 1, 1951, pp.1-13.

----, *The Venture of Islam*, Chicago, 1974.

Horovits, Joseph, "The Earliest Biographies of the Prophet and their Authors", in *Islamic Culture,* Vol. II, 1928, pp.22-50, pp.164-182 and pp.495-526.

Husain, S. Athar, *The Glorious Caliphate,* Lucknow (India), 1974.

Imamuddin, S.M., *A Political History of Muslim Spain,* Karachi, 1984.

Izutsu, Toshihiko, *Ethico-Religious Concepts in the Qur'an,* Montreal, 1966.

Jafri, S. Husayn M., *The Origins and Early Development of Shi'a Islam,* London, 1979.

Kaabi, Mongi, "Les origines Tahirides dans la da`wa `Abbaside", in *Arabica. Revue d'études arabes,* Vol. XIX, Fascicule 2, 1972, pp.145-164.

Kennedy, Hugh, *The Early 'Abbasid Caliphate,* London, 1981.

----, "Al-Mahdi", in *Encyclopaedia of Islam* (2), Vol. V, Leiden, 1985, pp.1238-1239.

----, *The Prophet and the Age of the Caliphates. The Islamic Near East from the Sixth to the Eleventh Century,* New York, 1986.

Al-Kharbutli, 'Ali Husni, *'Abd Allah Ibn al-Zubayr,* Cairo?, 1965?

Kister, M.J., "The Massacre of the Banu Qurayza. A Re-Examination of a Tradition", in *Jerusalem Studies in Arabic and Islam,* 8, 1986, pp.61-96.

----, "Mecca and the Tribes of Arabia: Some Notes on their Relations", in Moshe Sharon, *Studies in Islamic History and Civilization in Honour of Professor David Ayalon,* Jerusalem, Leiden, 1986, pp.33-57.

Kraus, P., "Zu Ibn al-Muqaffa`", in *Rivista degli Studi Orientali,* Vol. XIV, Fascicolo 1, 1933, pp.1-20.

Krenkow, F., "Kinda", in *Encyclopaedia of Islam* (1), Vol. II, Leyden, 1927, pp.1018-1019.

Lammens, H., "Djudham", in *Encyclopaedia of Islam* (1), Vol. I, Leyden, 1928, pp.1058-1059.

----,"Lakhm", in *Encyclopaedia of Islam* (1), Vol. III, Leyden, 1928, pp.11-12.

----, "Mo`awiya II ou le dernier Sofianides", in *Rivista degli Studi Orientali,* Vol. VII, Fascicolo 1, 1916, pp.1-49.

Laoust, Henri, "Ibn Katir historien", in *Arabica. Revue d'études arabes,* Vol. II, Fascicule 1, 1955, pp.42-88.

----, "La pensée politique d'Ibn Khaldun", in *Revue des études islamiques,* Vol. XLVIII, Fascicule 2, 1980, pp.133-153.

----, *Les schismes dans l'Islam,* Paris, 1977.

Lapidus, Ira M., "The Separation of State and Religion in the Development of Early Islamic Society, in *International Journal of Middle East Studies,* Vol. VI, Number 4, 1975, pp.363-385.

Lassner, Jacob, "Abu Muslim, Son of Salit: A Skeleton in the `Abbasid Closet?", in Moshe Sharon, *Studies in Islamic History and Civilization in Honour of Professor David Ayalon,* Jerusalem, Leiden, 1986, pp.91-104.

----, *Islamic Revolution and Historical Memory. An Inquiry into the Art of 'Abbasid Apologetics,* New Haven, 1986.

----,*The Shaping of the 'Abbasid Rule,* Princeton, 1980.

Lecker, Michael, "Muhammad at Medina: A Geographical Approach", in *Jerusalem Studies in Arabic and Islam,* 6, 1985, pp.29-62.

Le Strange, G., *Baghdad during the 'Abbasid Caliphate,* Oxford, 1900.

----, *The Lands of the Eastern Caliphate,* Cambridge, 1930.

----, *Palestine under the Muslims,* London, 1980.

Levi-Provençal, Evariste, *España Musulmana. Hasta la caída del Califato de Córdoba (711-1031),* in Ramón Menéndez Pidal, *Historia de España,* Madrid, 1950, Vol. IV.

----, *España Musulmana. Instituciones y vida social e intelectual,* in Ramón Menéndez Pidal, *Historia de España,* Madrid, 1957, Vol. V.

Levy, Reuben, "Persia and the Arabs", in John Arberry, *The Legacy of Persia,*

Oxford, 1953, pp.60-88.

Lewis, Bernard, "`Abbasids", in *Encyclopaedia of Islam* (2), Vol. I, Leiden, 1960, pp.15-23.

----, and Peter Holt, *Historians of the Middle East*, London, 1962.

----, *Islam in History*, London, 1973.

----, *The Origins of Isma'ilism. A Study of Historical Background of the Fatimid Caliphate*, Cambridge, 1940.

MacDonald, D.B., "Al-Mahdi", in *Shorter Encyclopaedia of Islam*, Leiden, 1974, pp.310-313.

Madelung, Wilferd, "Khurramiyyah", in *Encyclopaedia of Islam* (2), Vol. V, Leiden, 1979, pp.63-65.

----, *Religious Schools and Sects in Medieval Islam*, London, 1985.

----, *Religious Trends in Early Islamic Iran*, Albany, 1988.

----, "Das Imamat in der Frühen Ismailitischen Lehre", in *Der Islam*, XXXVII, 1961, pp.43-135.

Mahmud, Mu'in Ahmad, *Ta'rikh Madinat al-Quds*, n.p., 1979.

Margoliouth, D. S., "Mahdi", in *Encyclopaedia of Religion and Ethics*, Vol. III, 1964, pp.336-340.

----, "On Mahdis and Mahdiism", in *Proceedings of the British Academy*, 1915-1916, pp.213-223.

Marín-Guzmán, Roberto, "Algunas notas sobre el origen, la expansión y el desarrollo del Islam, in *Tiempo Actual*, Vol. VIII, Number 32, May 1984, pp.71-79.

----,"Las causas de la expansión islámica y los fundamentos del Imperio Musulmán", in *Revista Estudios*, Number 5, 1984, pp.29-67.

----, "Clasificación y tipología de los Movimientos Mesiánicos", in *Káñina*, Vol. VI, Numbers 1-2, 1982, pp.99-116.

----, *El Derrumbe del Viejo Orden en Irán. Ensayo histórico sobre la caída de la dinastía Pahlavi. (1925-1979)*, San José, Costa Rica, 1989.

----, "La Escatología Musulmana: Análisis del Mahdismo", in *Cuadernos de Historia*, Number 44, Publications of the University of Costa Rica, 1982.

----, "Ibn Khaldun y el método científico de la Historia", in *Cuadernos de Historia*, Number 43, Publications of the University of Costa Rica, 1982.

----, *Introducción a los Estudios Islámicos*, San José, Costa Rica, 1983.

----, *El Islam: Ideología e Historia*, San José, Costa Rica, 1986.

----, *El Islam: Religión y Política*, San José, Costa Rica, 1986.

----, "El Islam Shi`ita", in Roberto Marín-Guzmán, *Introducción a los Estudios Islámicos*, San José, Costa Rica, 1983, pp.173-183.

----, "El Islam, una religión", in *Crónica*, Number 3, 1982, pp.81-90.

----, "Periodización y Cronología del Mundo Islámico", in *Cuadernos de Historia*, Number 36, Publications of the University of Costa Rica, 1982.

----, "Razón y Revelación en el Islam", in *Revista de Filosofía*, Vol. XXII, Numbers 55-56, 1984, pp.133-150.

Marquet, Yves, "Le si`isme au IXe siècle à travers l'histoire de Ya`qubi (1ère partie)", in *Arabica. Revue d'études arabes*, Vol. XIX, Fascicule 1, 1972, pp.1-45.

----, "Le si`isme au IXe siècle à travers l'histoire de Ya`qubi (suite et fin), *Arabica. Revue d'études arabes*, Vol. XIX, Fascicule 2, 1972, pp.101-138.

Menéndez Pidal, Ramón, *La España del Cid*, Buenos Aires, 1939.

----, *Orígenes del español. Estado lingüístico de la Península Ibérica hasta el siglo XI*, Madrid, 1950.

Miquel, André, *L'Islam et sa civilisation, VIIe-XXe siècles*, Paris, 1977.

Moosa, Matti, *Extremist Shiites. The Ghulat Sects*, Syracuse, 1988.

Morony, Michael, *Iraq after the Muslim Conquest*, Princeton, 1984.

Moscati, Sabatino, "Le massacre des Umayyades dans l'histoire et dans les fragments poétiques, in *Archiv Orientální*, Vol. XVIII, Number 4, 1950, pp.88-115.

----, "Per una storia dell'antica Sia", in *Rivista degli Studi Orientali*, Vol. XXX, 1955, pp.251-267.

----, "Studi storici sul califfato di al-Mahdi", in *Orientalia*, Vol. XIV, Fascicoli 3-4, 1945, pp.300-354.

----, "Nuovi studi storici sul califfato di al-Mahdi", in *Orientalia*, Vol. XV, Fascicoli 1-2, 1946, pp.155-179.

----, "Studi su Abu Muslim. I-Abu Muslim e gli ʿAbbasidi", in *Rendiconti delle Sedute dell'Accademia Nazionale dei Lincei*, Vol. IV, Fascicoli 5-6, 1949, pp.323-325.

----, "Studi su Abu Muslim. II- Propaganda e politica religiosa di Abu Muslim", in *Rendiconti delle Sedute dell'Accademia Nazionale dei Lincei*, Vol. IV, Fascicoli 7-10, 1949, pp.474-495.

----, "Studi su Abu Muslim. III- La fine di Abu Muslim", in *Rendiconti delle Sedute dell'Accademia Nazionale dei Lincei*, Vol. V, Fascicoli 1-2, 1950, pp.89-105.

----,"Il testamento di Abu Hashim", in *Rivista degli Studi Orientali*, Vol. XXVII, Fascicoli 1-4, 1952, pp.28-46.

----, "Il tradimento di Wasit", in *Le Museon*, Vol. LXIV, 1951, pp.177-186.

Muir, William, *The Caliphate. Its Rise, Decline and Fall*, London, n.d.

Muranyi, M., "Die Ersten Muslime Von Mekka--Soziale Basis Einer Neuen Religion?", in *Jerusalem Studies in Arabic and Islam*, 8, 1986, pp.25-35.

Nadir, Albert Nasri, *Ahamm al-Firaq al-Islamiyyah*, Beirut, n.d.

Nallino, Carlo A., "Di una strana opinione attribuita ad al-Gahiz in torno al corano", in *Rivista degli Studi Orientali*, Vol. VII, Fascicolo 2, 1916, pp.421-428.

----, "Noterelle su Ibn al-Muqaffaʿ e suo figlio", in *Rivista degli Studi Orientali*, Vol. XIV, Fascicolo 2, 1933, pp.130-134.

----, "Rapporti fra la dogmatica Muʿtazila e quella degli Ibaditi dell'Africa Settentrionale", in *Rivista degli Studi Orientali*, Vol. VII, Fascicolo 2, 1916, pp.455-460.

----, "Sull' origine del nome dei Muʿtaziliti", in *Rivista degli Studi Orientali*, Vol. VII, Fascicolo 2, 1916, pp.429-454.

----, "Sul nome di Qadariti", in *Rivista degli Studi Orientali*, Vol.VII, Fascicolo 2, 1916, pp.461-466.

Nasr, Seyyed Hossein, *Shi'ism, Doctrines, Thought and Spirituality*, Albany, 1988.

Al-Nayfar, Muhammad al-Tahir, *Ahamm al-Firaq al-Islamiyyah*, Tunisia, 1974.

Nicholson, Reynold, *Los Místicos del Islam*, México, 1975.

Nyberg, H., "Al-Muʿtazila", in *Encyclopaedia of Islam* (1), Vol. III, Leyden, 1928, pp.787-793.

'Omar, Faruq, *Al-'Abbasiyun al-Awa'il*, Baghdad, 1977.

----, *Al-Khilafah al-'Abbasiyyah fi 'Asr al-Fawda al-'Askariyyah*, Baghdad, 1977.

----, "The Nature of the Iranian Revolts in the Early Islamic Period", in *Islamic Culture*, Vol. XLVIII, Number 1, 1974, pp.1-9.

----, "Politics and the Problem of Succession in the Early ʿAbbasid Caliphate", in *Islamic Culture*, Vol. XLVIII, 1974, pp.31-43.

Pareja, Félix, *Islamología*, Madrid, 1952-1954.

Parry, V.J. and M.E. Yapp, *War, Technology and Society in the Middle East*, London, 1975.

Pellat, Charles, *Études sur l'histoire socio-culturelle de l'Islam (VIIe-XVe s.)*, London, 1976.

----, "Gahiziana I. Le Kitab al-Tabassur bi-l-Tigara attribué à Gahiz", in *Arabica. Revue d'études arabes*, Vol. I, Fascicule 2, 1954, pp.153-165.

----, "Gahiz à Baghdad et à Samarra", in *Rivista degli Studi Orientali*, Vol. XXVII, 1952, pp.48-67.

----, *Langue et littérature arabes*, Paris, 1970.

----, *Le milieu basrien et la formation de Gahiz*, Paris, 1953.

Pinto, Olga, "Al-Fath b. Haqan favorito di al-Mutawakkil", in *Rivista degli Studi Orientali*, Vol. XIII, Fascicolo 2, 1931-1932, pp.133-149.

Pipes, Daniel, *Slave Soldiers and Islam. The Genesis of a Military System*, New Haven, 1981.

Poliak, A.N., "Classification of Lands in the Islamic Law and its Technical Terms", in *The American Journal of Semitic Languages and Literatures*, Vol. VII, Number 1, 1940, pp.50-62.

Pope, Arthur, *An Introduction to Persian Art since the Seventeenth Century*, London, 1930.

Rahman, Fazlur, *Prophecy in Islam. Philosophy and Orthodoxy*, London, 1958.

Al-Rayyis, Muhammad Diya' al-Din, *'Abd al-Malik b. Marwan wa Dawlat al-Umawiyyah*, Cairo?, 1969.

Ritter, Hellmut von, "Studien zur Geschichte der Islamischen Frömmigkeit I-Hasan al-Basri", in *Der Islam*, Vol. XXI, 1933, pp.1-83.

Rizzitano, Umberto, "Un nuovo trattatello attribuito ad Ibn al-Muqaffa`", in *Rivista degli Studi Orientali*, Vol. XXIV, Fascicoli 1-4, 1949, pp.25-30.

----, *Storia degli Arabi, dall'epoca preislamica ad oggi*, Palermo, 1971.

Ruwayhah, Mahmud Riyad, *Jabbar Thaqif: Al-Hajjaj Ibn Yusuf*, Beirut, 1963.

Rosenthal, F., "Dawlah", in *Encyclopaedia of Islam* (2), Vol. II, Leiden, 1965, pp.177-178.

----, *A History of Muslim Historiography*, Leiden, 1952.

Rothstein, G., *Die Dynastie der Lakhmiden in al-Hira*, Berlin, 1899.

Rubin, U., "Prophets and Progenitors in the Early Shi`a Tradition", in *Jerusalem Studies in Arabic and Islam*, Vol. I, 1979, pp.41-65.

Ruiz Figueroa, Manuel, "Imamah o autoridad en los primeros tiempos del Islam", in *Estudios Orientales*, Vol. IX, Numbers 1-2 (24-25), 1974, pp.61-82.

----, *El Islam Responde*, México, 1974.

Sabiq al-Sayyid, *Fiqh al-Sunnah*, Beirut, 1969.

Sachedina, Abdulaziz A., *Islamic Messianism. The Idea of the Mahdi in Twelver Shi'ism*, Albany, 1981.

Sadighi, G., *Les mouvements religieux Iraniens a IIe et au IIIe siècles de l'hégire*, Paris, 1938.

Al-Saghir, Muhammad Husayn 'Ali, *Ta'rikh al-Qur'an*, Beirut, 1983.

Al-Sa'ih, 'Abd al-Hamid, *Ahammiyyat al-Quds fi al-Islam*, 'Amman, 1979.

Al-Samarra'i, 'Abd Allah Sallum, *Al-Ghuluw wa al-Firaq al-Ghaliyah fi al-Hadarat al-Islamiyyah*, Baghdad, 1982.

Sánchez Albornoz, Claudio, *El Islam de España y el Occidente*, Madrid, 1974.

Santillana, D., *Istituzioni di diritto musulmano malichita con riguardo anche al sistema sciafiita*, Rome, 1926-1938.

Schaeder, Hans Heinrich, "Hasan al-Basri. Studien zur Frühgeschichte des Islam", in *Der Islam*, XIV, 1925, pp.1-75.

Schacht, Joseph, *An Introduction to Islamic Law*, Oxford, 1964.

----, *The Legacy of Islam*, Oxford, 1974.

----, *The Origins of Muhammadan Jurisprudence*, Oxford, 1950.

Schimmel, Annemarie, "The Primordial Dot. Some Thoughts About Sufi Letter Mysticism", in *Jerusalem Studies in Arabic and Islam*, 9, 1987, pp.350-356.

Shaban, M.A., *The 'Abbasid Revolution*, Cambridge, 1970.

----, *El Islam*, Madrid, 1976.

----, "The Social and Political Background of the `Abbasid Revolution in

Khurasan", Ph.D. dissertation, Harvard University, 1960.

Shahid, Irfan, "Lakhmids", in *Encyclopaedia of Islam* (2), Vol. V, Leiden, 1986, pp.632-634.

Shalaq, 'Ali, '*Abd al-Malik b. Marwan*, Beirut, 1980.

Sharon, Moshe, "Ahl al-Bayt--People of the House", in *Jerusalem Studies in Arabic and Islam*, 8, 1986, pp.169-184.

----, *Black Banners from the East. The Establishment of the 'Abbasid State. Incubation of a Revolt*, Jerusalem and Leiden, 1983.

----, "The Development of the Debate around Legitimacy of Authority in Early Islam", in *Jerusalem Studies in Arabic and Islam*, 5, 1984, pp.121-142.

----, "The Military Reforms of Abu Muslim, their Background and Consequences", in Moshe Sharon, *Studies in Islamic History and Civilization in Honour of Professor David Ayalon*, Jerusalem and Leiden, 1986, pp.105-143.

Shoufani, Elias, *Al-Riddah and the Muslim Conquest of Arabia*, Toronto, 1973.

Van Sievers, Peter, "Military Merchants and Nomads. The Social Evolution of the Syrian Cities and Countryside in the Classical Period", in *Der Islam*, Vol. LVI, Number 2, 1979, pp.206-244.

Sourdel, Domique, La biographie d' Ibn al-Muqaffa' d'après les sources anciennes", in *Arabica. Revue d'études arabes*, Vol. I, Fascicule 3, 1954, pp.307-323.

----, "L'imamisme vu par le Cheikh al-Mufid", in *Revue des études islamiques*, Vol. XL, Fascicule 2, 1972, pp.217-296.

----, "La Syrie au temps des premiers califes `Abbassides (132/750-264/878)", in *Revue des études islamiques*, Vol. XLVII, Fascicule 2, 1980, pp.155-175.

----, *Le Vizirat 'Abbaside, de 749 à 936*, Damascus, 1959-1960.

Sourdel, Dominique and Janine Sourdel-Thomine, *La civilisation de l'Islam classique*, Paris, 1968.

Spuler, Bertold, *Geschichte der Islamischen Länder*, Leiden, 1959.

----, *Iran in Früh-Islamischer Zeit*, Wiesbaden, 1952.

Stehly, Ralph, "Un problème de théologie islamique: la définition des fautes graves (kaba'ir), in *Revue des études islamiques*, Vol. LXV, Fascicule 2, 1977, pp.165-181.

Strothman, R., "Al-Zaidiya", in *Shorter Encyclopaedia of Islam*, Ithaca, 1961, pp.651-652.

Sviri, Sara, "Between Fear and Hope. On the Coincidence of Opposites in Islamic Mysticism", in *Jerusalem Studies in Arabic and Islam*, 9, 1987, pp.316-349.

Tabataba'i, 'Allamah, "The Shi'i View of Revelation and Prophecy", in Seyyed Hossein Nasr, *Shi'ism, Doctrines, Thought, and Spirituality*, Albany, 1988, pp.127-137.

Tabataba'i, Husayn, *Shi'ite Islam*, Houston, 1979.

----, "Shi`ism, Zaydism, Isma`ilism and Shaykhism", in Seyyed Hossein Nasr, *Shi`ism, Doctrines, Thought and Spirituality*, Albany, 1988, pp.85-86.

----, "Taqiyyah", in Seyyed Hossein Nasr, *Shi`ism, Doctrines, Thought and Spirituality*, Albany, 1988, pp.204-205.

Taha, 'Abd al-Wahid Dhannun, *Al-'Iraq fi 'Asr al-Hajjaj Ibn Yusuf al-Thaqafi*, Mosul, 1985.

Thabit, N., *Al-Jundiyyah fi al-Dawlah al-'Abbasiyyah*, Baghdad, 1358/1939.

Vadet, Jean-Claude, "Le Karramisme de la Haute-Asie au carrefour de trois sects rivales", in *Revue des études islamiques*, Vol. XLVIII, Fascicule 1, 1980, pp.25-50.

Vajda, Georges, "Les zindiqs en pays d'Islam au début de la période `Abbaside", in *Rivista degli Studi Orientali*, Vol. XVII, 1938, pp.173-229.

Veccia Vaglieri, Laura, "Sulla denominazione Hawarig", in *Rivista degli Studi Orientali*, Vol. XXVI, Fascicoli 1-4, 1951, pp.41-46.

----, "Le vicende del Harigismo in epoca Abbaside", in *Rivista degli Studi Orientali*, Vol. XXIV, Fascicoli 1-4, 1949, pp.31-44.

Van Vloten, Gerlof, *De Opkomst der Abbasiden im Chorasan*, Leiden, 1890.

----, *Recherches sur la domination arabe, le Chiitisme, et les croyances messianiques sous le Khalifat Omayedes*, Asmterdam, 1894.

Watt, Montgomery, "The Beginning of the Islamic Theological Schools", in *Revue des études islamiques*, Vol. XLIV, 1976, pp.15-21.

----, *The Formative Period of Islamic Thought*, Edinburgh, 1973.

----, *Free Will and Predestination in Early Islam*, London, 1948.

----, *Historia de la España Islámica*, Madrid, 1980.

----, *Islam and the Integration of Society*, London, 1961.

----, *Islamic Philosophy and Theology*, Edinburgh, 1979.

----, "Kharijite Thought in the Umayyad Period", in *Der Islam*, Vol. XXXVI, Number 3, 1961, pp.215-232.

----, *Mahoma, Profeta y Hombre de Estado*, Buenos Aires, 1973.

----, *The Majesty that Was Islam; the Islamic World, 661-1100*, New York, 1974.

----, *Muhammad at Mecca*, Oxford, 1960.

----, *Muhammad at Medina*, Oxford, 1956.

----, *Muhammad's Mecca: History in the Qur'an*, Edinburgh, 1988.

Wellhausen, Julius, *The Arab Kingdom and its Fall*, English translation by Margaret Graham Weir, Beirut, 1963.

----, *Die Religiös-Politischen Oppositionsparteien im Alten Islam*, Göttingen, 1901.

Wendell, Charles, "Baghdad: Imago Mundi, and Other Foundation-Lore", in *International Journal of Middle East Studies*, Vol. II, Number 2, 1971, pp.99-128.

Wensink, Arent Jan, *Muhammad and the Jews of Medina*, Freiburg, 1975.

Al-Zabidi, Muhammad Husayn, *Al-Hayah al-Ijtima'iyah wa al-Iqtisadiyah fi al-Kufah fi al-Qarn al-Awwal al-Hijri*, Cairo, 1970.

# *INDEX*